Trick 'r Treat

DAYS OF THE DEAD

LEGENDARY

A **LEGENDARY COMICS** PRODUCTION
PRESENTED BY **MICHAEL DOUGHERTY**

TRICK 'R TREAT
DAYS OF THE DEAD

STORY BY
MICHAEL DOUGHERTY, TODD CASEY & ZACH SHIELDS

WRITTEN BY
MICHAEL DOUGHERTY, TODD CASEY,
ZACH SHIELDS & MARC ANDREYKO

SEED
ART BY
FIONA STAPLES
COLORS BY
JOSE VILLARRUBIA

CORN MAIDEN
ART & COLORS BY
STEPHEN BYRNE

ECHOES
ART BY
STUART SAYGER
COLORS BY
GUY MAJOR

MONSTER MASH
ART & COLORS BY
ZID
COLORS BY
RICCARDO RULLO

LETTERING BY
TROY PETERI

COVER ART BY
ZID

BOOK DESIGNED BY
JOHN J. HILL

EDITED BY
ROBERT NAPTON

SPECIAL THANKS TO **ALEX GARCIA, BARNABY LEGG, SHIRIT BRADLEY, & BENJAMIN WRIGHT**

LEGENDARY

THOMAS TULL Chairman and Chief Executive Officer
JON JASHNI President and Chief Creative Officer   **MARTY WILLHITE** Chief Operating Officer & General Counsel
EMILY CASTEL Chief Marketing Officer   **JESSICA KANTOR** VP, Business and Legal Affairs
BARNABY LEGG VP, Theatrical Marketing   **DANIEL FEINBERG** Director, Business & Legal Affairs
PEARL WIBLE Director, Digital Content   **MANSI PATEL** Creative Services Director

LEGENDARY COMICS
BOB SCHRECK Senior Vice President, Editor-in-Chief   **ROBERT NAPTON** Vice President, Editorial Director
DAVID SADOVE Publishing Operations Coordinator   **GREG TUMBARELLO** Editor

Published by **LEGENDARY COMICS** - 2900 West Alameda Ave Suite 1500 Burbank, CA 91505

INTRODUCTION

Seven years ago this month I was delivered the unfortunate news that TRICK 'R TREAT wouldn't be getting theatrical distribution. It obviously wasn't the most ideal decision but it was one that I accepted and decided to make the best of. Thankfully, the forces of darkness agreed to help, and when it was finally unleashed, the film quickly grew to become a cult favorite. But this didn't happen overnight and didn't happen because of some cash-fueled marketing campaign, it was strictly through the word of mouth of fans like you. Fans who eagerly embraced Sam and introduced the movie to their friends every Halloween like a long-forgotten tradition.

And now, seven years later, that enthusiasm has only grown. I've seen your costumes, your tattoos (sometimes a little too up close and personal), and I've heard the cries for a sequel. And while I'd love nothing more than to go trick-or-treating with Sam one more time, my cohorts and I have been busy helping another pagan holiday demon make his way to the big screen (KRAMPUS, in theaters in December!). But even while surrounded by dark Christmas carols and cloven hoofed monsters, the sights and sounds of Halloween night were always lurking in the background, dying for more time in the moonlight.

I still don't know exactly when TRICK 'R TREAT 2 will rise from the pumpkin patch, but hopefully the book you're holding in your hands will tide you over until it does. Like the original film, we have four interconnected stories all centered around the best night of the year. But instead of taking place on the same All Hallow's Eve, these tales span the centuries, depicting a variety of characters, creatures, and cultures, going all the way back to the holiday's roots in ancient Ireland. There are tales of witchcraft, tragic romance, detective mystery, and even an eerie story set in the Old West.

And this time I'm not trick or treating alone. I've picked up a few friends along the way, including my KRAMPUS co-writers Todd Casey and Zach Shields, and the supremely talented Marc Andreyko, who helped pen the original TRICK 'R TREAT comic adaptation. Also returning from the original book is the lovely Fiona Staples, who has made quite a name for herself in recent years as a co-creator of SAGA with Brian K. Vaughan. Also providing artwork are Stephen Byrne, an up and coming comic artist, animator, and mutual Buffy fanatic, as well as Stuart Sayger whose work looks as if it was literally painted with shadows, and finally Zid, who can best be described as Norman Rockwell meets Norman Bates.

Again, a proper sequel is very much on the agenda after KRAMPUS finally arrives this Christmas, but hopefully Sam and his menagerie of monsters can keep you company on the printed page until that day comes. And hopefully it won't be another seven years…

Happy Halloween.
Michael Dougherty
July 2015

SEED

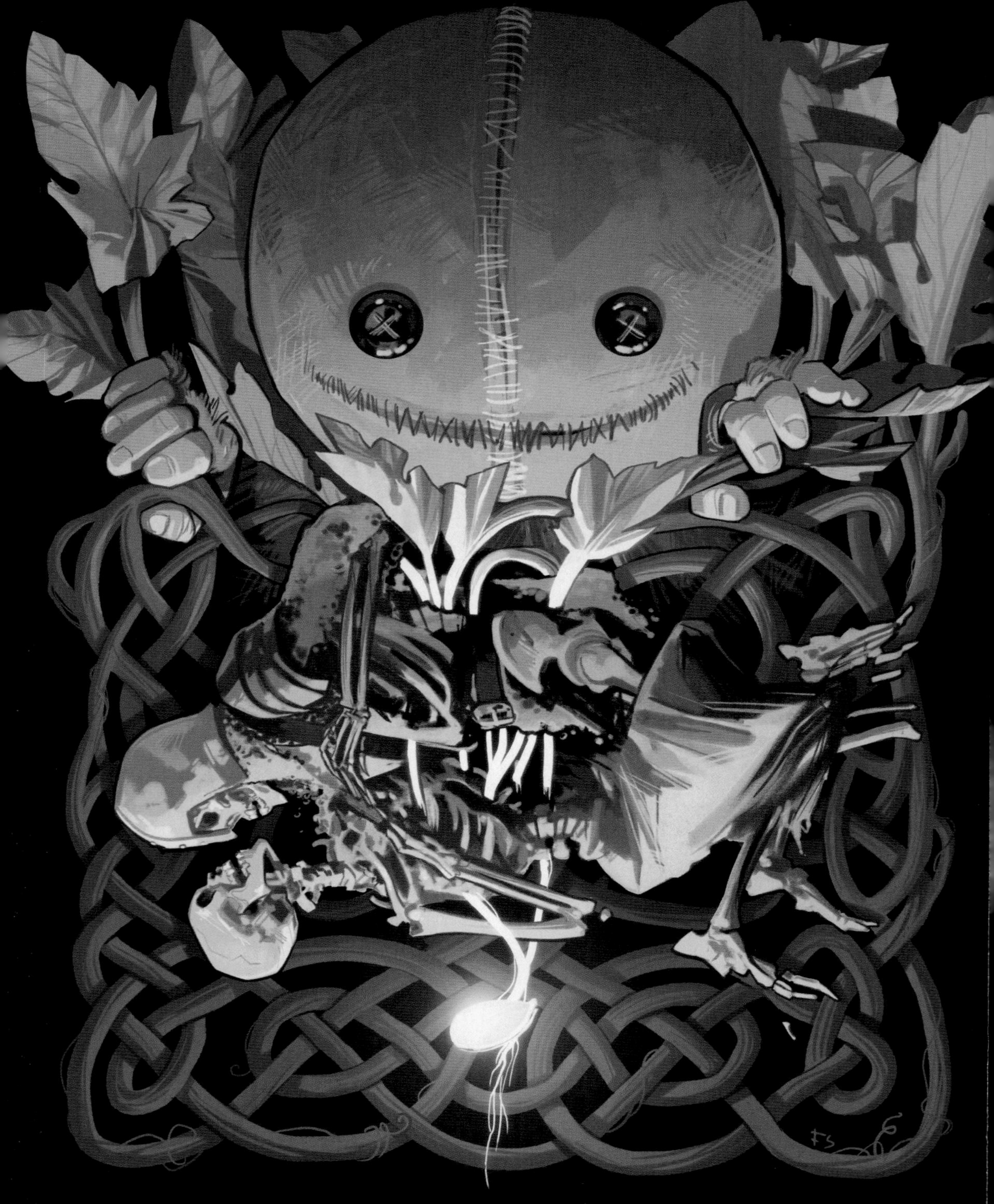

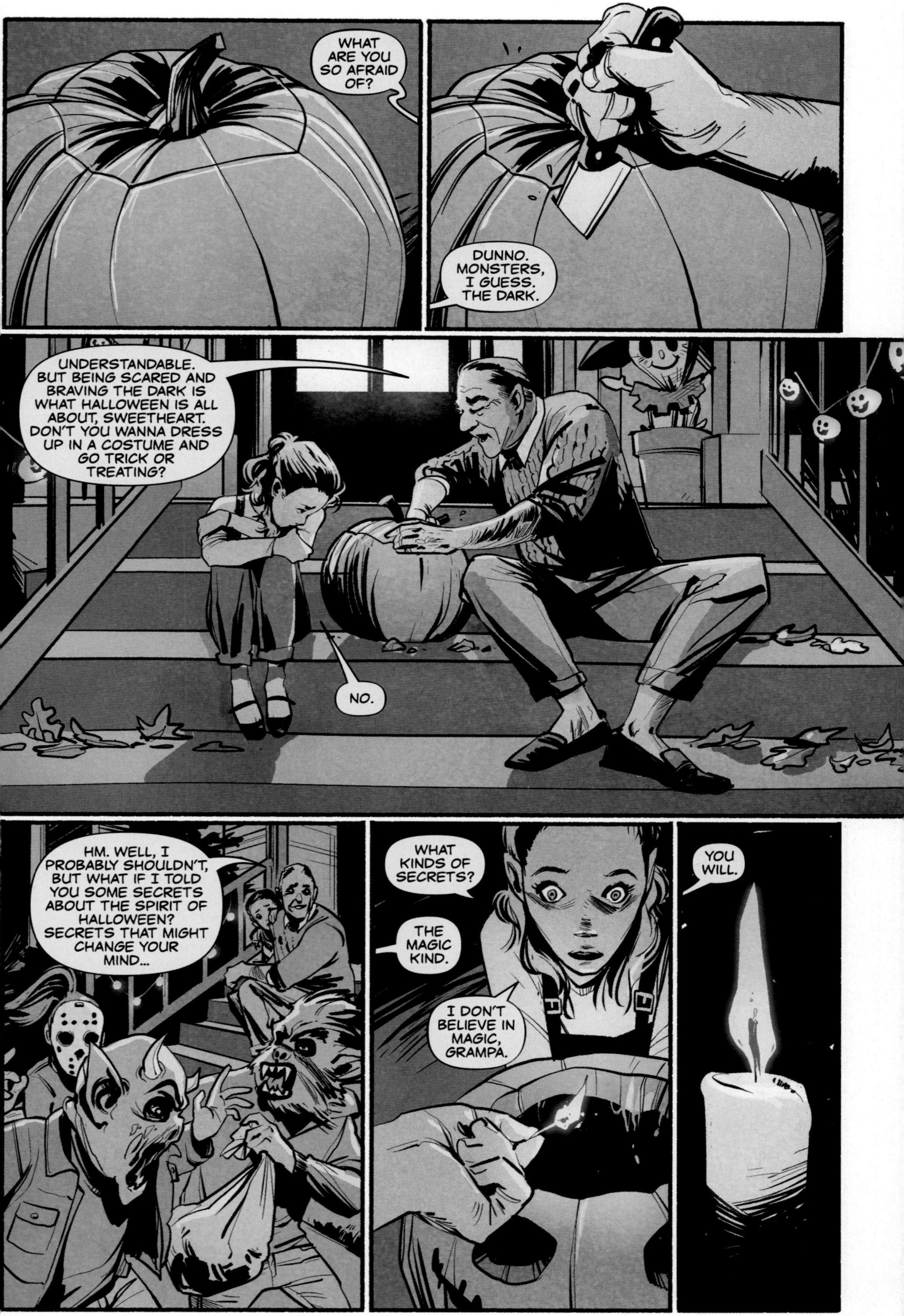
WHAT ARE YOU SO AFRAID OF?
DUNNO. MONSTERS, I GUESS. THE DARK.
UNDERSTANDABLE. BUT BEING SCARED AND BRAVING THE DARK IS WHAT HALLOWEEN IS ALL ABOUT, SWEETHEART. DON'T YOU WANNA DRESS UP IN A COSTUME AND GO TRICK OR TREATING?
NO.
HM. WELL, I PROBABLY SHOULDN'T, BUT WHAT IF I TOLD YOU SOME SECRETS ABOUT THE SPIRIT OF HALLOWEEN? SECRETS THAT MIGHT CHANGE YOUR MIND...
WHAT KINDS OF SECRETS?
THE MAGIC KIND.
I DON'T BELIEVE IN MAGIC, GRAMPA.
YOU WILL.

IRELAND. OCTOBER 24, 1640.

ETERNAL REST, GRANT UNTO THEM, O LORD, AND LET PERPETUAL LIGHT SHINE UPON THEM...

MAY THE SOULS OF THE FAITHFUL DEPARTED THROUGH THE MERCY OF GOD REST IN PEACE.

SURELY YOUR PRAYER IS FOR THE CHILDREN THEY'VE SLAUGHTERED?

BECAUSE ONLY A FOOL WOULD BELIEVE GOD WOULD GRANT MERCY ON SUCH CREATURES.

THESE SOULLESS HEATHENS BROUGHT THE PLAGUE UPON US, THOMAS. AND LIKE ALL PLAGUES, THEY MUST BE CLEANSED. DO NOT WASTE YOUR SYMPATHIES ON THEM.

PERHAPS IT IS THOSE WITHOUT SOULS WHO NEED OUR PRAYERS THE MOST, COMMANDER WOLFRIC.

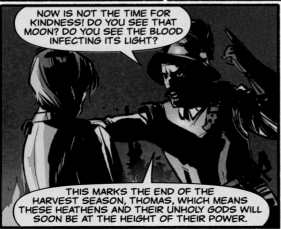

NOW IS NOT THE TIME FOR KINDNESS! DO YOU SEE THAT MOON? DO YOU SEE THE BLOOD INFECTING ITS LIGHT?

THIS MARKS THE END OF THE HARVEST SEASON, THOMAS, WHICH MEANS THESE HEATHENS AND THEIR UNHOLY GODS WILL SOON BE AT THE HEIGHT OF THEIR POWER.

GOD NEEDS SOLDIERS TO WIN HIS WAR, NOT PRAYERS. BUT IF YOU CAN'T STOMACH THE EXECUTIONS, THEN PERHAPS SOME TIME IN THE INTERROGATION TENTS WILL TOUGHEN YOU UP.

YES, COMMANDER.

BUT REMEMBER...

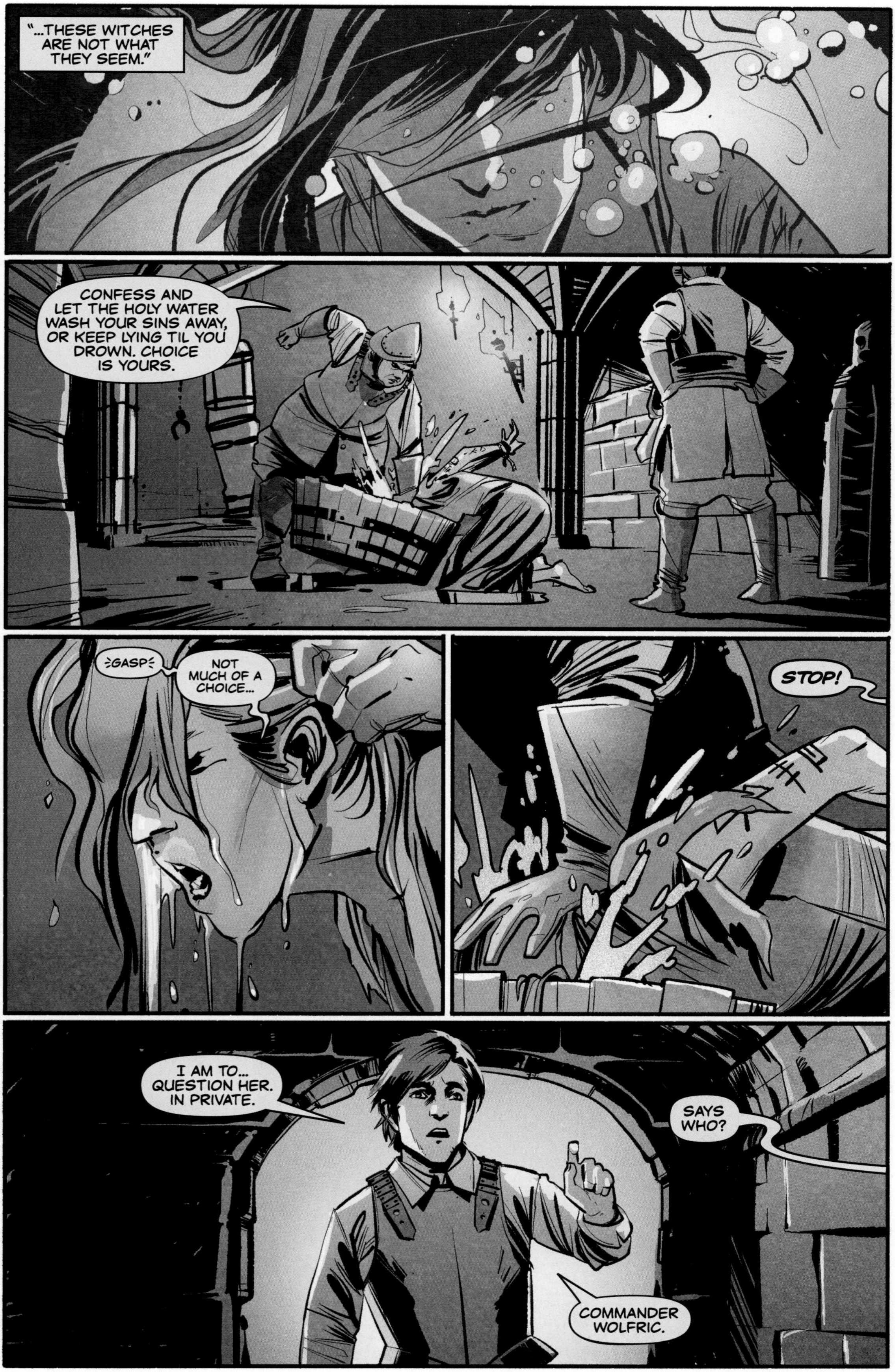
"...THESE WITCHES ARE NOT WHAT THEY SEEM."
CONFESS AND LET THE HOLY WATER WASH YOUR SINS AWAY, OR KEEP LYING TIL YOU DROWN. CHOICE IS YOURS.
GASP
NOT MUCH OF A CHOICE...
STOP!
I AM TO... QUESTION HER. IN PRIVATE.
SAYS WHO?
COMMANDER WOLFRIC.

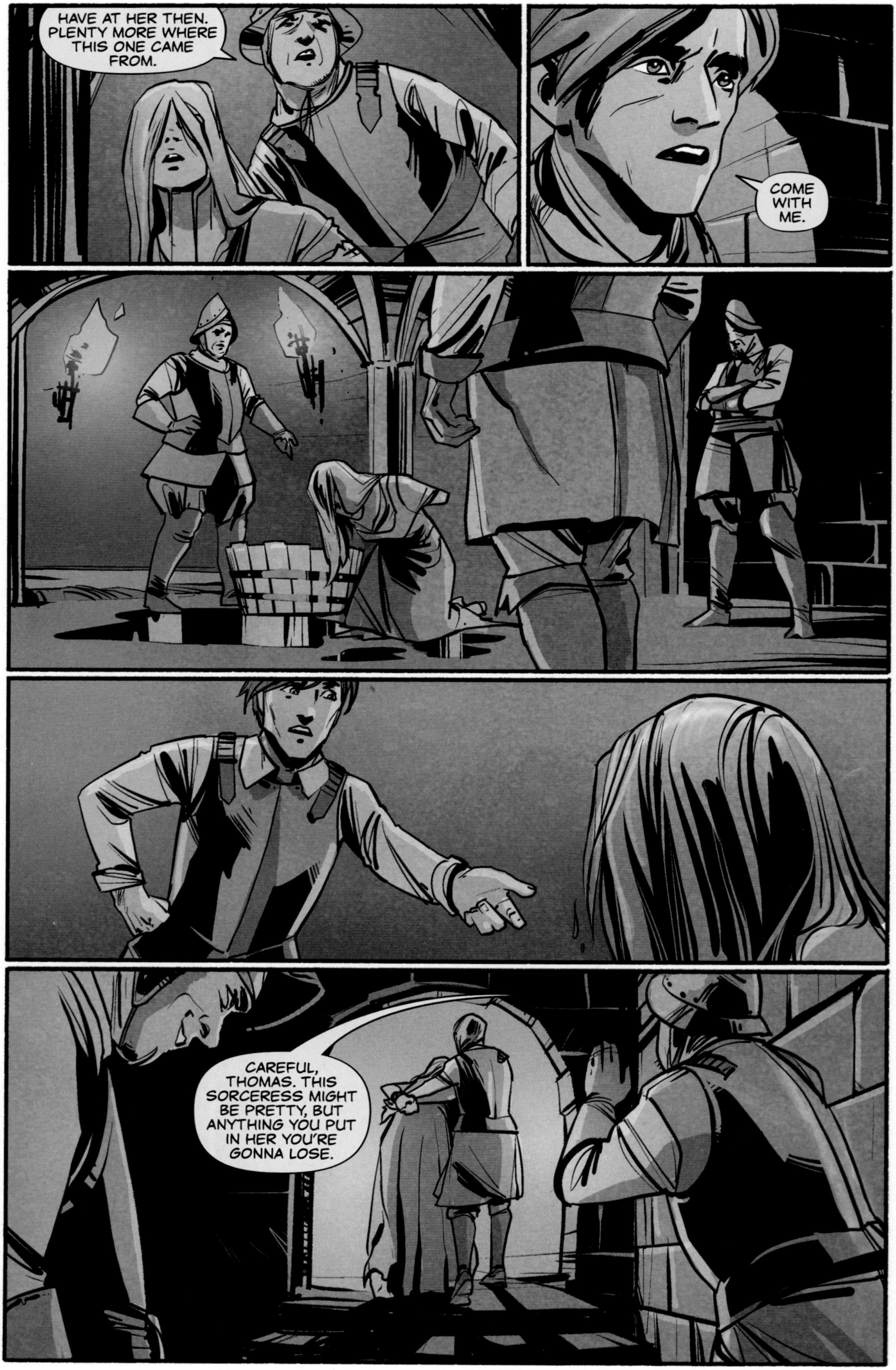
HAVE AT HER THEN. PLENTY MORE WHERE THIS ONE CAME FROM.
COME WITH ME.
CAREFUL, THOMAS. THIS SORCERESS MIGHT BE PRETTY, BUT ANYTHING YOU PUT IN HER YOU'RE GONNA LOSE.

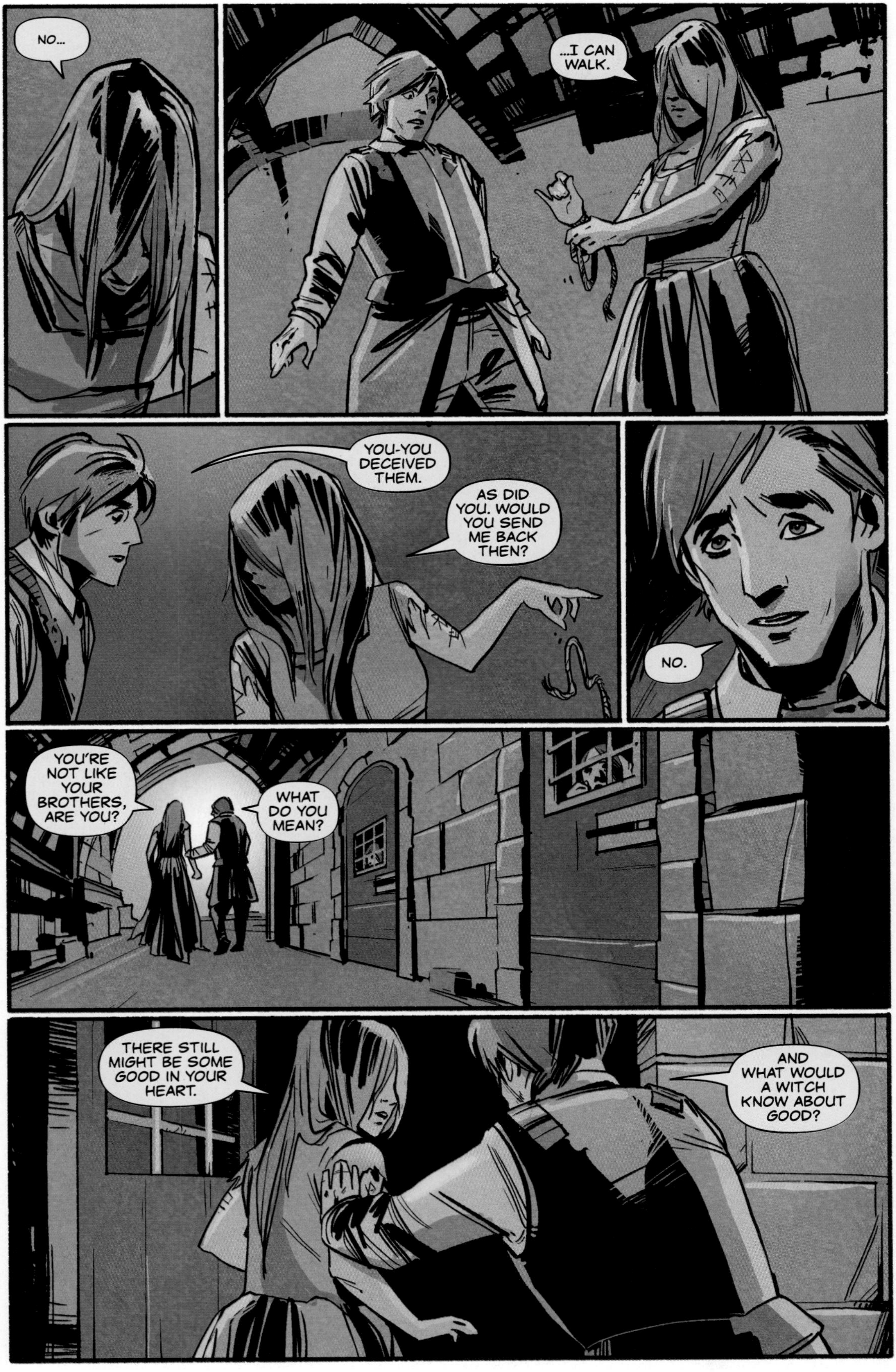
NO...
...I CAN WALK.
YOU-YOU DECEIVED THEM.
AS DID YOU. WOULD YOU SEND ME BACK THEN?
NO.
YOU'RE NOT LIKE YOUR BROTHERS, ARE YOU?
WHAT DO YOU MEAN?
THERE STILL MIGHT BE SOME GOOD IN YOUR HEART.
AND WHAT WOULD A WITCH KNOW ABOUT GOOD?

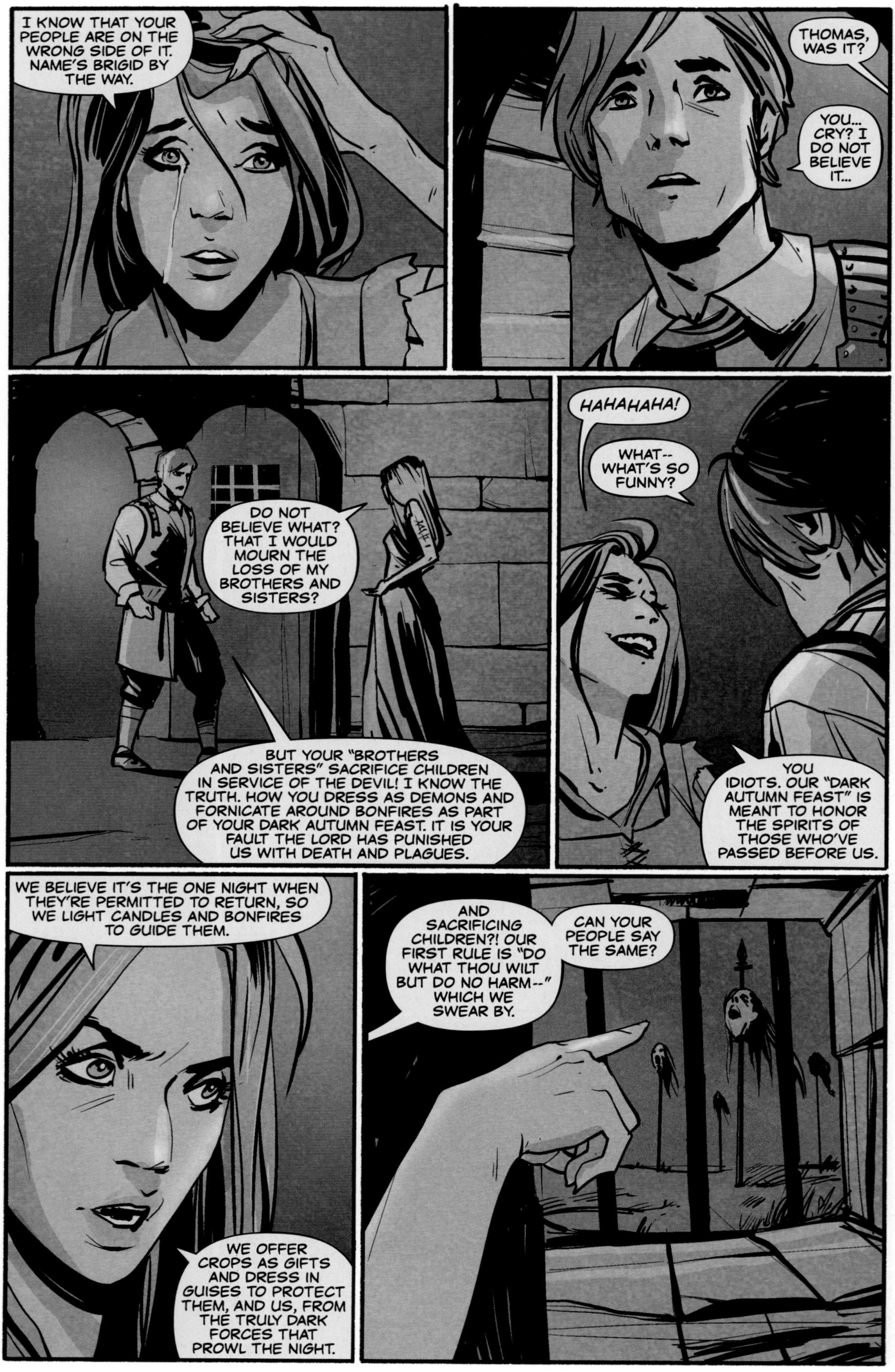
I KNOW THAT YOUR PEOPLE ARE ON THE WRONG SIDE OF IT. NAME'S BRIGID BY THE WAY.
THOMAS, WAS IT?
YOU... CRY? I DO NOT BELIEVE IT...
DO NOT BELIEVE WHAT? THAT I WOULD MOURN THE LOSS OF MY BROTHERS AND SISTERS?
BUT YOUR "BROTHERS AND SISTERS" SACRIFICE CHILDREN IN SERVICE OF THE DEVIL! I KNOW THE TRUTH. HOW YOU DRESS AS DEMONS AND FORNICATE AROUND BONFIRES AS PART OF YOUR DARK AUTUMN FEAST. IT IS YOUR FAULT THE LORD HAS PUNISHED US WITH DEATH AND PLAGUES.
HAHAHAHA!
WHAT-- WHAT'S SO FUNNY?
YOU IDIOTS. OUR "DARK AUTUMN FEAST" IS MEANT TO HONOR THE SPIRITS OF THOSE WHO'VE PASSED BEFORE US.
WE BELIEVE IT'S THE ONE NIGHT WHEN THEY'RE PERMITTED TO RETURN, SO WE LIGHT CANDLES AND BONFIRES TO GUIDE THEM.
WE OFFER CROPS AS GIFTS AND DRESS IN GUISES TO PROTECT THEM, AND US, FROM THE TRULY DARK FORCES THAT PROWL THE NIGHT.
AND SACRIFICING CHILDREN?! OUR FIRST RULE IS "DO WHAT THOU WILT BUT DO NO HARM--" WHICH WE SWEAR BY.
CAN YOUR PEOPLE SAY THE SAME?

YOUR BROTHERS INFECT YOU WITH LIES BY ACCUSING US OF THE VERY CRIMES THEY COMMIT.

THEN WHAT IS THE TRUTH?

WE BELIEVE THAT ALL LIFE IS SACRED.

THAT DIVINITY, THE GODS, CAN BE FOUND IN EVERY CORNER OF THE WORLD. BE IT IN OURSELVES, IN OTHERS...

...OR EVEN WITHIN A TINY SEED.

THAT'S A RATHER SMALL PLACE FOR A GOD TO LIVE.

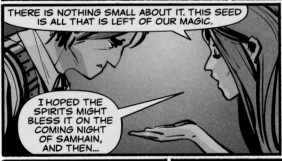

THERE IS NOTHING SMALL ABOUT IT. THIS SEED IS ALL THAT IS LEFT OF OUR MAGIC.

I HOPED THE SPIRITS MIGHT BLESS IT ON THE COMING NIGHT OF SAMHAIN, AND THEN...

AND THEN WHAT?

I WAS TO TAKE IT TO THE NEW WORLD... SO THAT OUR MAGIC, THE OLD WAYS, MIGHT SURVIVE.

I AM MOVED BY YOUR PASSION, BUT MAGIC SEEDS ARE THE STUFF OF FAIRY TALES.

ONE MAN'S FAIRYTALE IS ANOTHER MAN'S RELIGION.

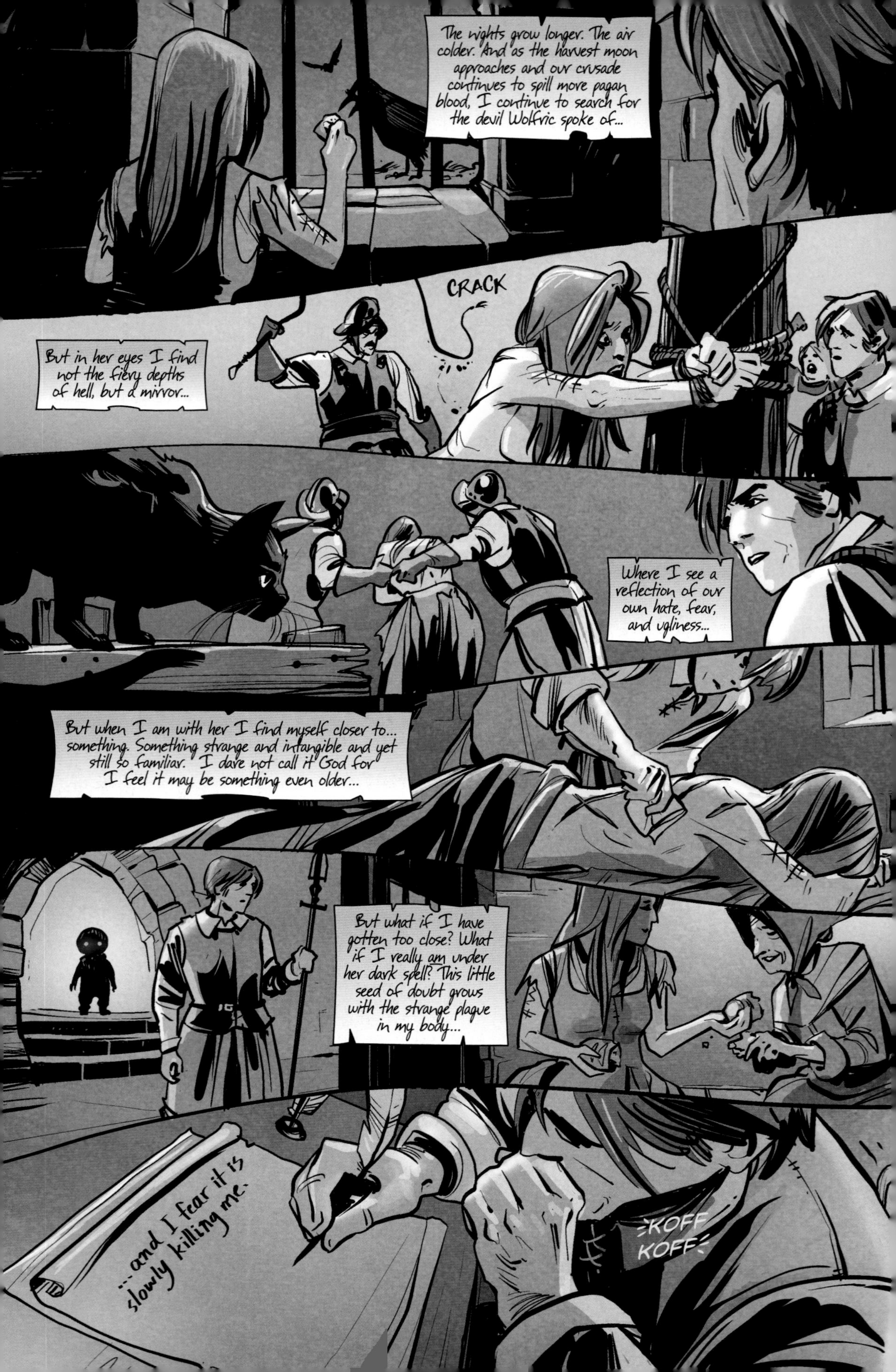
The nights grow longer. The air colder. And as the harvest moon approaches and our crusade continues to spill more pagan blood, I continue to search for the devil Wolfric spoke of...
CRACK
But in her eyes I find not the fiery depths of hell, but a mirror...
Where I see a reflection of our own hate, fear, and ugliness...
But when I am with her I find myself closer to... something. Something strange and intangible and yet still so familiar. I dare not call it God for I feel it may be something even older...
But what if I have gotten too close? What if I really am under her dark spell? This little seed of doubt grows with the strange plague in my body...
...and I fear it is slowly killing me.
KOFF KOFF

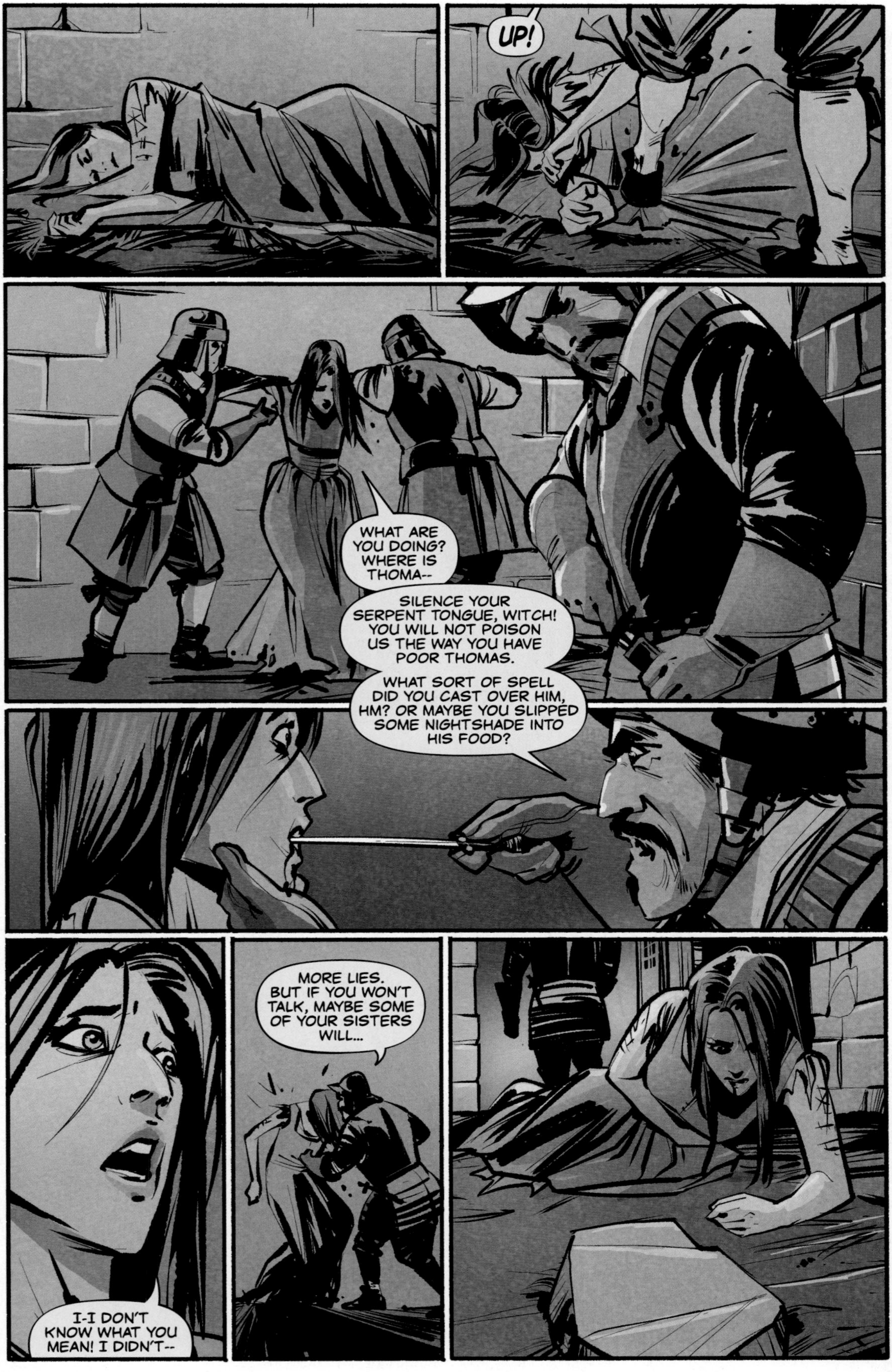
UP!
WHAT ARE YOU DOING? WHERE IS THOMA--
SILENCE YOUR SERPENT TONGUE, WITCH! YOU WILL NOT POISON US THE WAY YOU HAVE POOR THOMAS.
WHAT SORT OF SPELL DID YOU CAST OVER HIM, HM? OR MAYBE YOU SLIPPED SOME NIGHTSHADE INTO HIS FOOD?
I-I DON'T KNOW WHAT YOU MEAN! I DIDN'T--
MORE LIES. BUT IF YOU WON'T TALK, MAYBE SOME OF YOUR SISTERS WILL...

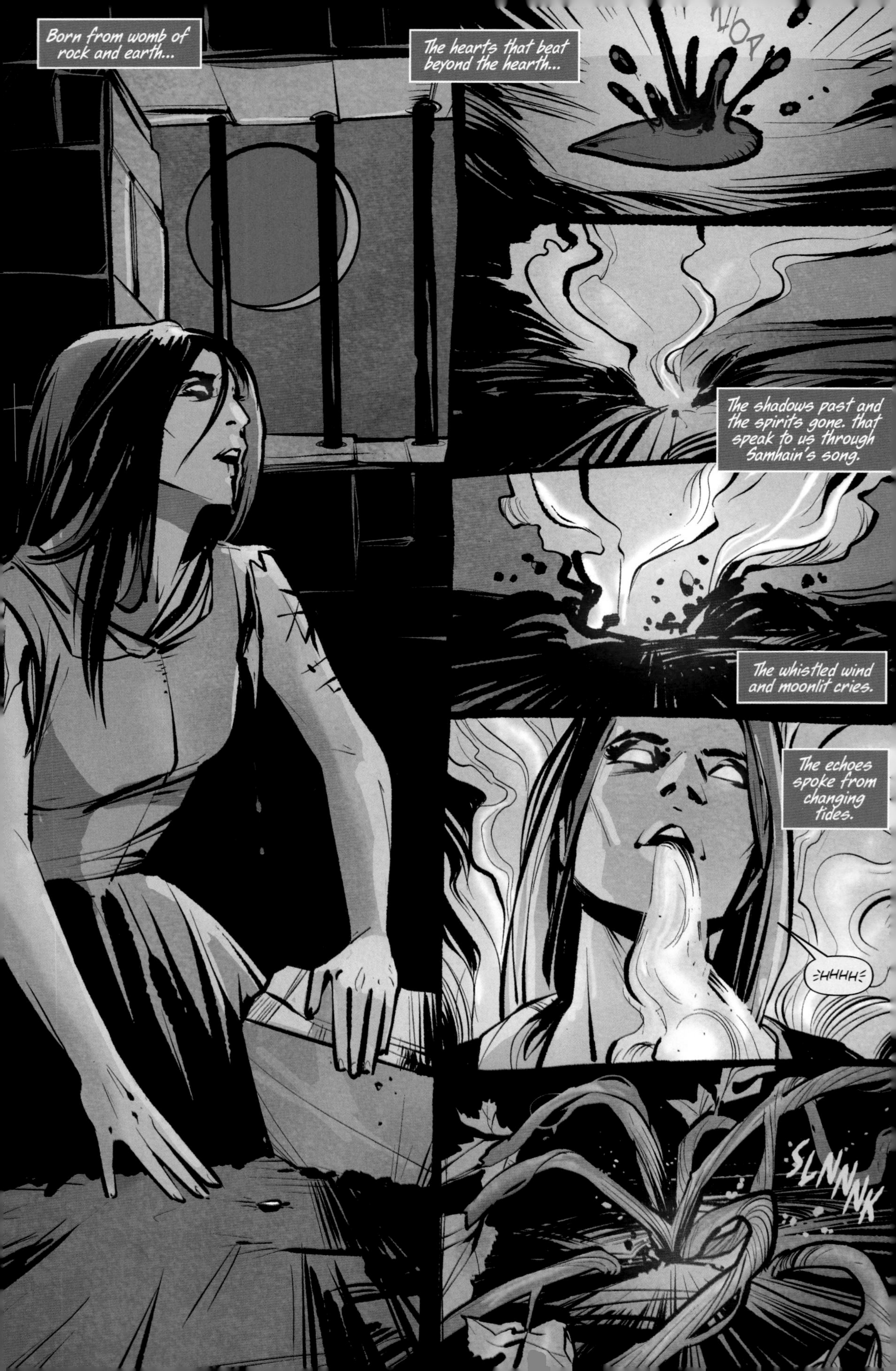

Born from womb of rock and earth...
The hearts that beat beyond the hearth...
The shadows past and the spirits gone. that speak to us through Samhain's song.
The whistled wind and moonlit cries.
The echoes spoke from changing tides.
HHHH
SLNNNK

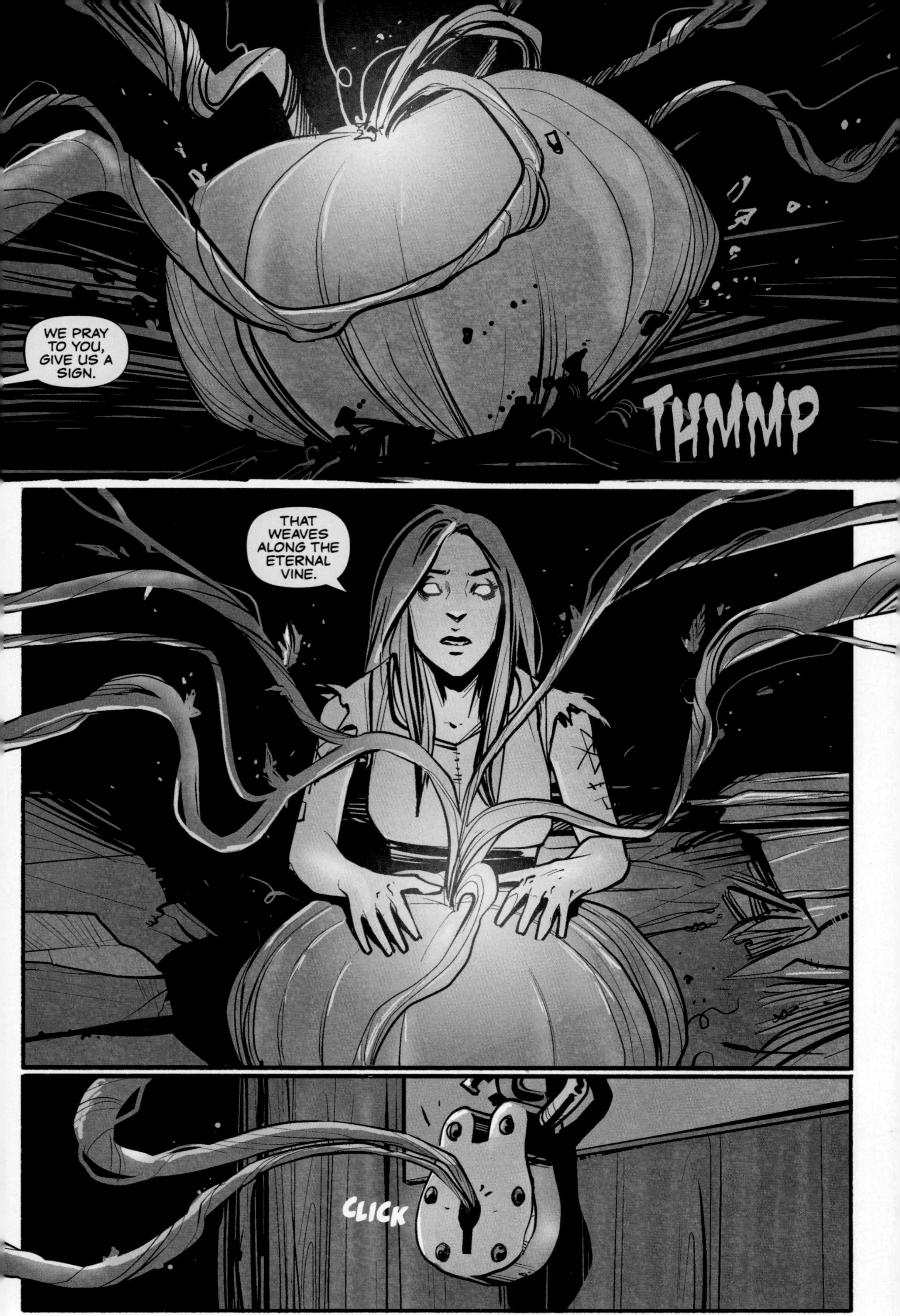
WE PRAY TO YOU, GIVE US A SIGN.
THMMP
THAT WEAVES ALONG THE ETERNAL VINE.
CLICK

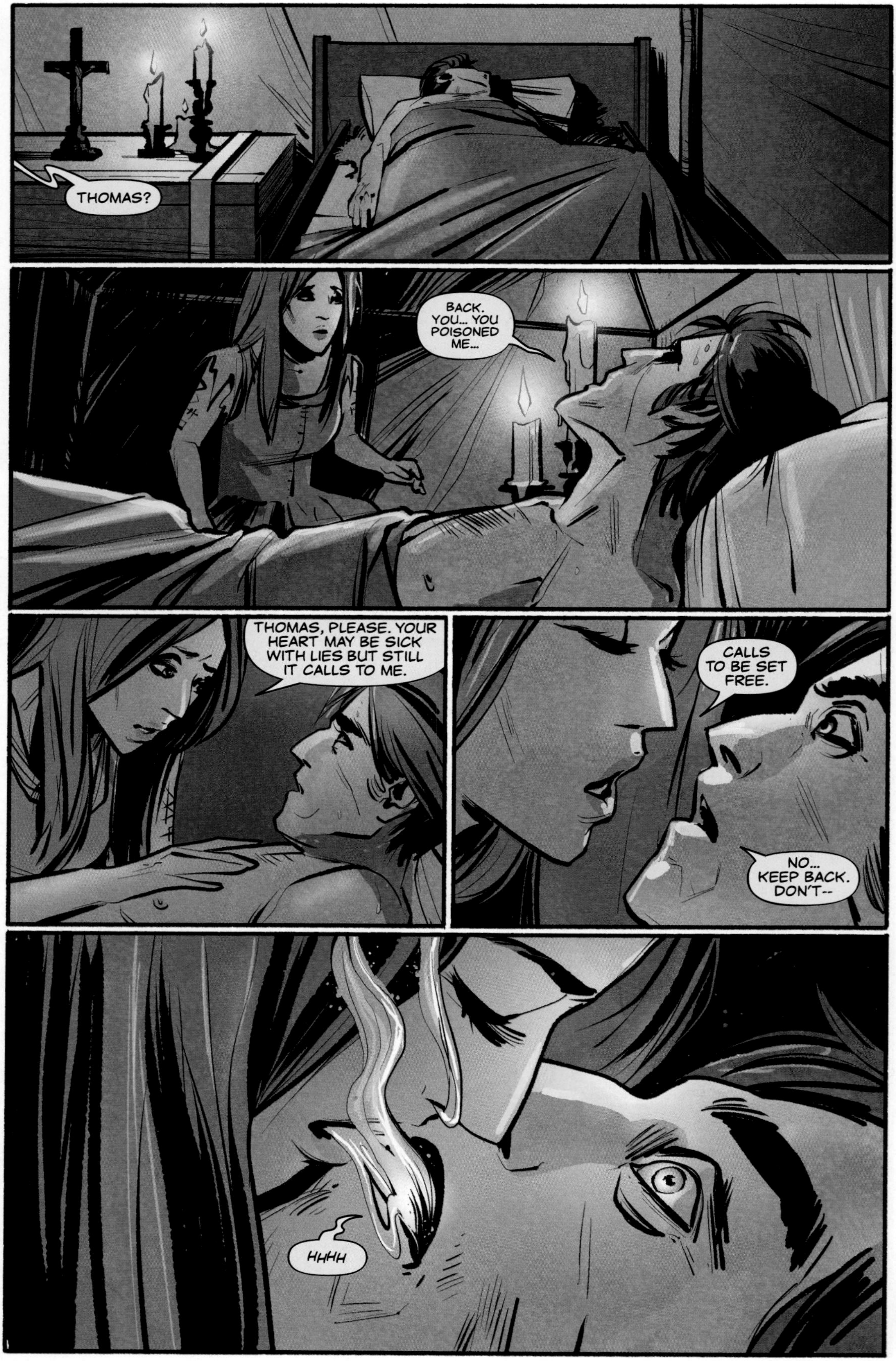
THOMAS?
BACK. YOU... YOU POISONED ME...
THOMAS, PLEASE. YOUR HEART MAY BE SICK WITH LIES BUT STILL IT CALLS TO ME.
CALLS TO BE SET FREE.
NO... KEEP BACK. DON'T--
HHHH

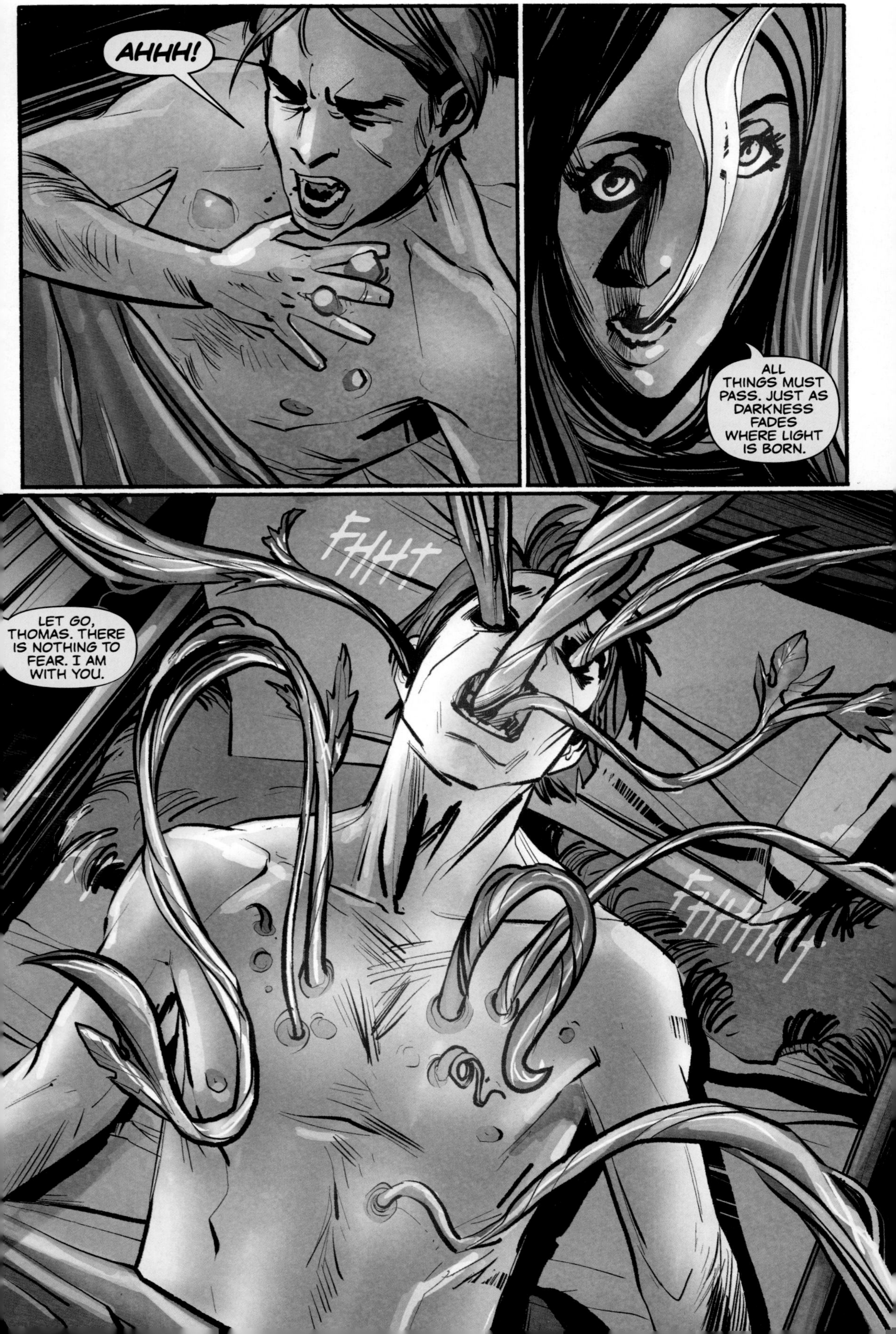
AHHH!
ALL THINGS MUST PASS. JUST AS DARKNESS FADES WHERE LIGHT IS BORN.
FHHT
LET GO, THOMAS. THERE IS NOTHING TO FEAR. I AM WITH YOU.

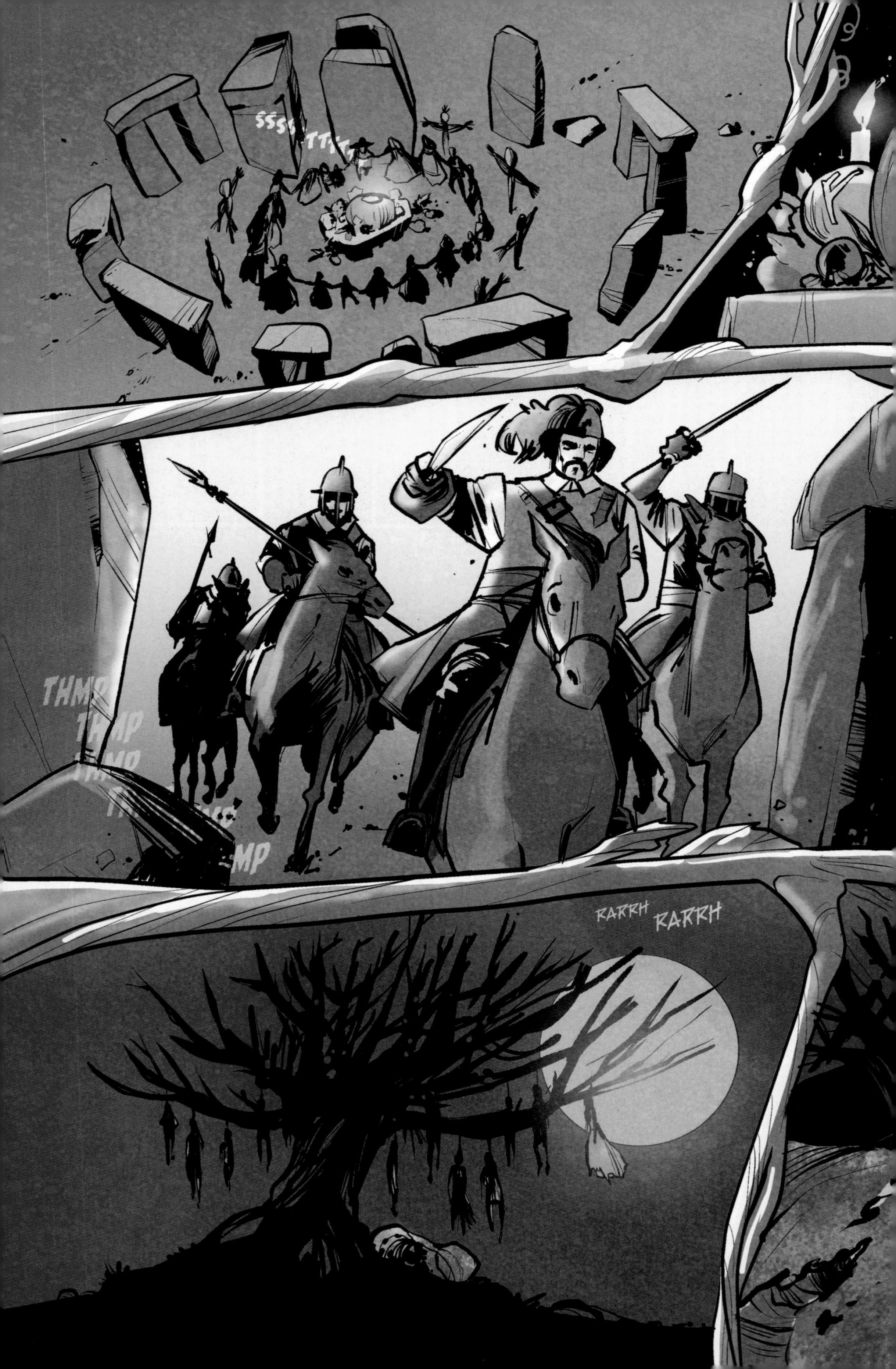
SSSSTTTT
THMP
THMP
THMP
THMP
THMP
RARRH RARRH

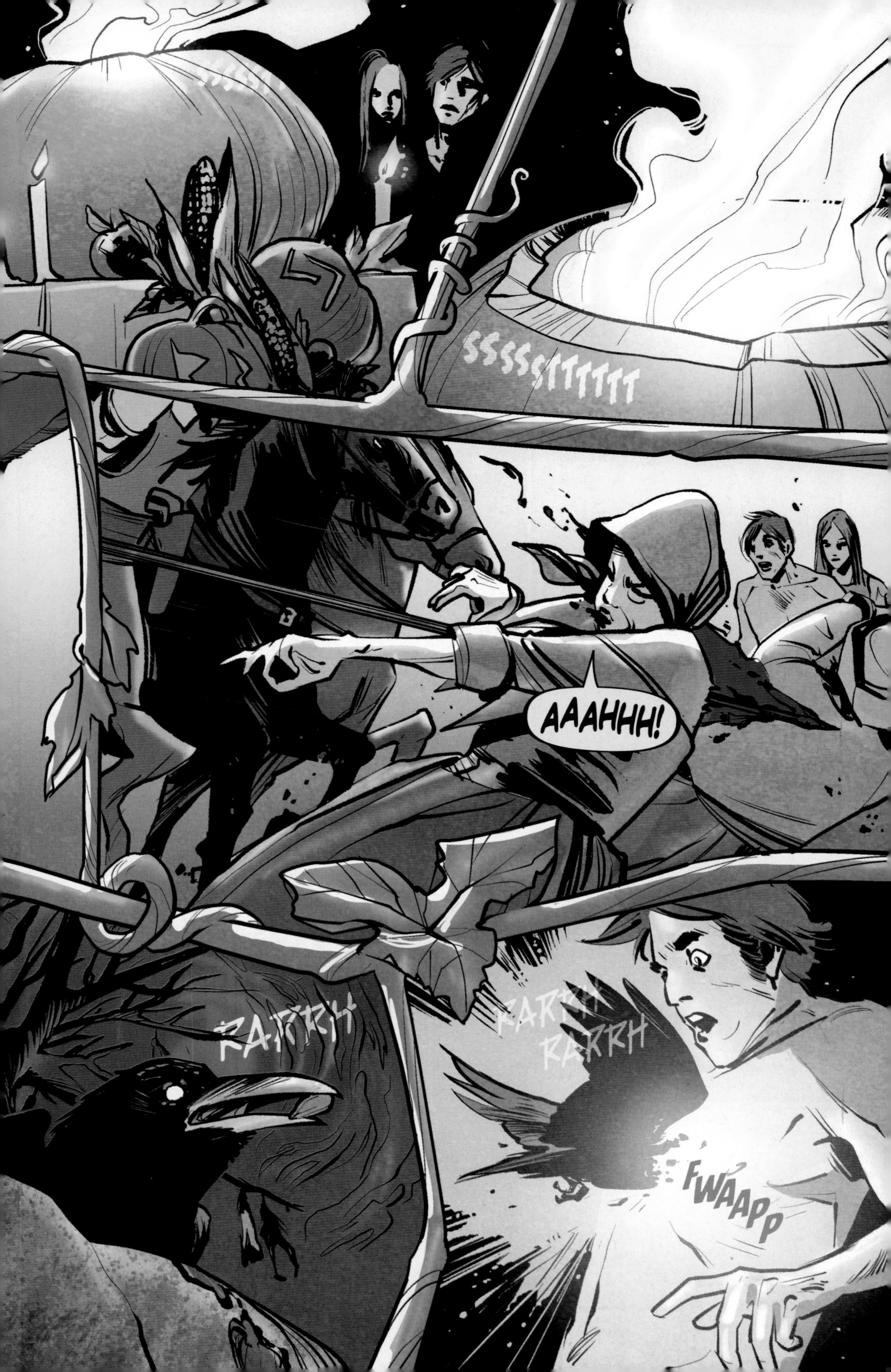
SSSSSIT
SSSSSITTTTTT
AAAHHH!
RARRH
RARRH
RARRH
FWAAPP

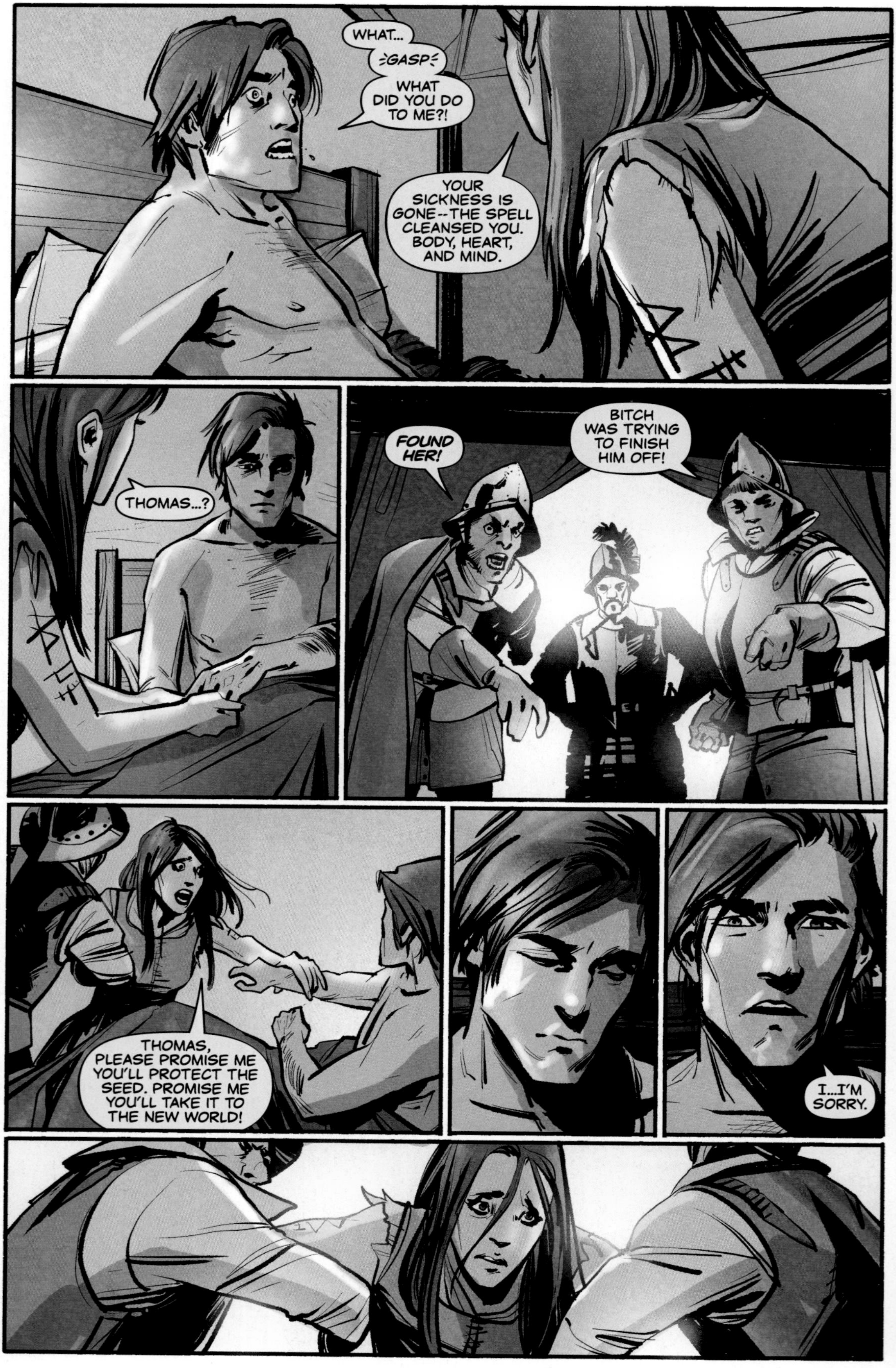
WHAT...
GASP
WHAT DID YOU DO TO ME?!
YOUR SICKNESS IS GONE--THE SPELL CLEANSED YOU. BODY, HEART, AND MIND.
THOMAS...?
FOUND HER!
BITCH WAS TRYING TO FINISH HIM OFF!
THOMAS, PLEASE PROMISE ME YOU'LL PROTECT THE SEED. PROMISE ME YOU'LL TAKE IT TO THE NEW WORLD!
I...I'M SORRY.

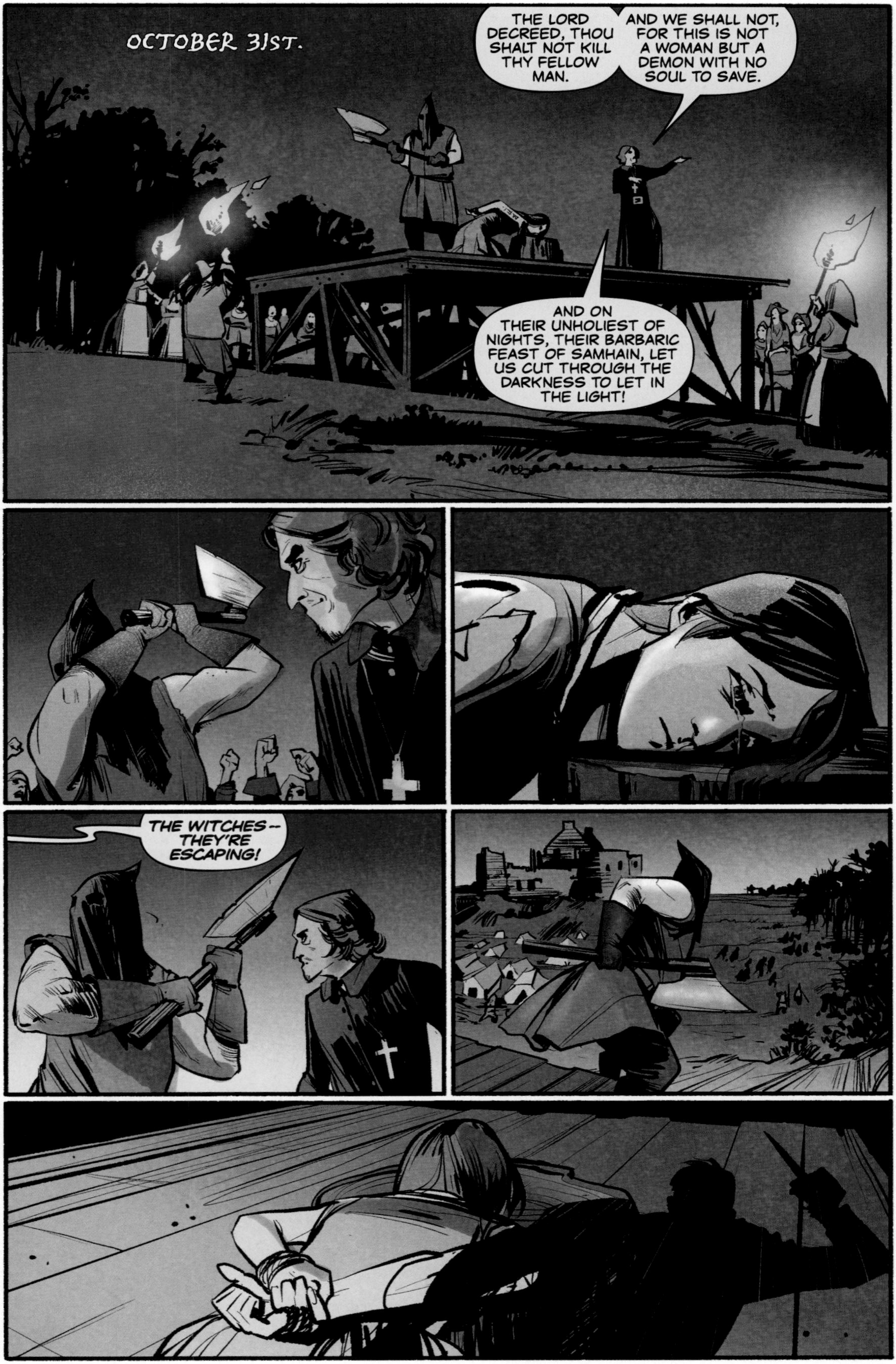
OCTOBER 31ST.
THE LORD DECREED, THOU SHALT NOT KILL THY FELLOW MAN.
AND WE SHALL NOT, FOR THIS IS NOT A WOMAN BUT A DEMON WITH NO SOUL TO SAVE.
AND ON THEIR UNHOLIEST OF NIGHTS, THEIR BARBARIC FEAST OF SAMHAIN, LET US CUT THROUGH THE DARKNESS TO LET IN THE LIGHT!
THE WITCHES-- THEY'RE ESCAPING!

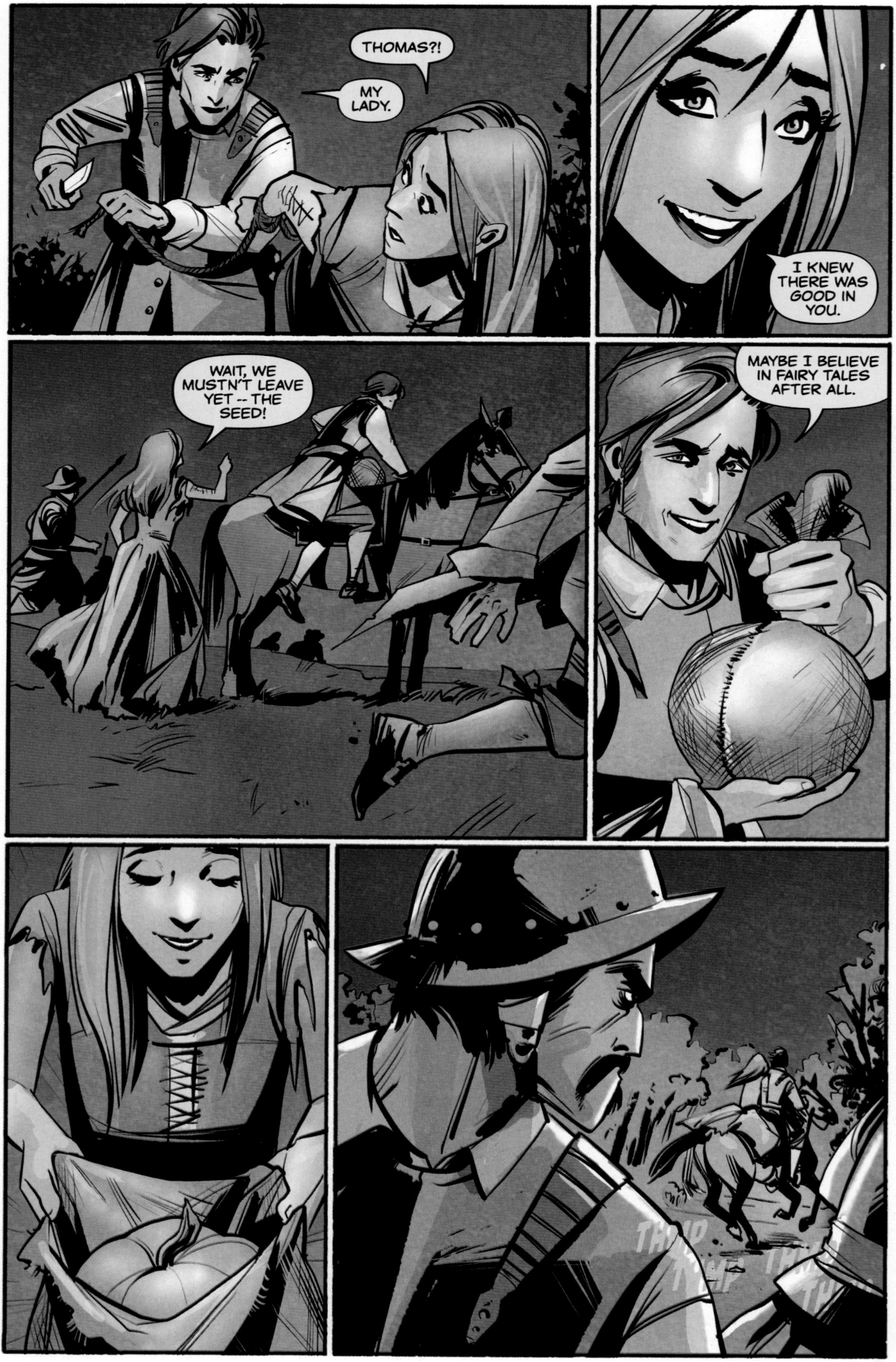
THOMAS?!
MY LADY.
I KNEW THERE WAS GOOD IN YOU.
WAIT, WE MUSTN'T LEAVE YET -- THE SEED!
MAYBE I BELIEVE IN FAIRY TALES AFTER ALL.

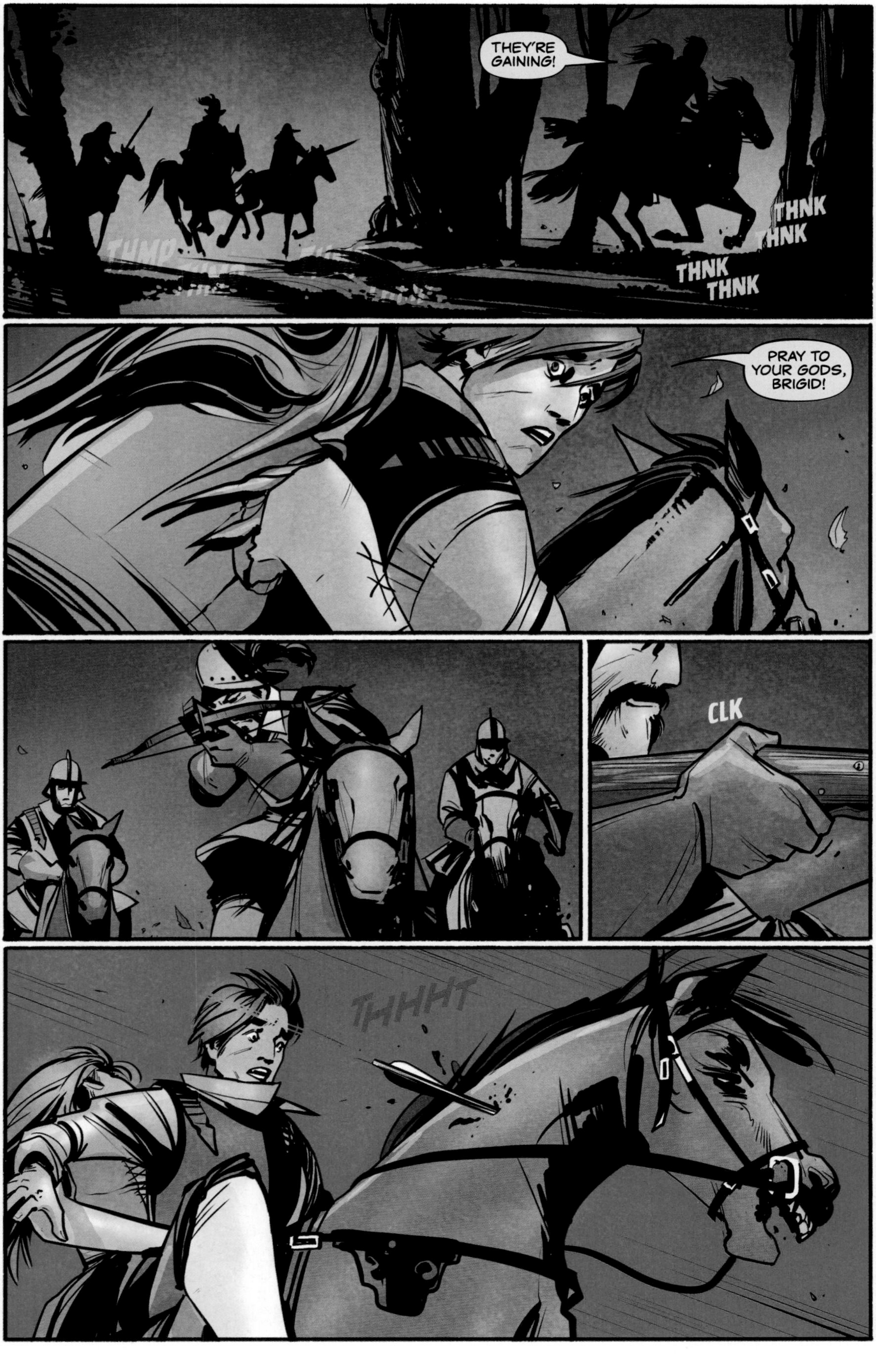
THEY'RE GAINING!
THMP
THNK
THNK
THNK
THNK
PRAY TO YOUR GODS, BRIGID!
CLK
THHHT

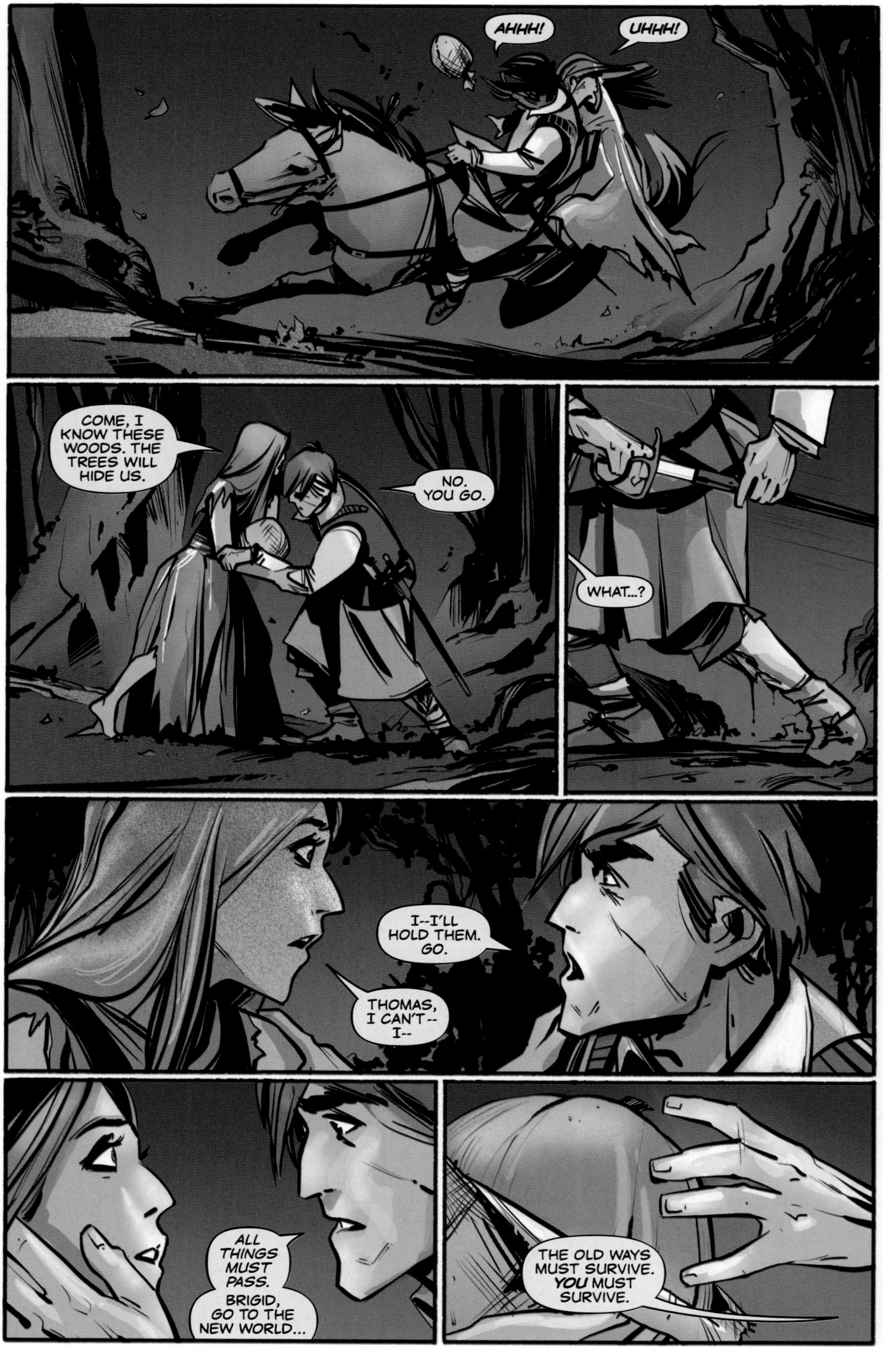
AHHH!
UHHH!
COME, I KNOW THESE WOODS. THE TREES WILL HIDE US.
NO. YOU GO.
WHAT...?
I--I'LL HOLD THEM. GO.
THOMAS, I CAN'T-- I--
ALL THINGS MUST PASS.
BRIGID, GO TO THE NEW WORLD...
THE OLD WAYS MUST SURVIVE. *YOU* MUST SURVIVE.

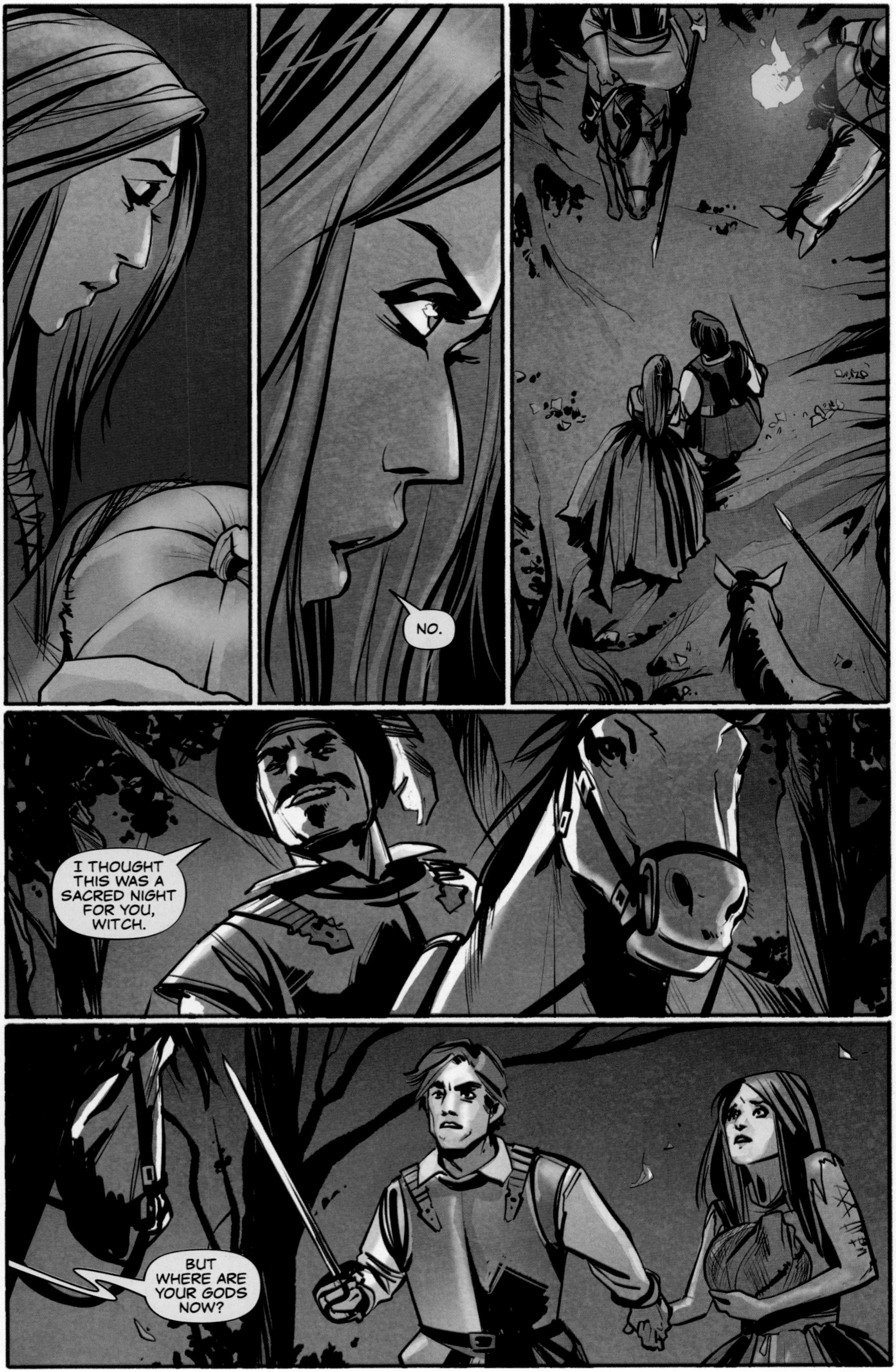
NO.
I THOUGHT THIS WAS A SACRED NIGHT FOR YOU, WITCH.
BUT WHERE ARE YOUR GODS NOW?

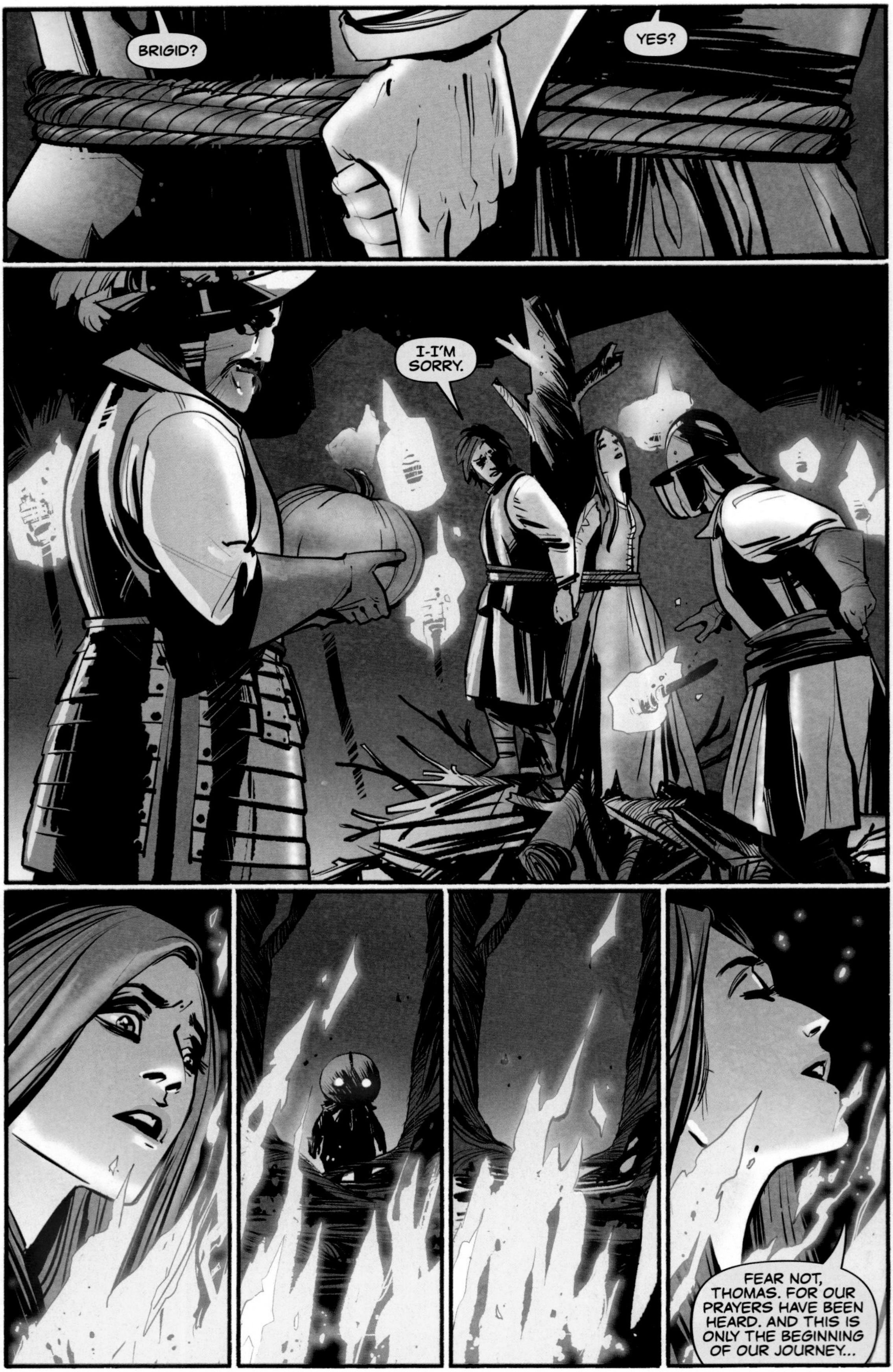
BRIGID?
YES?
I-I'M SORRY.
FEAR NOT, THOMAS. FOR OUR PRAYERS HAVE BEEN HEARD. AND THIS IS ONLY THE BEGINNING OF OUR JOURNEY...

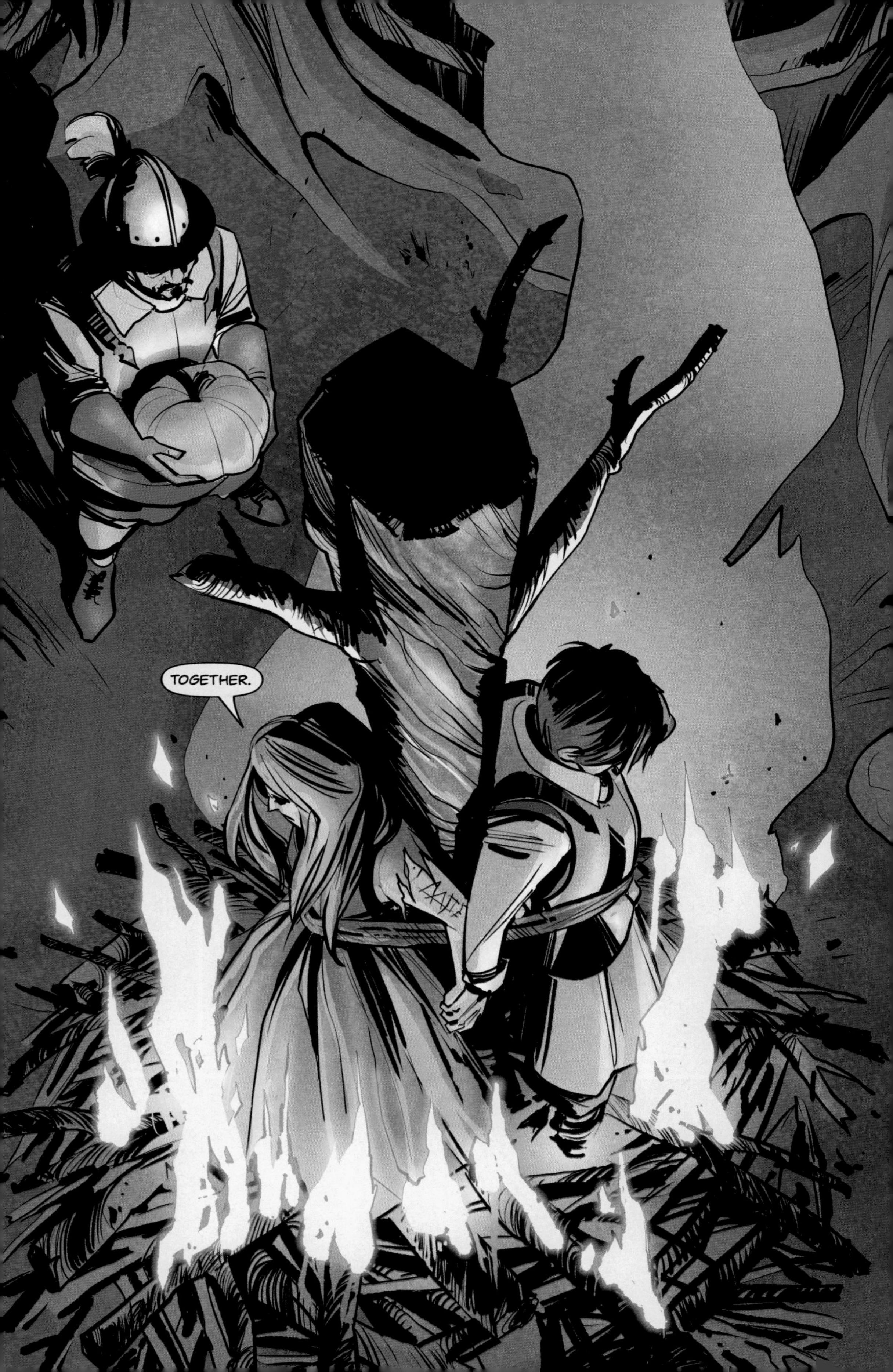
TOGETHER.

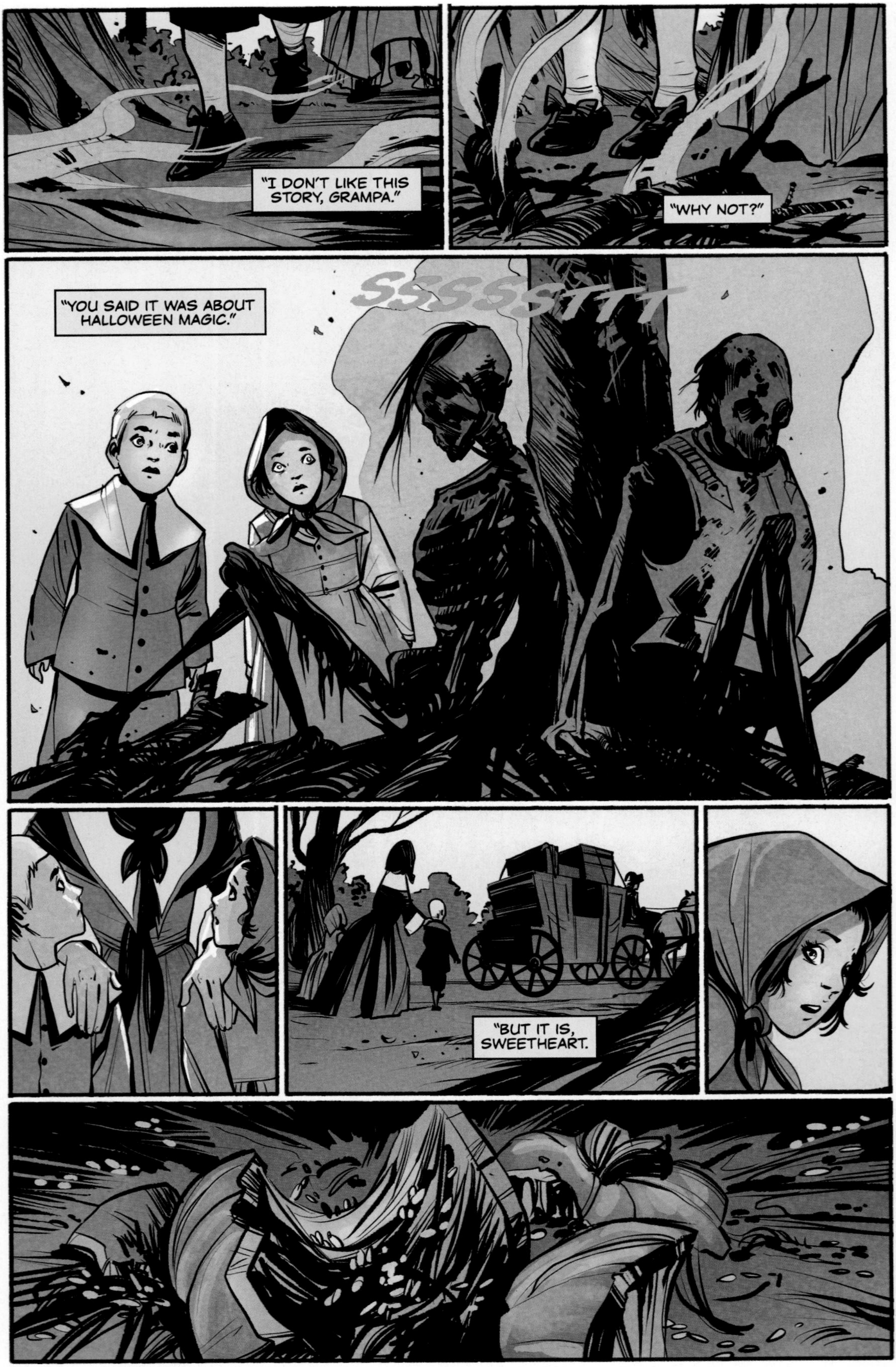
"I DON'T LIKE THIS STORY, GRAMPA."
"WHY NOT?"
"YOU SAID IT WAS ABOUT HALLOWEEN MAGIC."
SSSSSTTT
"BUT IT IS, SWEETHEART.

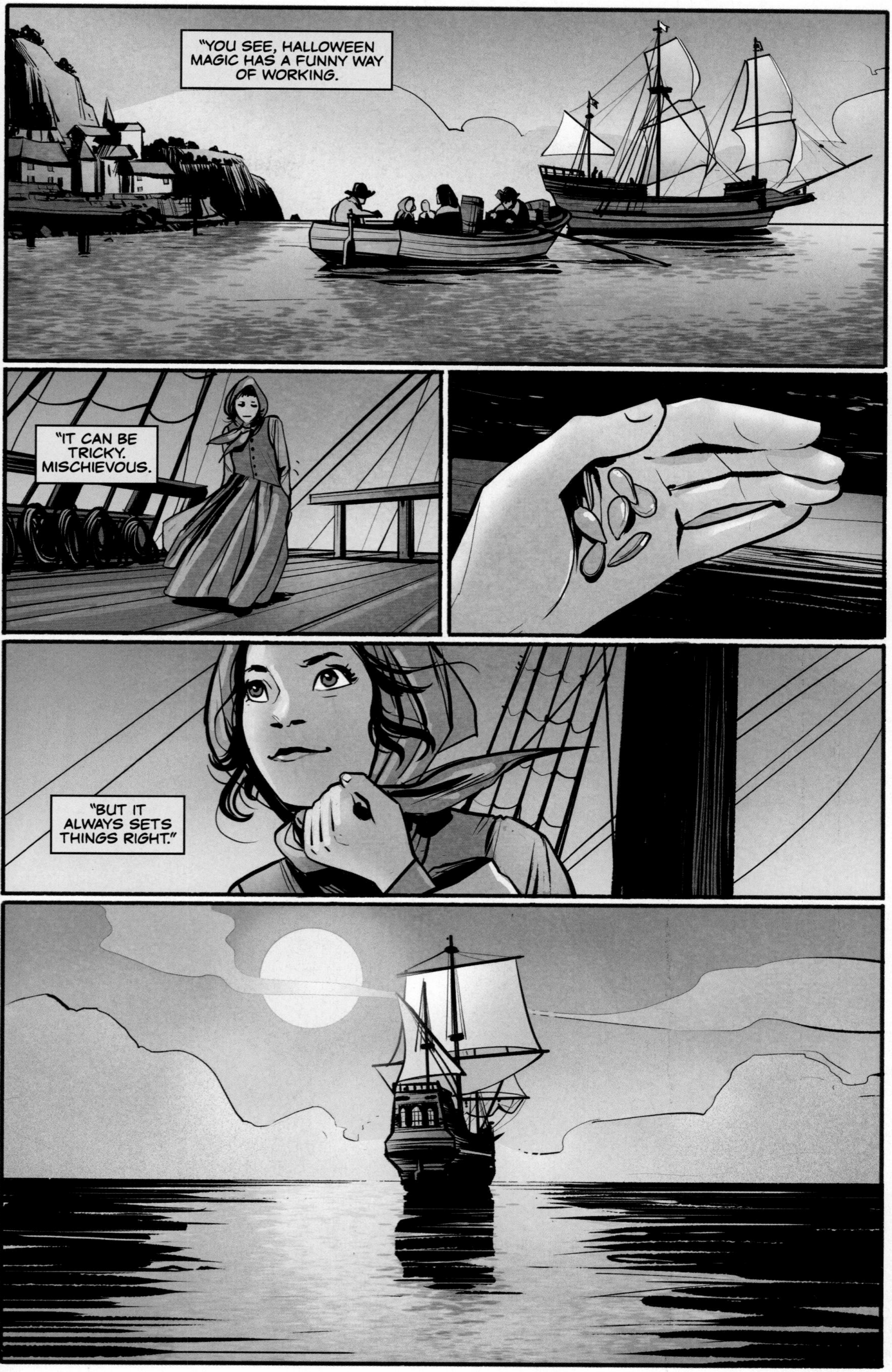
"YOU SEE, HALLOWEEN MAGIC HAS A FUNNY WAY OF WORKING.
"IT CAN BE TRICKY. MISCHIEVOUS.
"BUT IT ALWAYS SETS THINGS RIGHT."

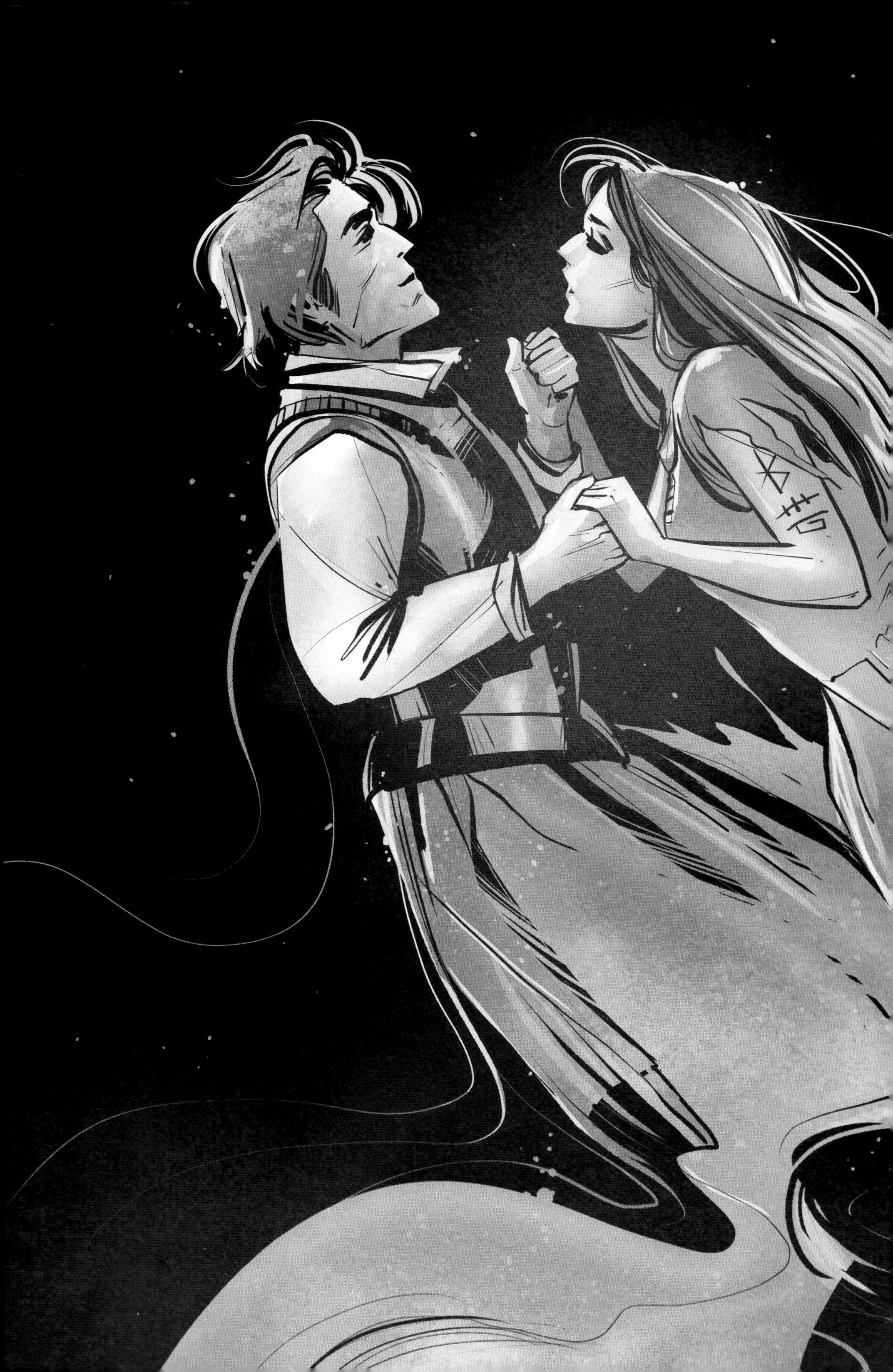

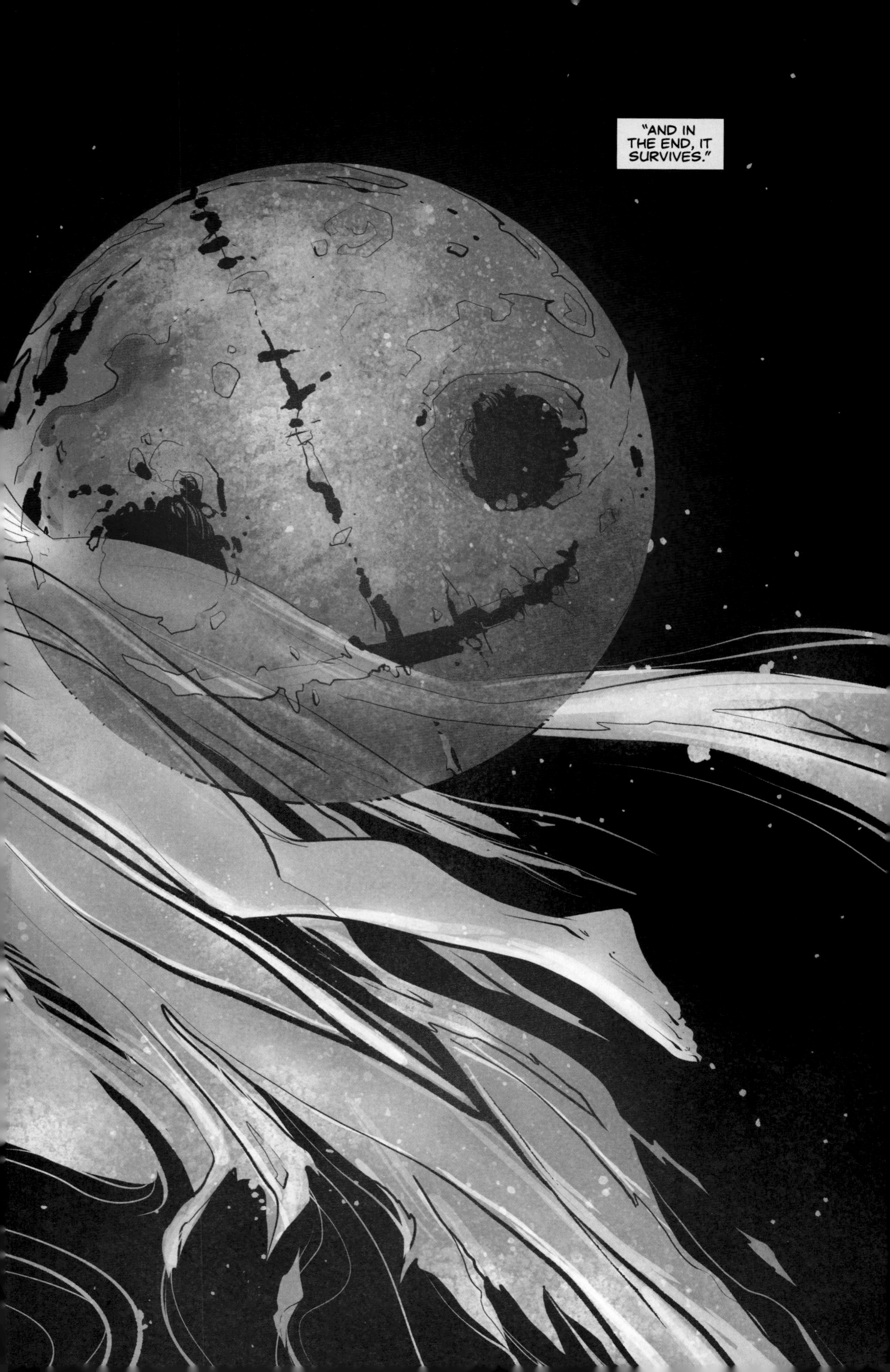
"AND IN THE END, IT SURVIVES."

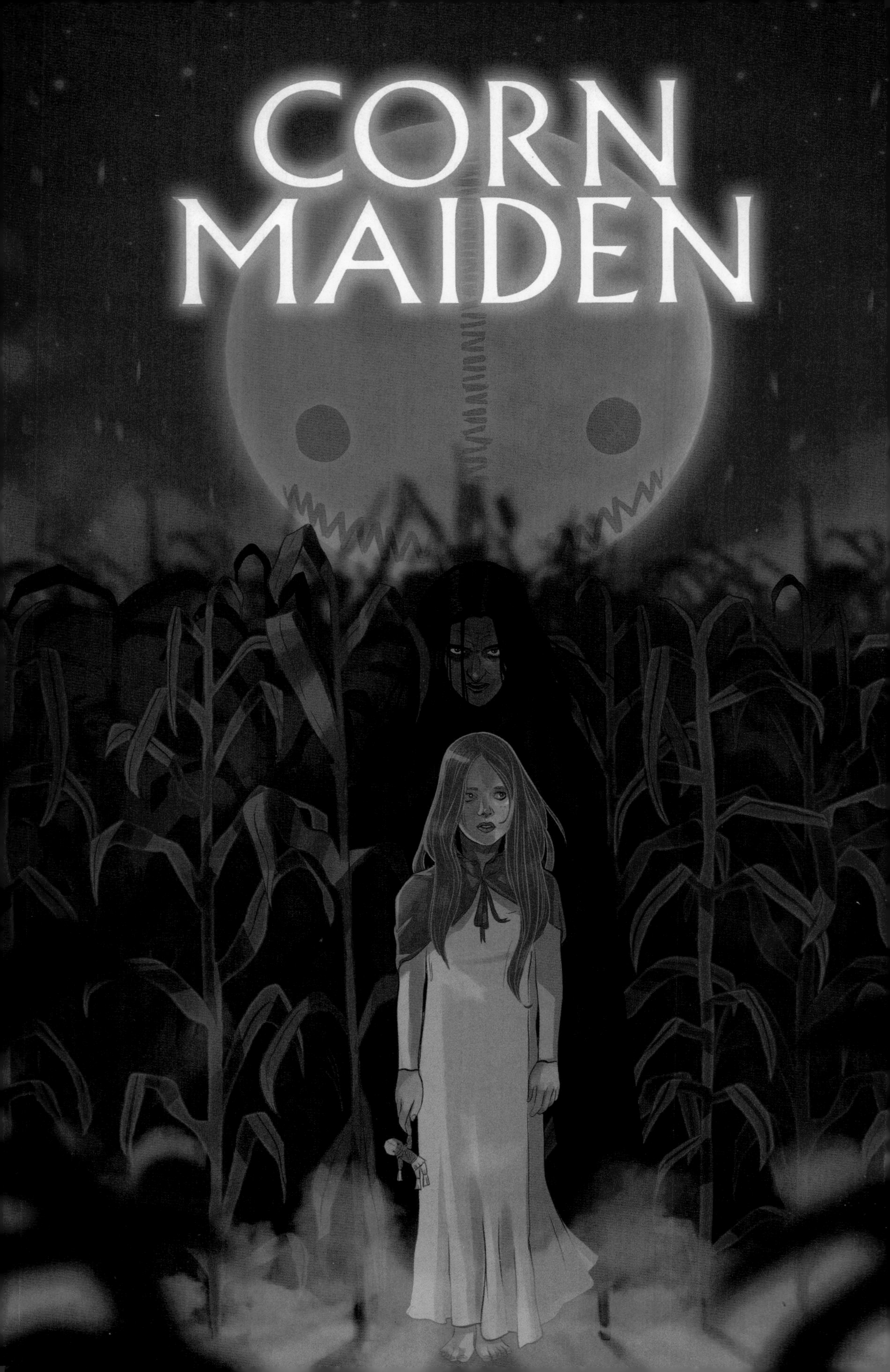
CORN
MAIDEN

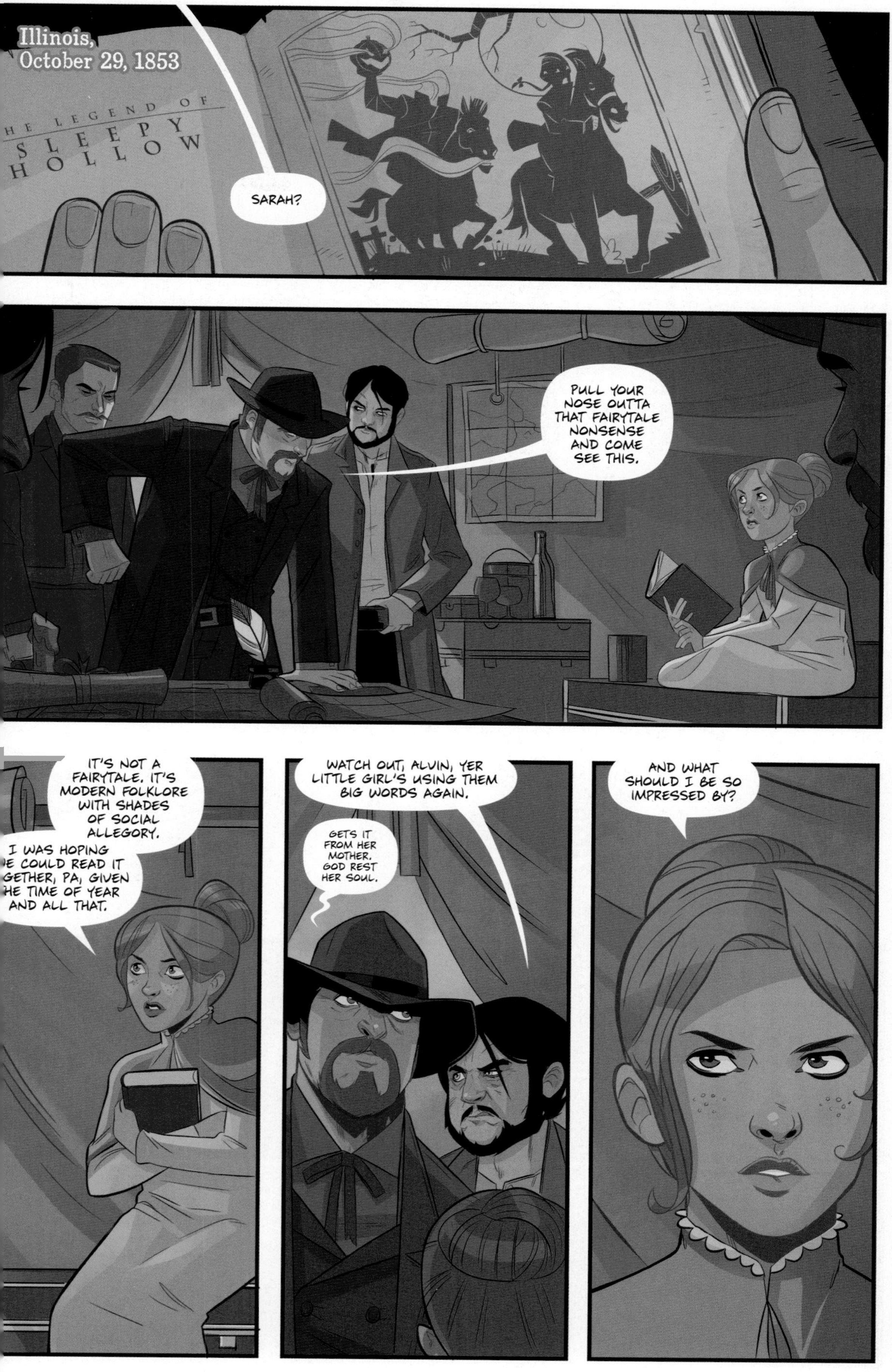
Illinois, October 29, 1853
HE LEGEND OF SLEEPY HOLLOW
SARAH?
PULL YOUR NOSE OUTTA THAT FAIRYTALE NONSENSE AND COME SEE THIS.
IT'S NOT A FAIRYTALE. IT'S MODERN FOLKLORE WITH SHADES OF SOCIAL ALLEGORY.
I WAS HOPING E COULD READ IT GETHER, PA, GIVEN HE TIME OF YEAR AND ALL THAT.
WATCH OUT, ALVIN, YER LITTLE GIRL'S USING THEM BIG WORDS AGAIN.
GETS IT FROM HER MOTHER. GOD REST HER SOUL.
AND WHAT SHOULD I BE SO IMPRESSED BY?

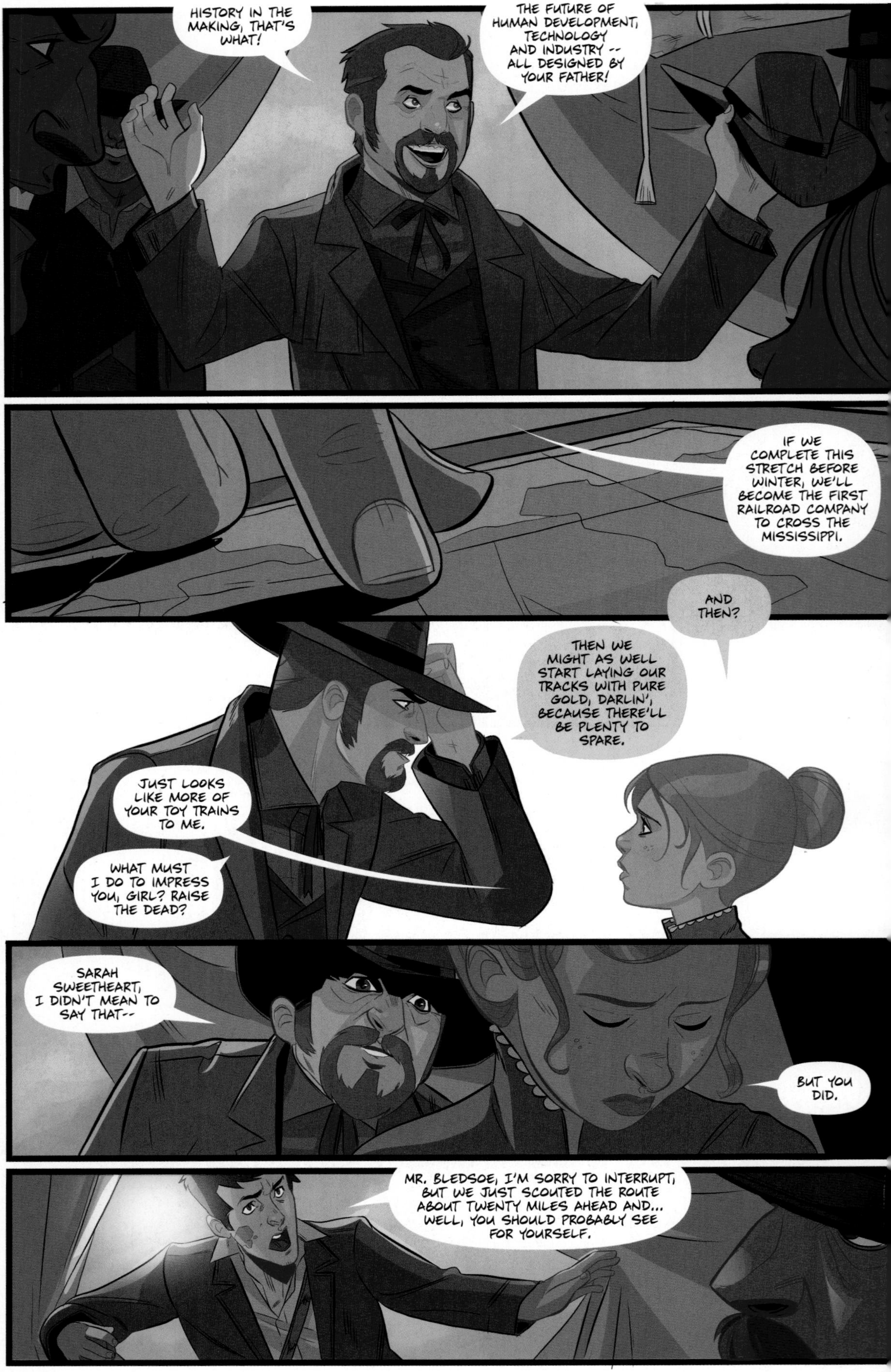
HISTORY IN THE MAKING, THAT'S WHAT!
THE FUTURE OF HUMAN DEVELOPMENT, TECHNOLOGY AND INDUSTRY -- ALL DESIGNED BY YOUR FATHER!
IF WE COMPLETE THIS STRETCH BEFORE WINTER, WE'LL BECOME THE FIRST RAILROAD COMPANY TO CROSS THE MISSISSIPPI.
AND THEN?
THEN WE MIGHT AS WELL START LAYING OUR TRACKS WITH PURE GOLD, DARLIN', BECAUSE THERE'LL BE PLENTY TO SPARE.
JUST LOOKS LIKE MORE OF YOUR TOY TRAINS TO ME.
WHAT MUST I DO TO IMPRESS YOU, GIRL? RAISE THE DEAD?
SARAH SWEETHEART, I DIDN'T MEAN TO SAY THAT--
BUT YOU DID.
MR. BLEDSOE, I'M SORRY TO INTERRUPT, BUT WE JUST SCOUTED THE ROUTE ABOUT TWENTY MILES AHEAD AND... WELL, YOU SHOULD PROBABLY SEE FOR YOURSELF.

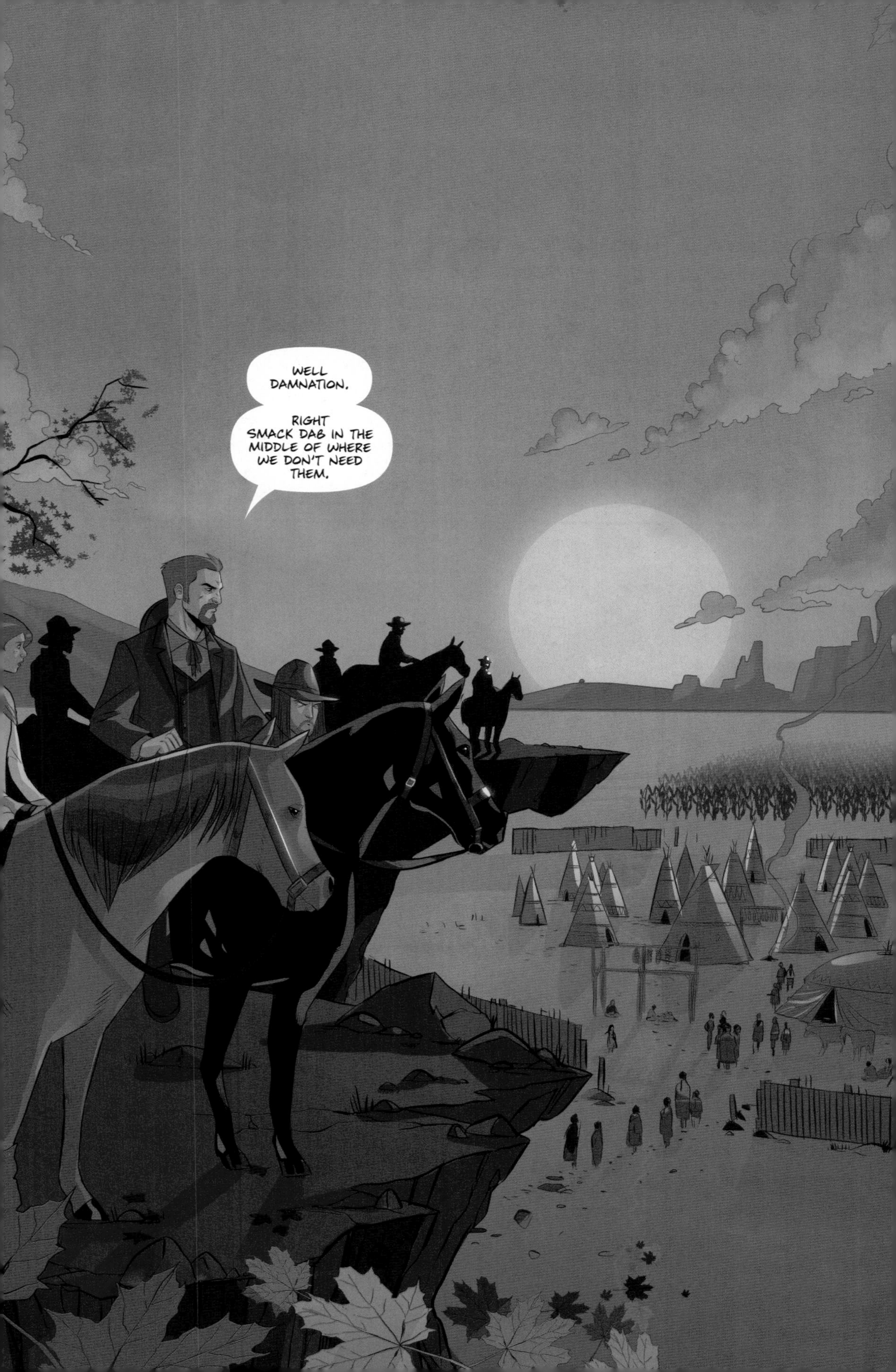
WELL DAMNATION.
RIGHT SMACK DAB IN THE MIDDLE OF WHERE WE DON'T NEED THEM.

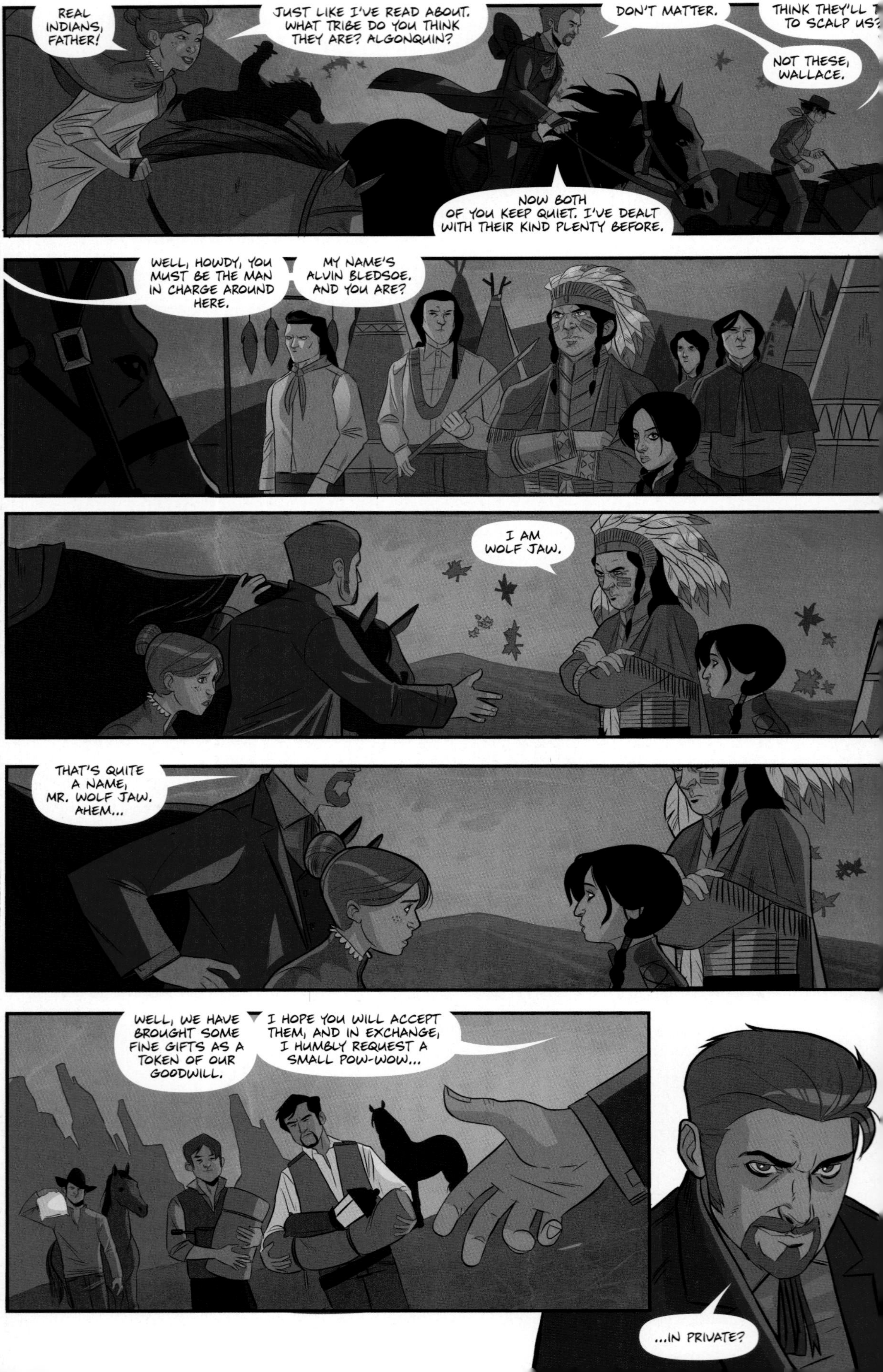
REAL INDIANS, FATHER!
JUST LIKE I'VE READ ABOUT. WHAT TRIBE DO YOU THINK THEY ARE? ALGONQUIN?
DON'T MATTER.
THINK THEY'LL
TO SCALP US?
NOT THESE, WALLACE.
NOW BOTH OF YOU KEEP QUIET. I'VE DEALT WITH THEIR KIND PLENTY BEFORE.
WELL, HOWDY, YOU MUST BE THE MAN IN CHARGE AROUND HERE.
MY NAME'S ALVIN BLEDSOE. AND YOU ARE?
I AM WOLF JAW.
THAT'S QUITE A NAME, MR. WOLF JAW. AHEM...
WELL, WE HAVE BROUGHT SOME FINE GIFTS AS A TOKEN OF OUR GOODWILL.
I HOPE YOU WILL ACCEPT THEM, AND IN EXCHANGE, I HUMBLY REQUEST A SMALL POW-WOW...
...IN PRIVATE?

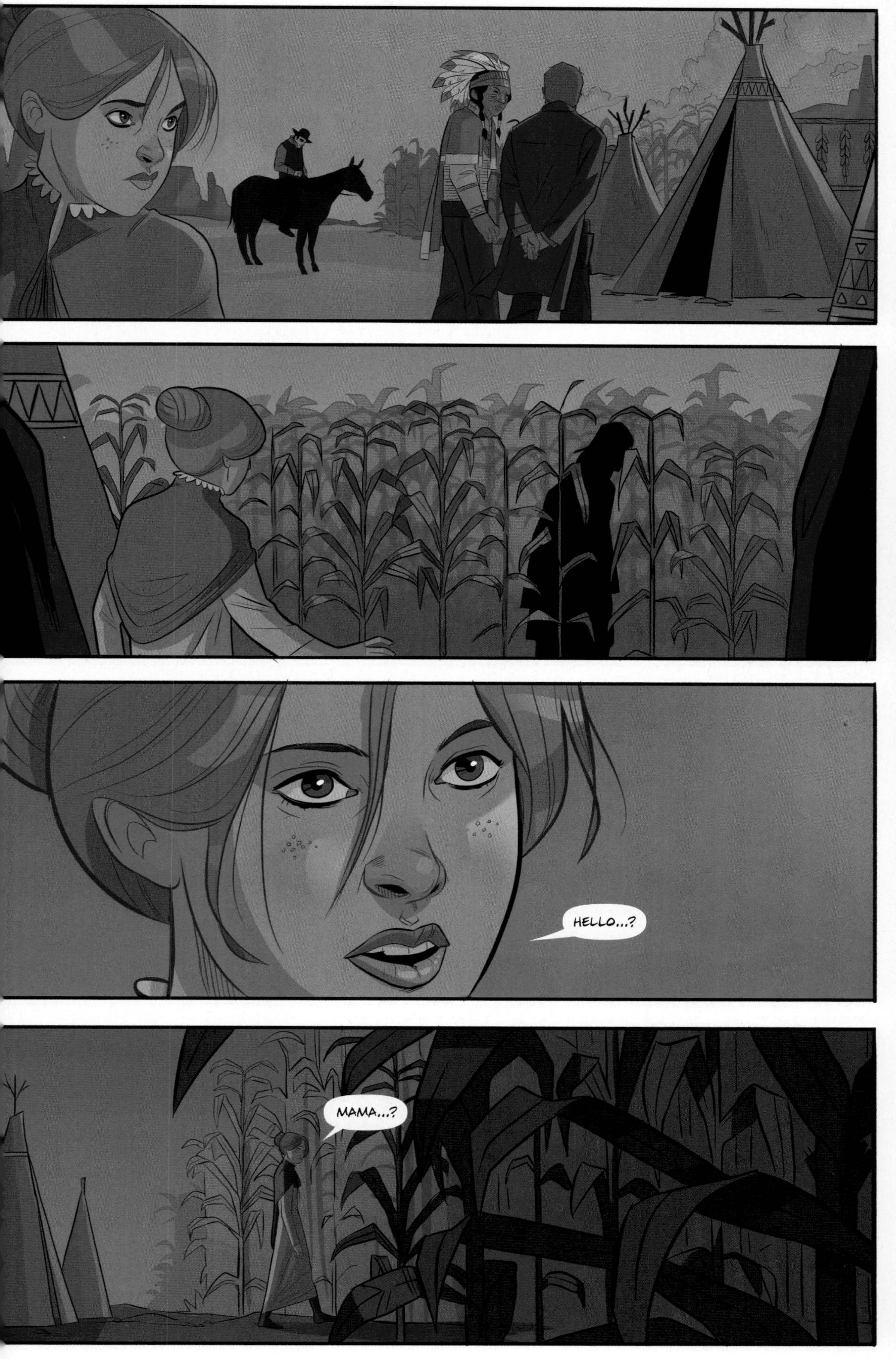
HELLO...?
MAMA...?

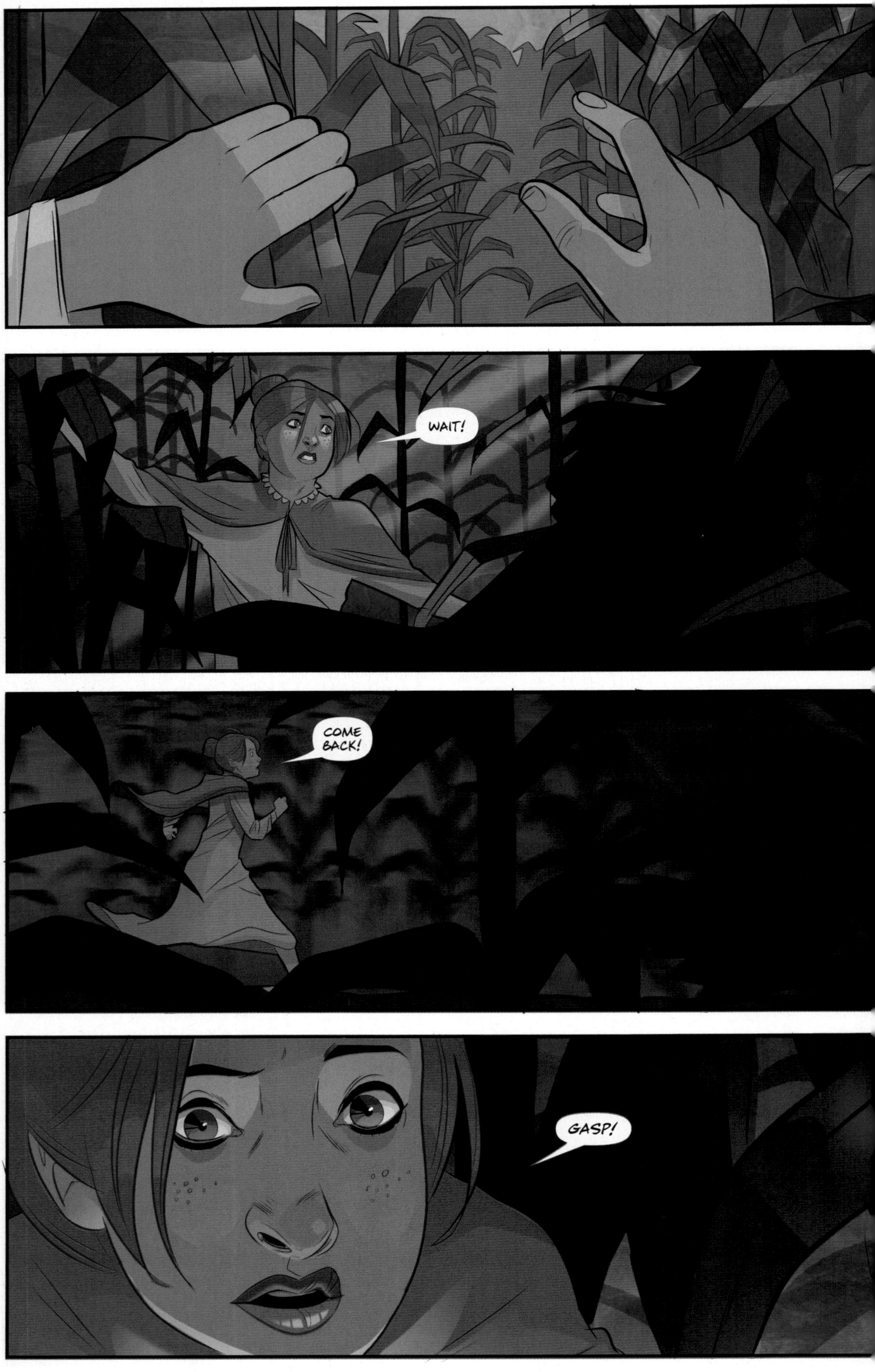
WAIT!
COME BACK!
GASP!

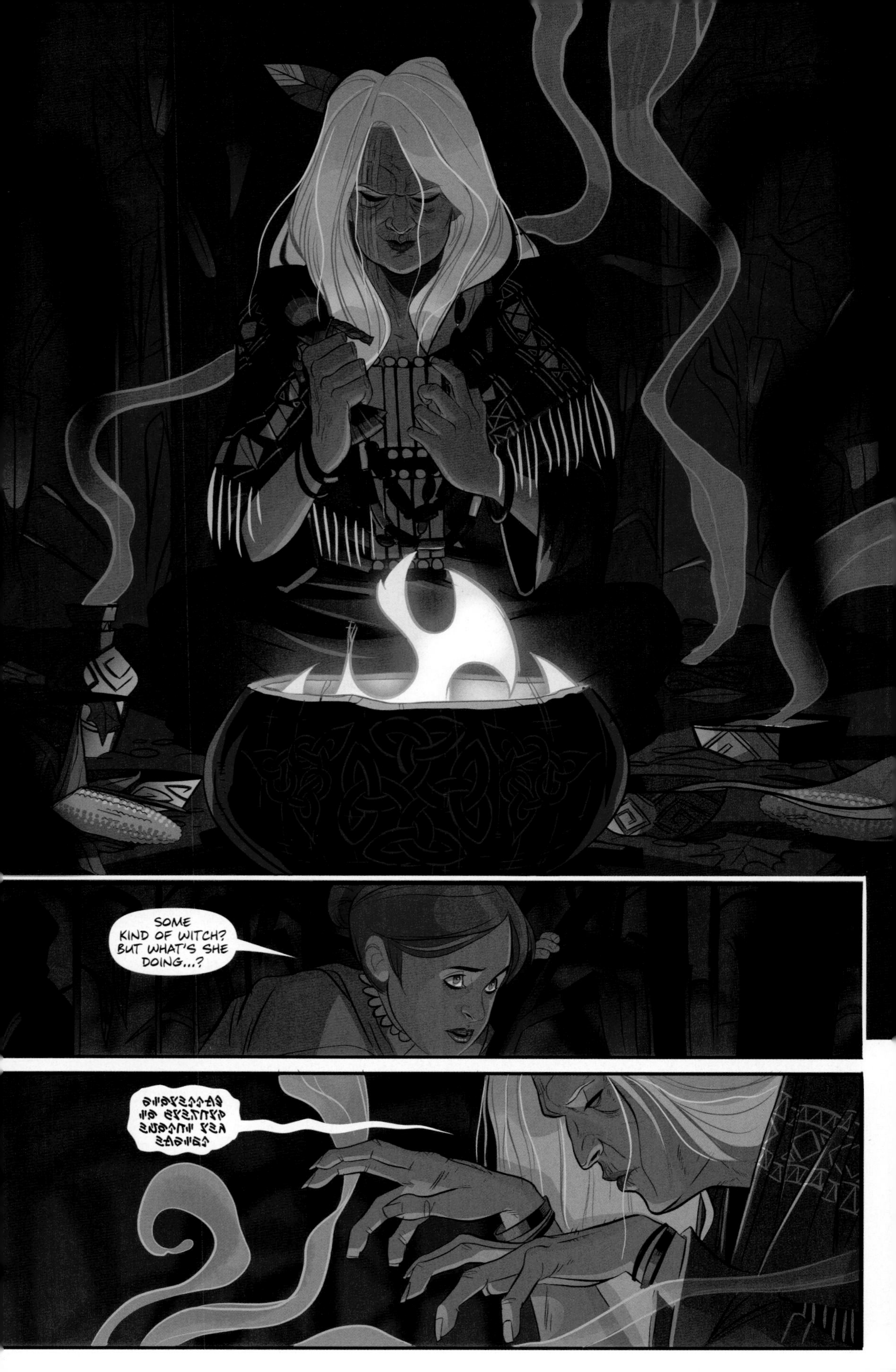
SOME KIND OF WITCH? BUT WHAT'S SHE DOING...?

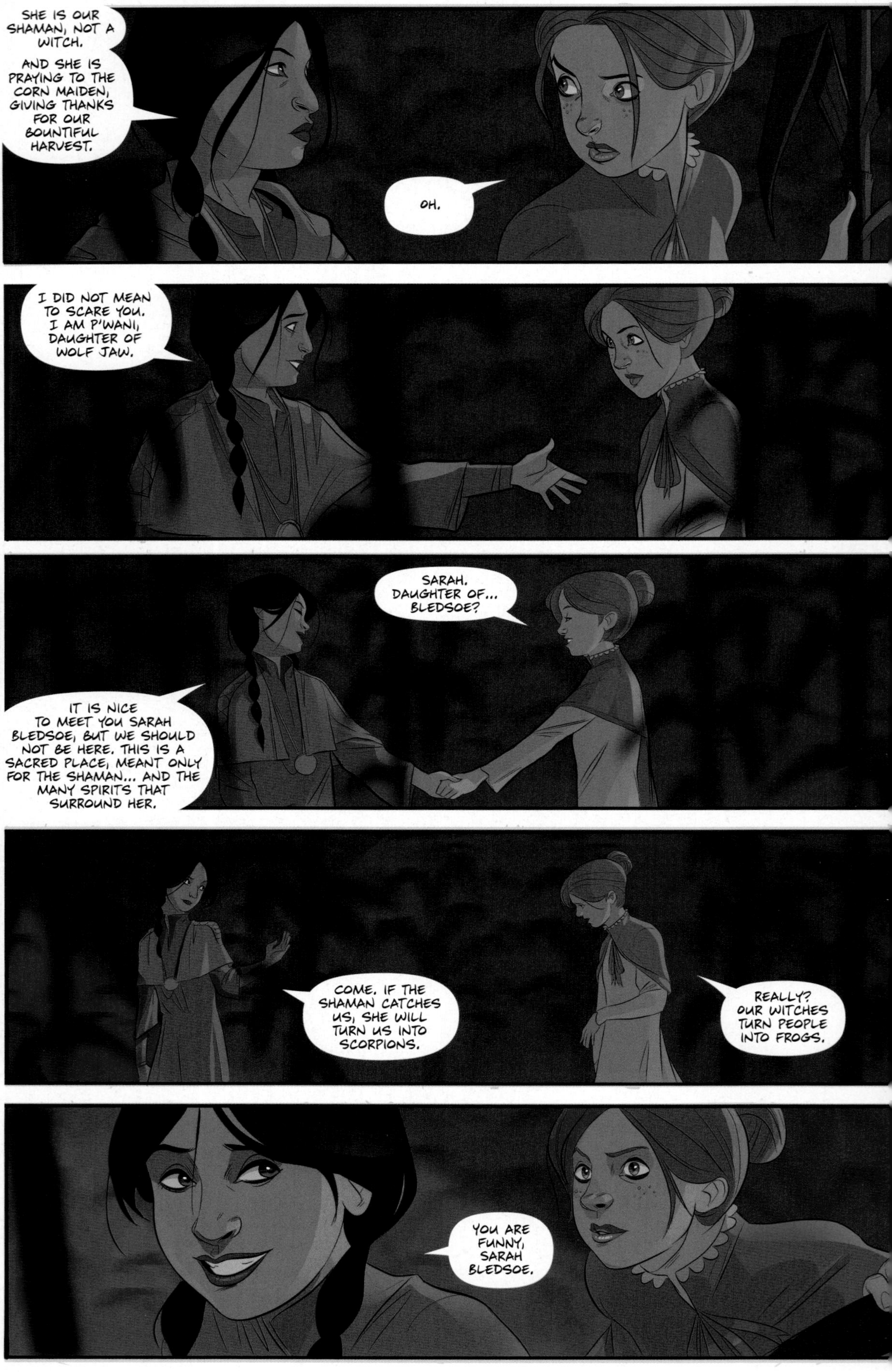
SHE IS OUR SHAMAN, NOT A WITCH.
AND SHE IS PRAYING TO THE CORN MAIDEN, GIVING THANKS FOR OUR BOUNTIFUL HARVEST.
OH.
I DID NOT MEAN TO SCARE YOU. I AM P'WANI, DAUGHTER OF WOLF JAW.
SARAH. DAUGHTER OF... BLEDSOE?
IT IS NICE TO MEET YOU SARAH BLEDSOE, BUT WE SHOULD NOT BE HERE. THIS IS A SACRED PLACE, MEANT ONLY FOR THE SHAMAN... AND THE MANY SPIRITS THAT SURROUND HER.
COME. IF THE SHAMAN CATCHES US, SHE WILL TURN US INTO SCORPIONS.
REALLY? OUR WITCHES TURN PEOPLE INTO FROGS.
YOU ARE FUNNY, SARAH BLEDSOE.

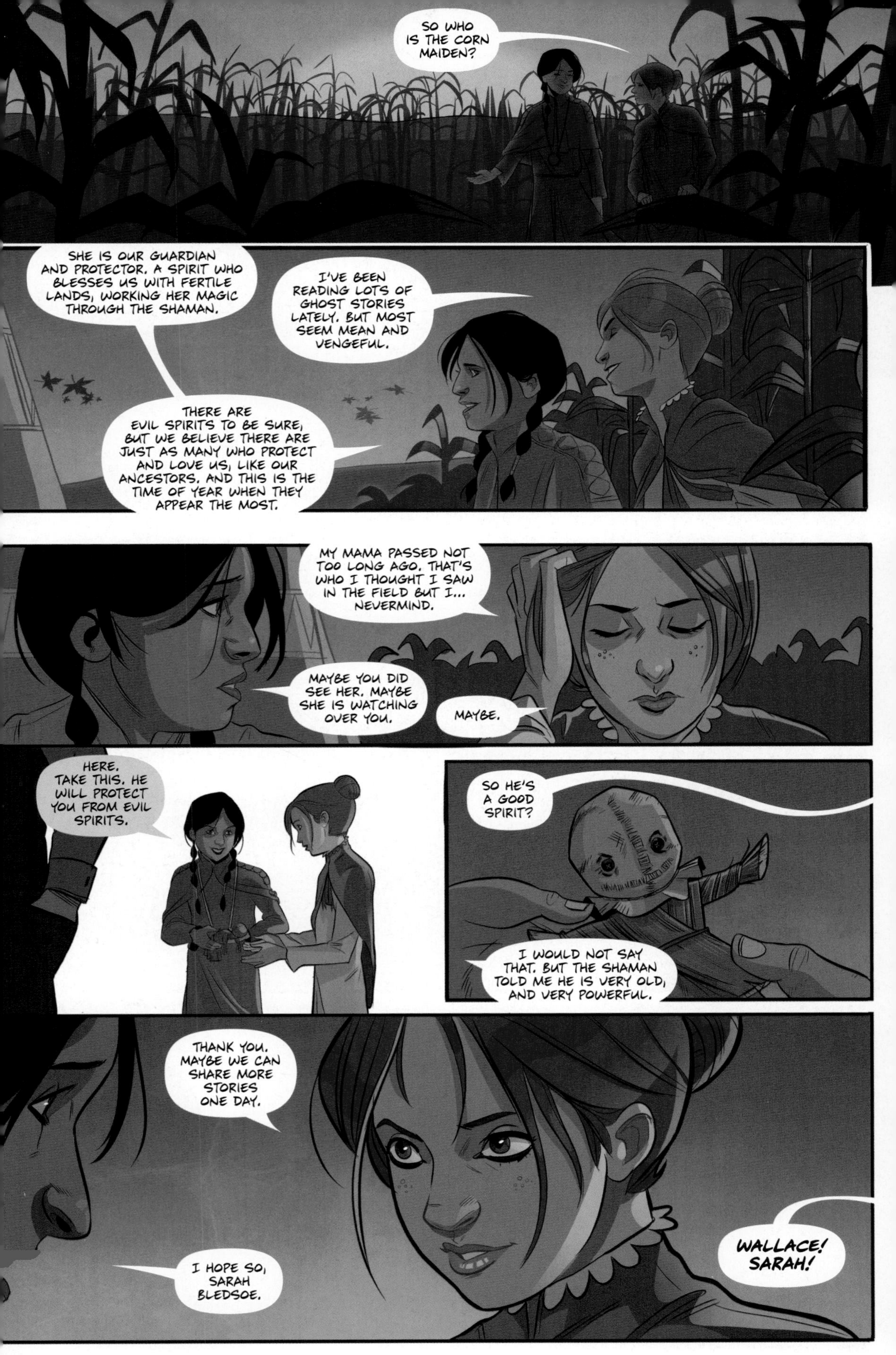
SO WHO IS THE CORN MAIDEN?
SHE IS OUR GUARDIAN AND PROTECTOR. A SPIRIT WHO BLESSES US WITH FERTILE LANDS, WORKING HER MAGIC THROUGH THE SHAMAN.
I'VE BEEN READING LOTS OF GHOST STORIES LATELY. BUT MOST SEEM MEAN AND VENGEFUL.
THERE ARE EVIL SPIRITS TO BE SURE, BUT WE BELIEVE THERE ARE JUST AS MANY WHO PROTECT AND LOVE US, LIKE OUR ANCESTORS. AND THIS IS THE TIME OF YEAR WHEN THEY APPEAR THE MOST.
MY MAMA PASSED NOT TOO LONG AGO. THAT'S WHO I THOUGHT I SAW IN THE FIELD BUT I... NEVERMIND.
MAYBE YOU DID SEE HER. MAYBE SHE IS WATCHING OVER YOU.
MAYBE.
HERE. TAKE THIS. HE WILL PROTECT YOU FROM EVIL SPIRITS.
SO HE'S A GOOD SPIRIT?
I WOULD NOT SAY THAT. BUT THE SHAMAN TOLD ME HE IS VERY OLD, AND VERY POWERFUL.
THANK YOU. MAYBE WE CAN SHARE MORE STORIES ONE DAY.
I HOPE SO, SARAH BLEDSOE.
WALLACE! SARAH!

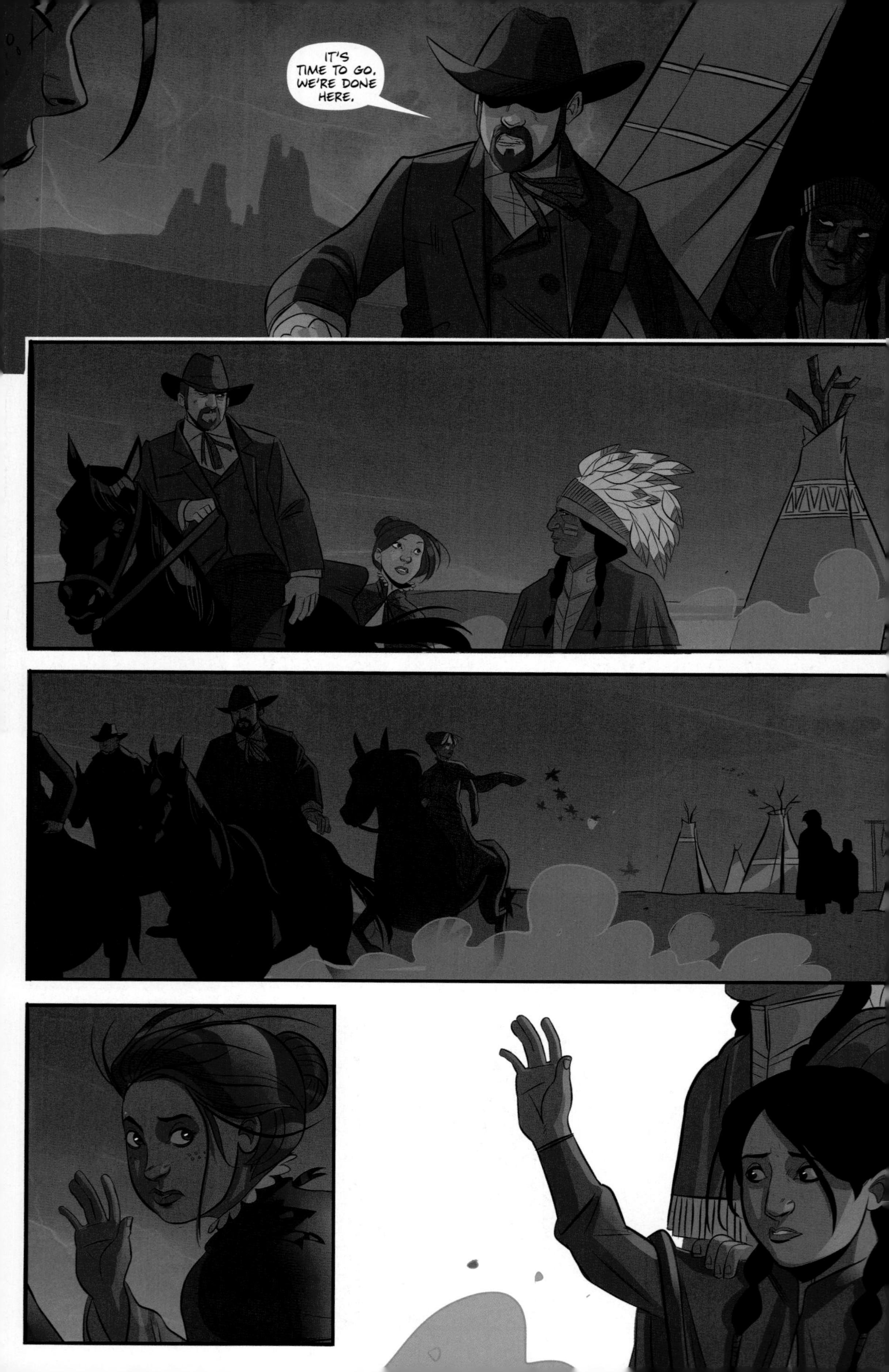
IT'S
TIME TO GO.
WE'RE DONE
HERE.

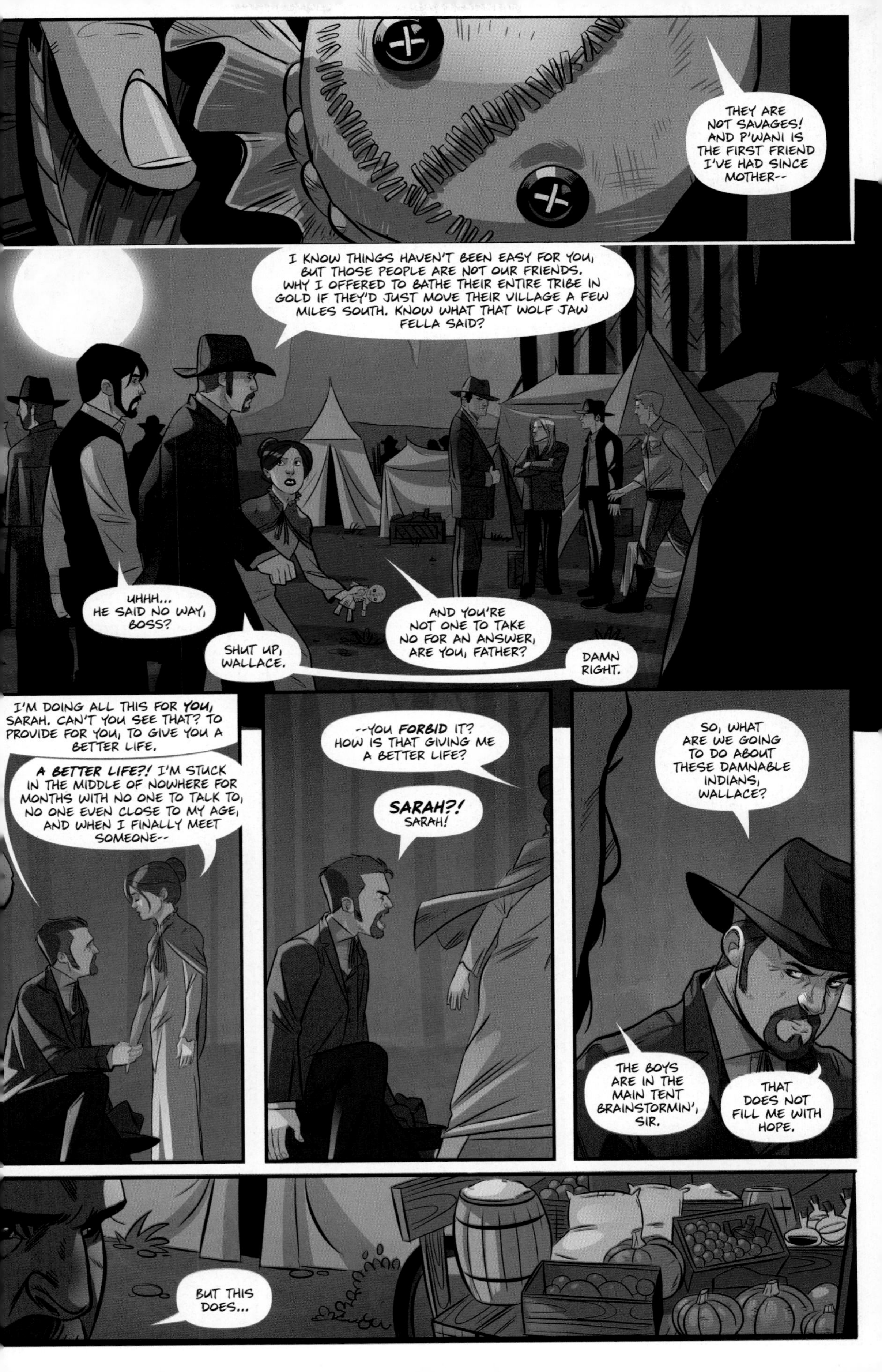
THEY ARE NOT SAVAGES! AND P'WANI IS THE FIRST FRIEND I'VE HAD SINCE MOTHER--
I KNOW THINGS HAVEN'T BEEN EASY FOR YOU, BUT THOSE PEOPLE ARE NOT OUR FRIENDS. WHY I OFFERED TO BATHE THEIR ENTIRE TRIBE IN GOLD IF THEY'D JUST MOVE THEIR VILLAGE A FEW MILES SOUTH. KNOW WHAT THAT WOLF JAW FELLA SAID?
UHHH... HE SAID NO WAY, BOSS?
SHUT UP, WALLACE.
AND YOU'RE NOT ONE TO TAKE NO FOR AN ANSWER, ARE YOU, FATHER?
DAMN RIGHT.
I'M DOING ALL THIS FOR YOU, SARAH. CAN'T YOU SEE THAT? TO PROVIDE FOR YOU, TO GIVE YOU A BETTER LIFE.
A BETTER LIFE?! I'M STUCK IN THE MIDDLE OF NOWHERE FOR MONTHS WITH NO ONE TO TALK TO, NO ONE EVEN CLOSE TO MY AGE, AND WHEN I FINALLY MEET SOMEONE--
--YOU FORBID IT? HOW IS THAT GIVING ME A BETTER LIFE?
SARAH?! SARAH!
SO, WHAT ARE WE GOING TO DO ABOUT THESE DAMNABLE INDIANS, WALLACE?
THE BOYS ARE IN THE MAIN TENT BRAINSTORMIN', SIR.
THAT DOES NOT FILL ME WITH HOPE.
BUT THIS DOES...

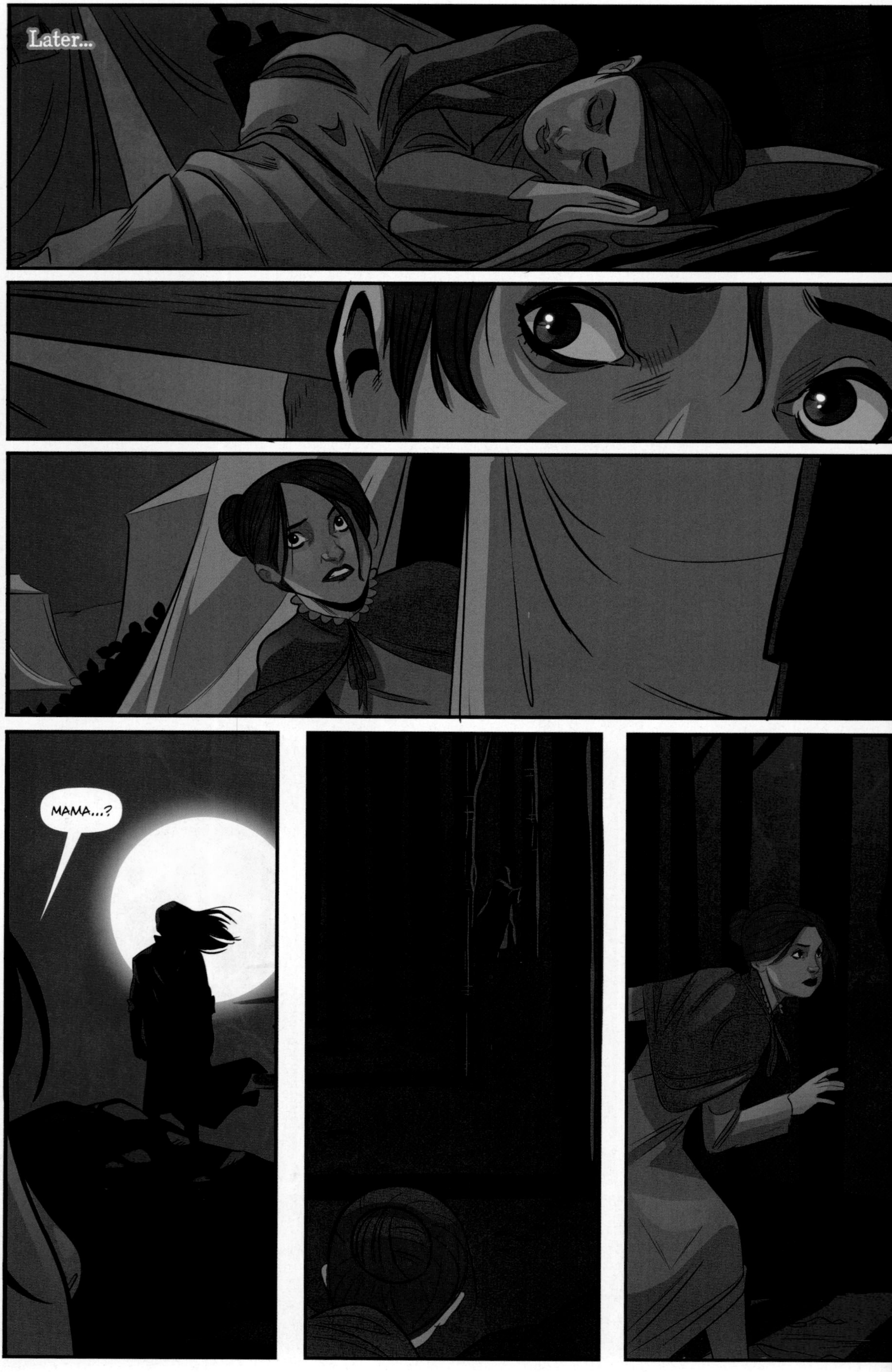
Later...
MAMA...?

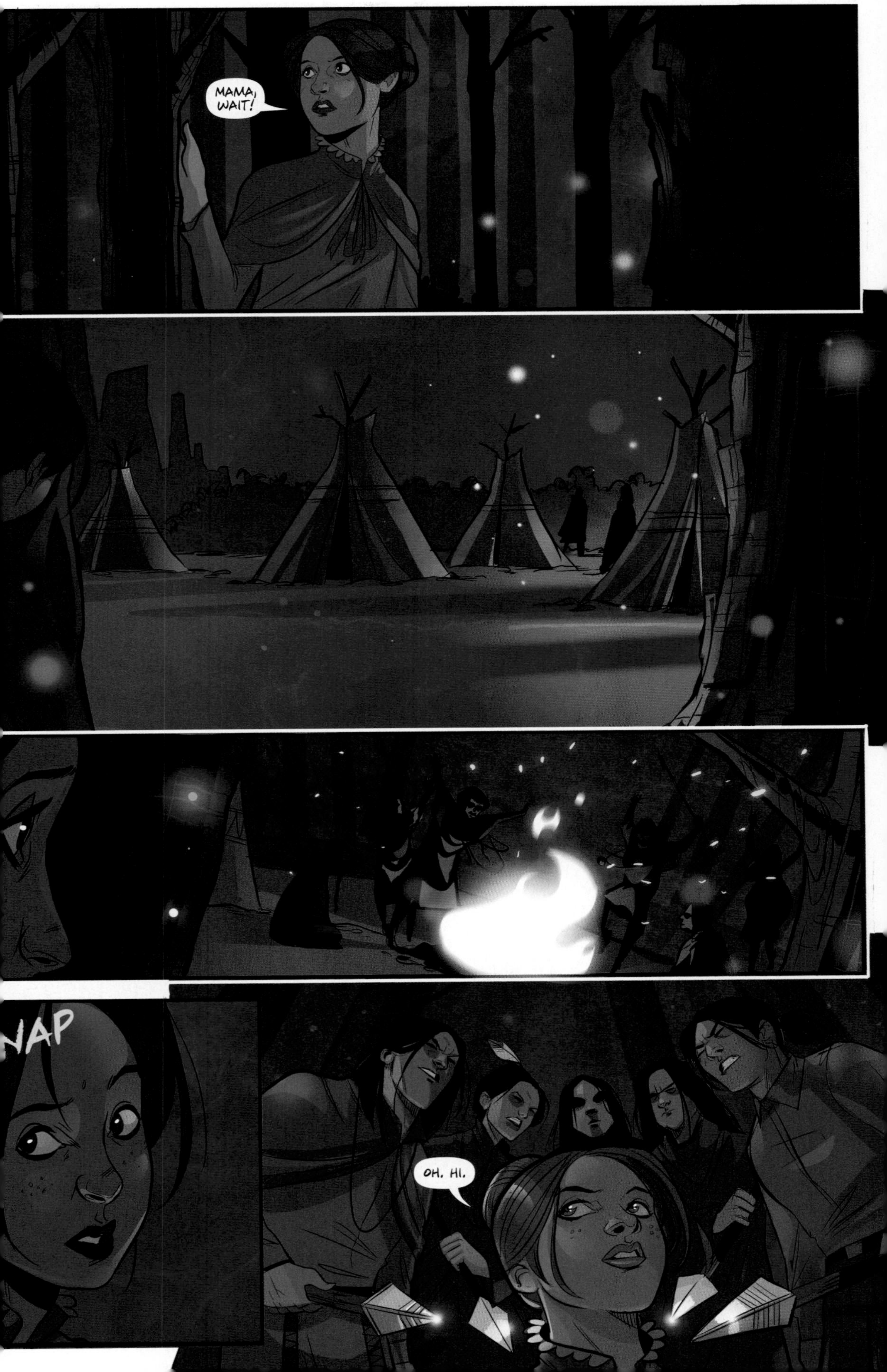
MAMA, WAIT!
NAP
OH. HI.

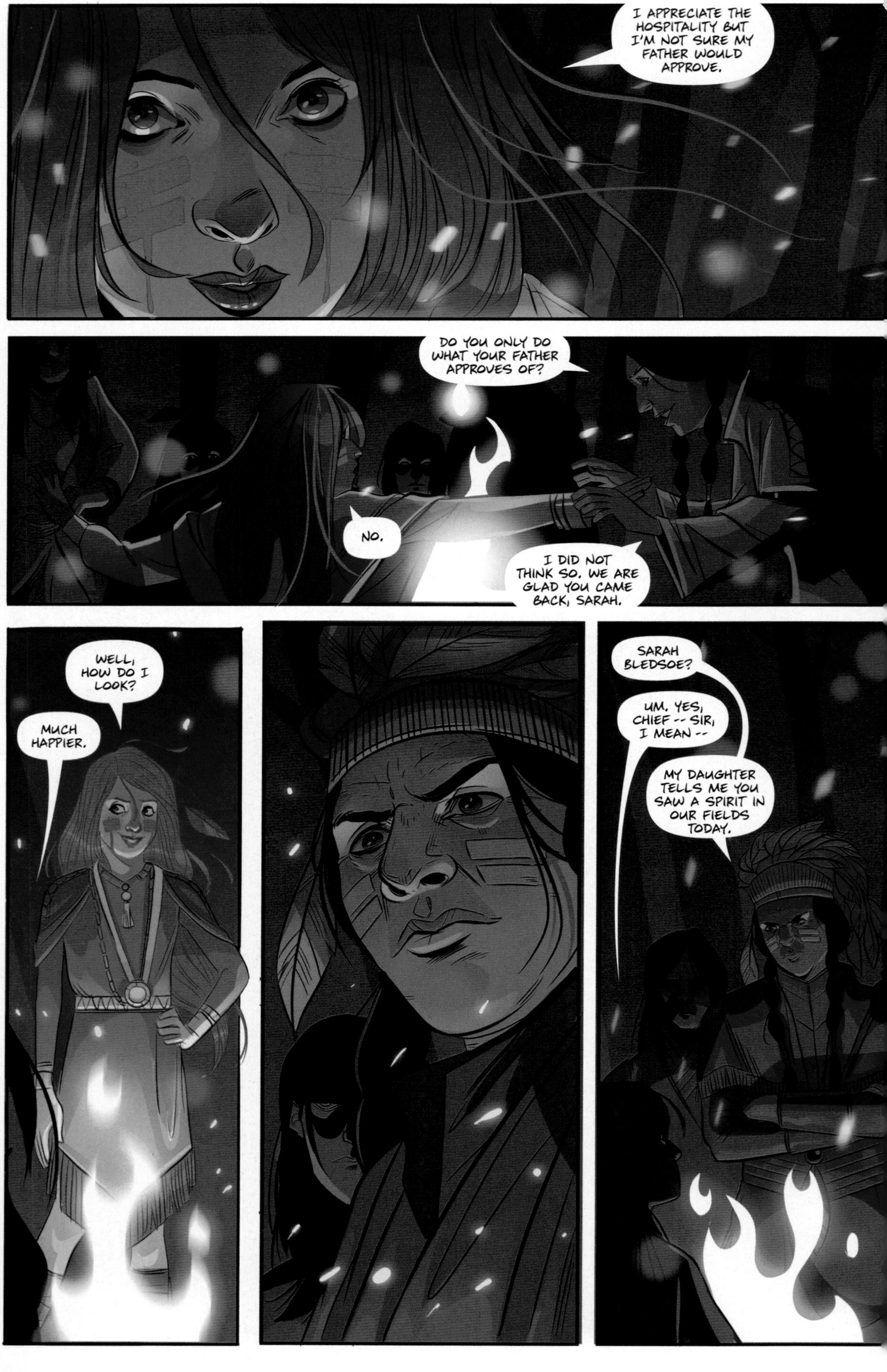
I APPRECIATE THE HOSPITALITY BUT I'M NOT SURE MY FATHER WOULD APPROVE.
DO YOU ONLY DO WHAT YOUR FATHER APPROVES OF?
NO.
I DID NOT THINK SO. WE ARE GLAD YOU CAME BACK, SARAH.
WELL, HOW DO I LOOK?
MUCH HAPPIER.
SARAH BLEDSOE?
UM, YES, CHIEF -- SIR, I MEAN --
MY DAUGHTER TELLS ME YOU SAW A SPIRIT IN OUR FIELDS TODAY.

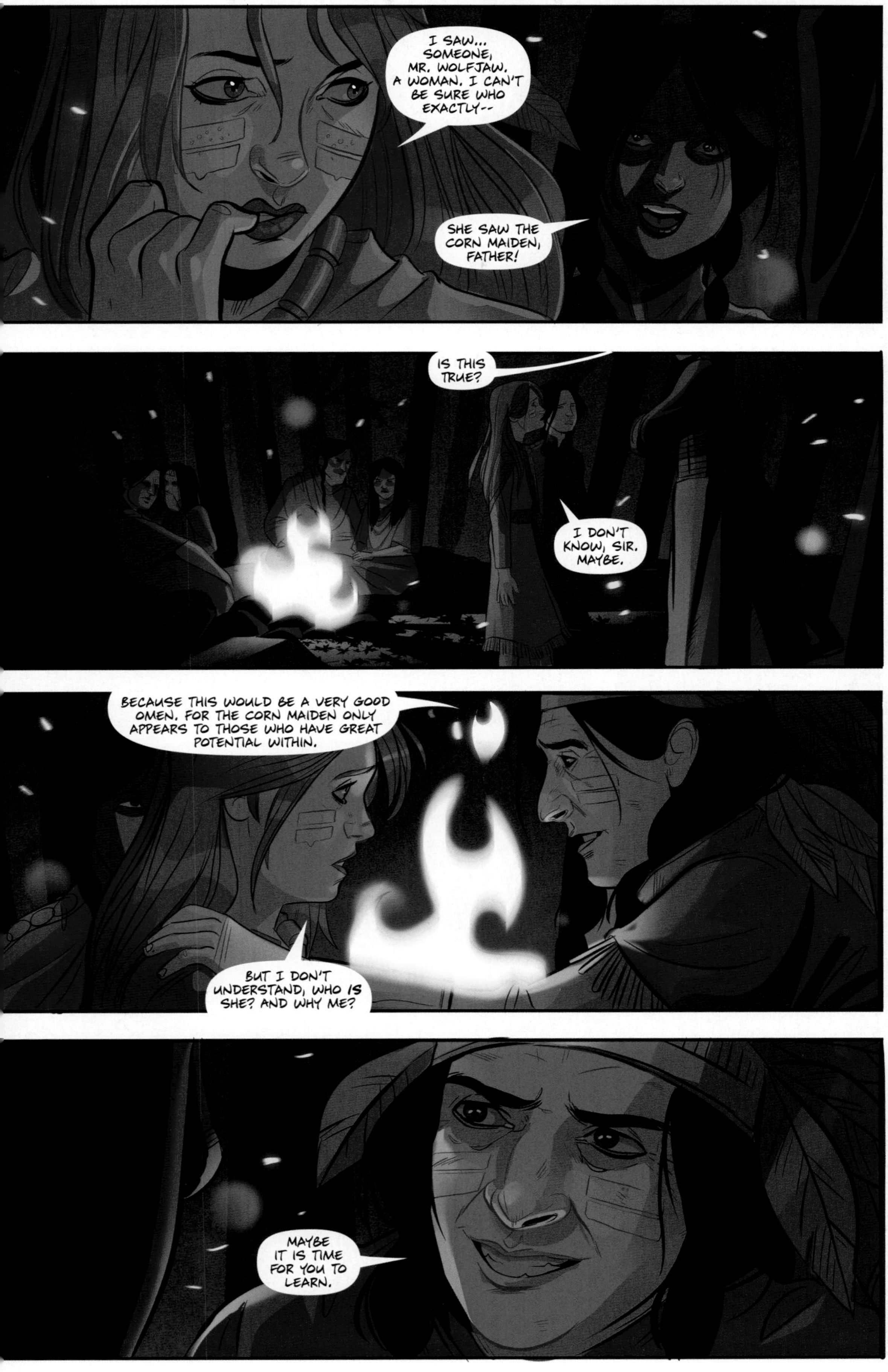
I SAW... SOMEONE, MR. WOLFJAW. A WOMAN. I CAN'T BE SURE WHO EXACTLY--
SHE SAW THE CORN MAIDEN, FATHER!
IS THIS TRUE?
I DON'T KNOW, SIR. MAYBE.
BECAUSE THIS WOULD BE A VERY GOOD OMEN. FOR THE CORN MAIDEN ONLY APPEARS TO THOSE WHO HAVE GREAT POTENTIAL WITHIN.
BUT I DON'T UNDERSTAND, WHO IS SHE? AND WHY ME?
MAYBE IT IS TIME FOR YOU TO LEARN.

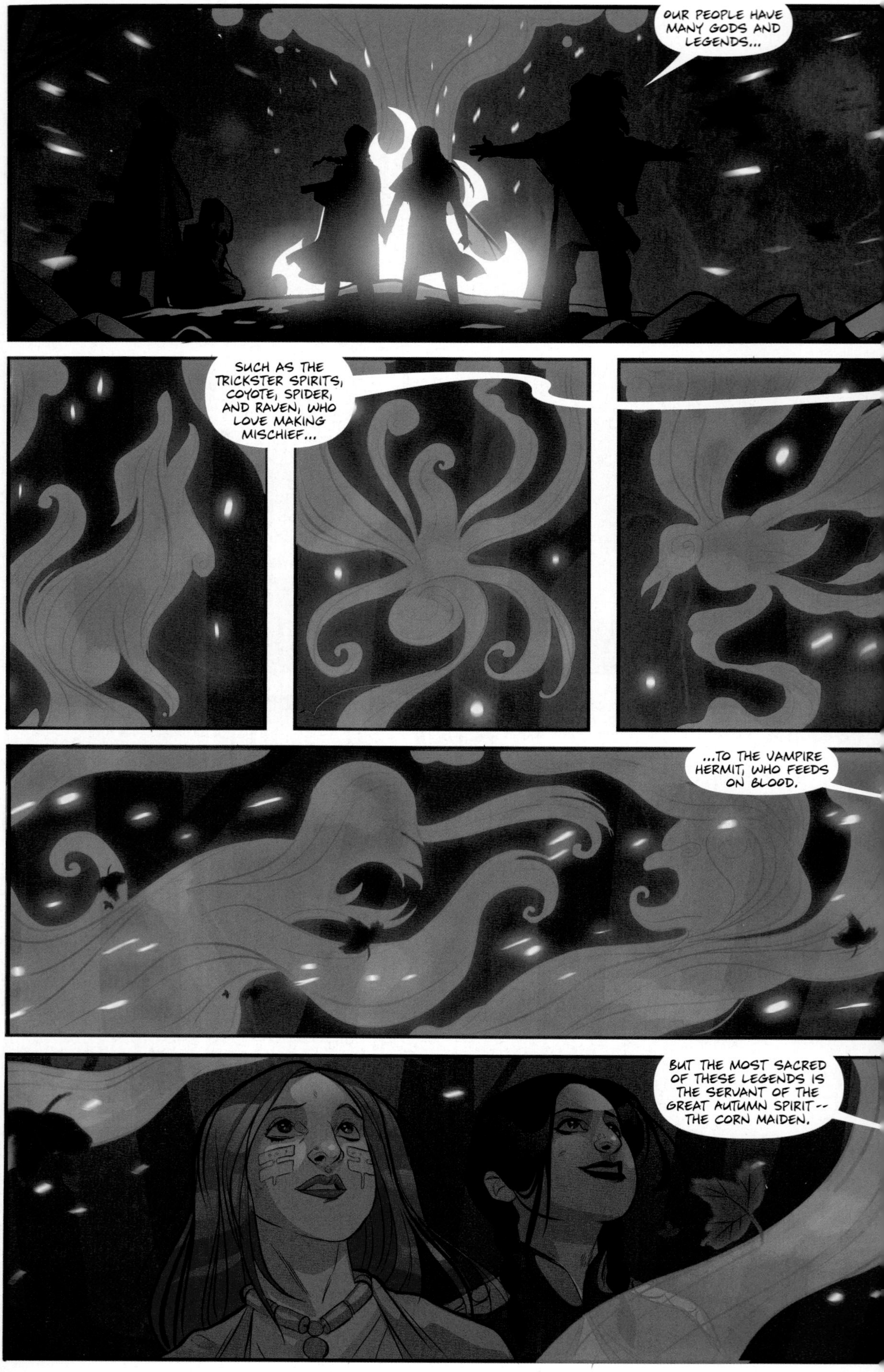
OUR PEOPLE HAVE MANY GODS AND LEGENDS...
SUCH AS THE TRICKSTER SPIRITS, COYOTE, SPIDER, AND RAVEN, WHO LOVE MAKING MISCHIEF...
...TO THE VAMPIRE HERMIT, WHO FEEDS ON BLOOD.
BUT THE MOST SACRED OF THESE LEGENDS IS THE SERVANT OF THE GREAT AUTUMN SPIRIT-- THE CORN MAIDEN.

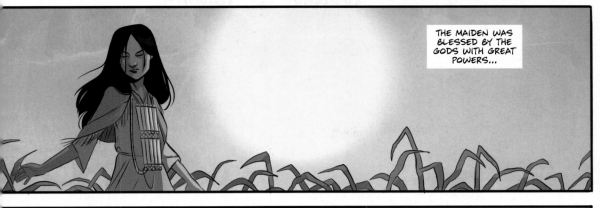

THE MAIDEN WAS BLESSED BY THE GODS WITH GREAT POWERS...

HER TOUCH BROUGHT LIFE.

AND PROVIDED CROPS FOR MANY TRIBES.

THE PEOPLE LOVED HER, AND SHE, IN TURN, LOVED THEM AS IF THEY WERE HER OWN CHILDREN.

UNTIL THE DAY THEY ARRIVED...

THE GOLD SEEKERS.

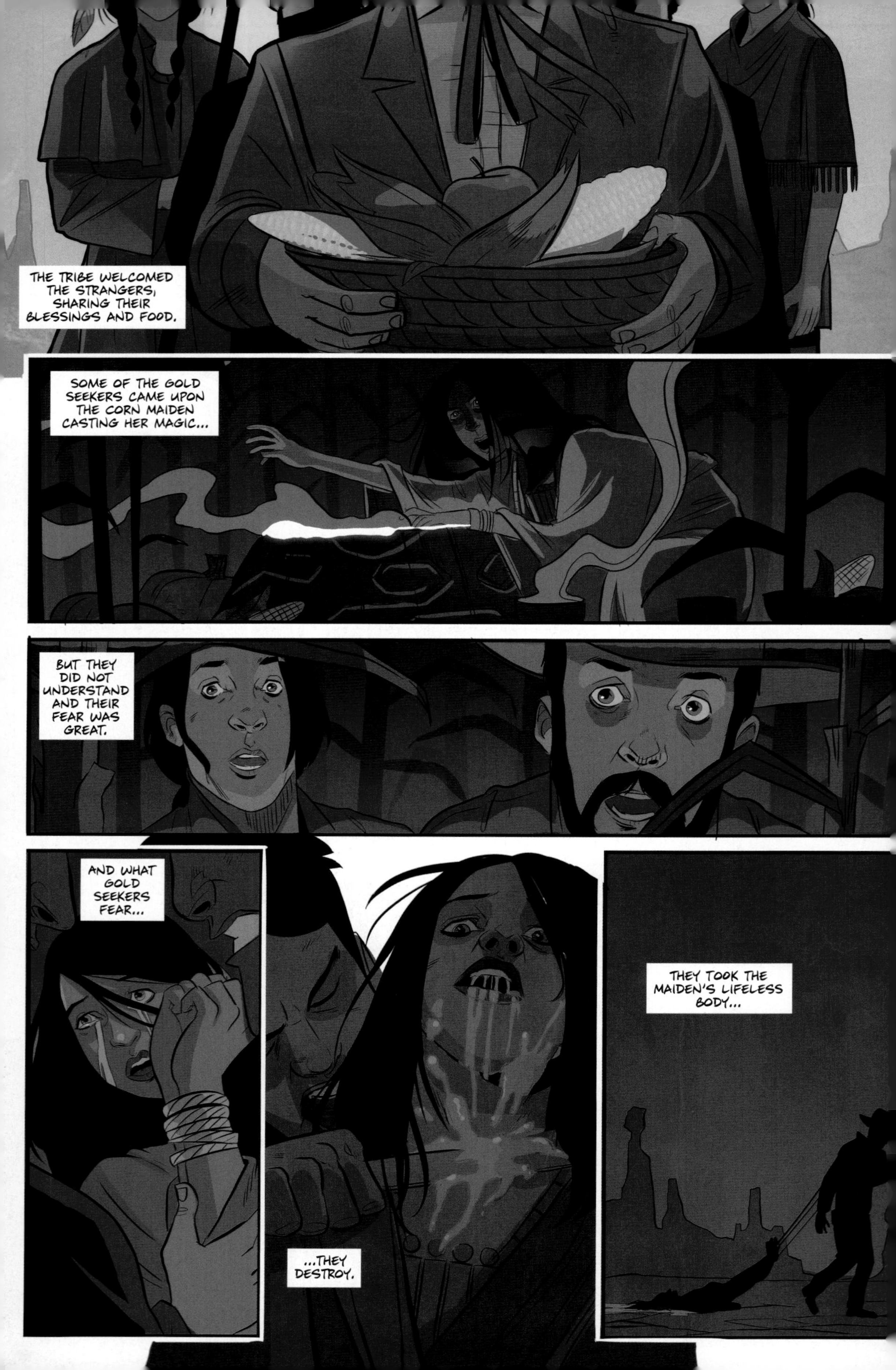
THE TRIBE WELCOMED THE STRANGERS, SHARING THEIR BLESSINGS AND FOOD.
SOME OF THE GOLD SEEKERS CAME UPON THE CORN MAIDEN CASTING HER MAGIC...
BUT THEY DID NOT UNDERSTAND AND THEIR FEAR WAS GREAT.
AND WHAT GOLD SEEKERS FEAR...
...THEY DESTROY.
THEY TOOK THE MAIDEN'S LIFELESS BODY...

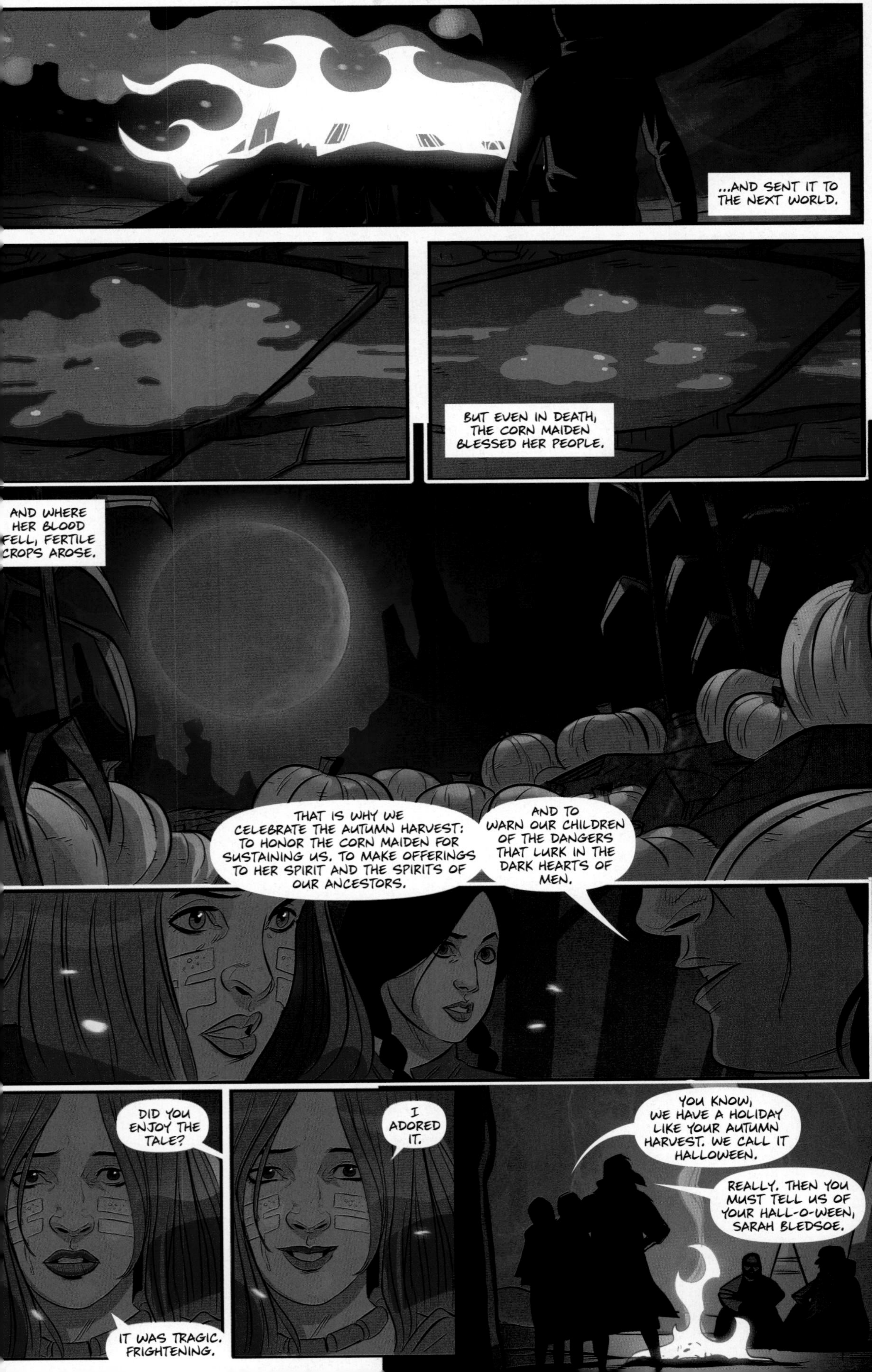
...AND SENT IT TO THE NEXT WORLD.
BUT EVEN IN DEATH, THE CORN MAIDEN BLESSED HER PEOPLE.
AND WHERE HER BLOOD FELL, FERTILE CROPS AROSE.
THAT IS WHY WE CELEBRATE THE AUTUMN HARVEST: TO HONOR THE CORN MAIDEN FOR SUSTAINING US. TO MAKE OFFERINGS TO HER SPIRIT AND THE SPIRITS OF OUR ANCESTORS.
AND TO WARN OUR CHILDREN OF THE DANGERS THAT LURK IN THE DARK HEARTS OF MEN.
DID YOU ENJOY THE TALE?
IT WAS TRAGIC. FRIGHTENING.
I ADORED IT.
YOU KNOW, WE HAVE A HOLIDAY LIKE YOUR AUTUMN HARVEST. WE CALL IT HALLOWEEN.
REALLY. THEN YOU MUST TELL US OF YOUR HALL-O-WEEN, SARAH BLEDSOE.

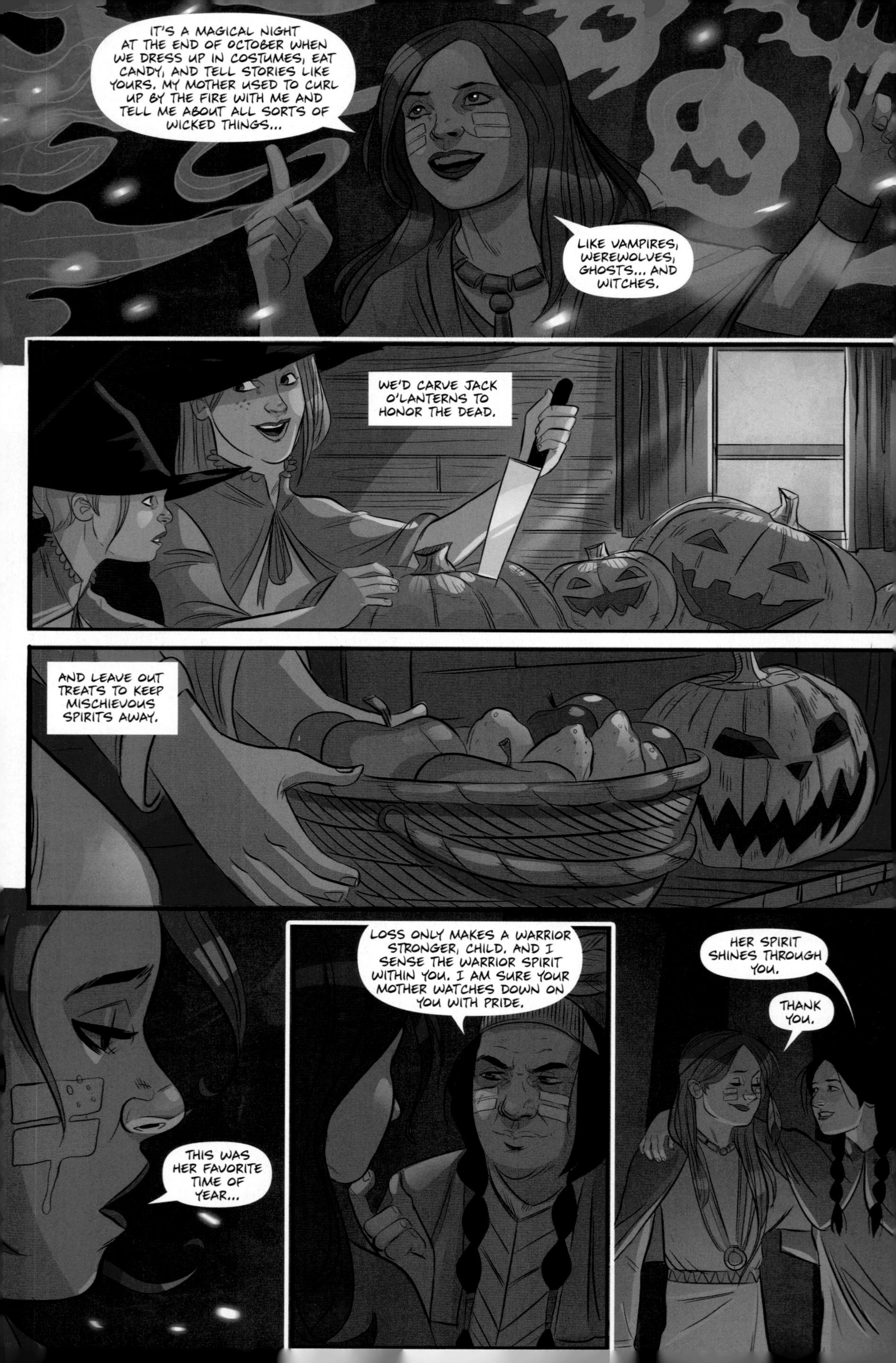
IT'S A MAGICAL NIGHT AT THE END OF OCTOBER WHEN WE DRESS UP IN COSTUMES, EAT CANDY, AND TELL STORIES LIKE YOURS. MY MOTHER USED TO CURL UP BY THE FIRE WITH ME AND TELL ME ABOUT ALL SORTS OF WICKED THINGS...
LIKE VAMPIRES, WEREWOLVES, GHOSTS... AND WITCHES.
WE'D CARVE JACK O'LANTERNS TO HONOR THE DEAD.
AND LEAVE OUT TREATS TO KEEP MISCHIEVOUS SPIRITS AWAY.
THIS WAS HER FAVORITE TIME OF YEAR...
LOSS ONLY MAKES A WARRIOR STRONGER, CHILD. AND I SENSE THE WARRIOR SPIRIT WITHIN YOU. I AM SURE YOUR MOTHER WATCHES DOWN ON YOU WITH PRIDE.
HER SPIRIT SHINES THROUGH YOU.
THANK YOU.

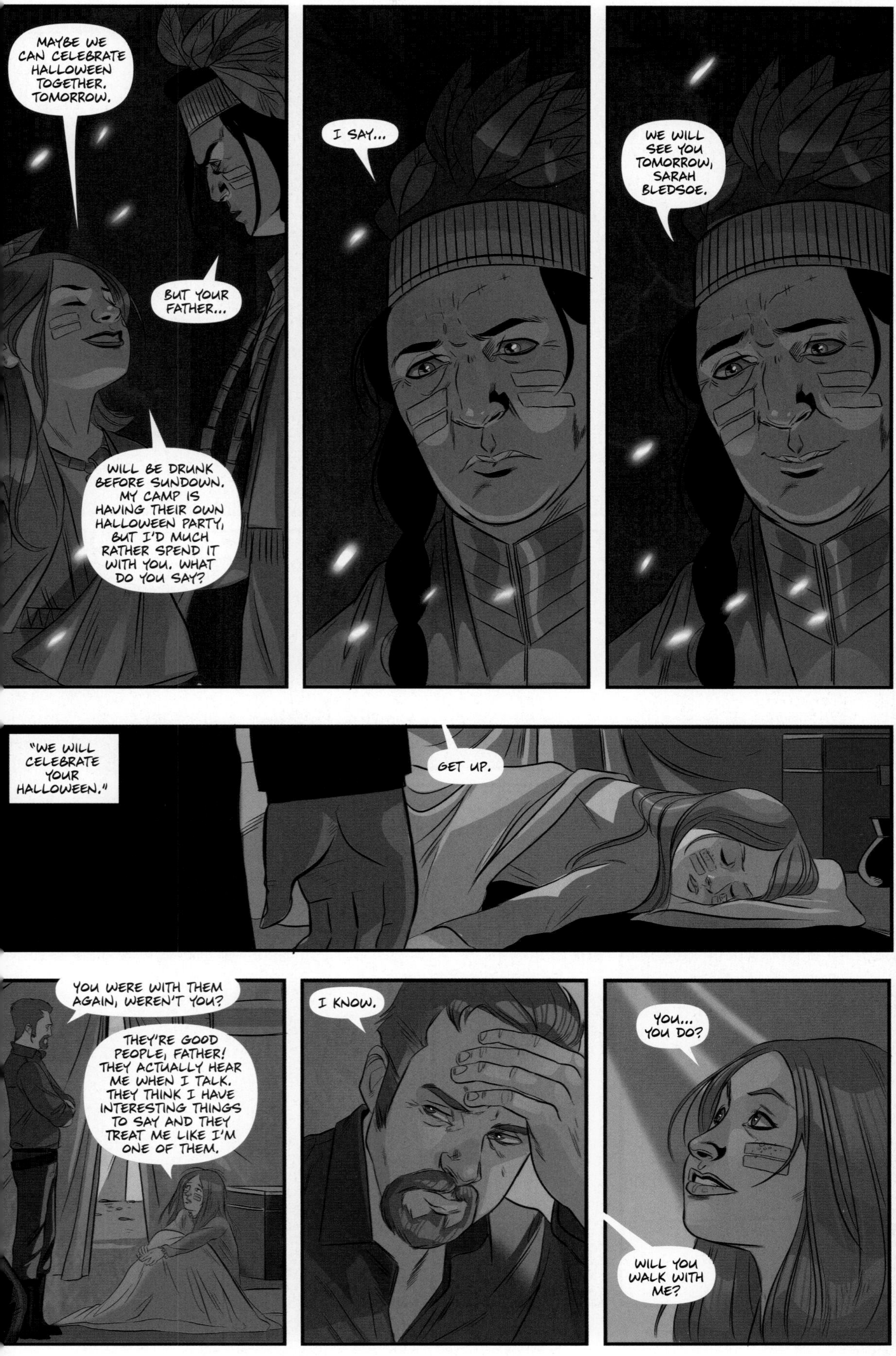
MAYBE WE CAN CELEBRATE HALLOWEEN TOGETHER. TOMORROW.
BUT YOUR FATHER...
WILL BE DRUNK BEFORE SUNDOWN. MY CAMP IS HAVING THEIR OWN HALLOWEEN PARTY, BUT I'D MUCH RATHER SPEND IT WITH YOU. WHAT DO YOU SAY?
I SAY...
WE WILL SEE YOU TOMORROW, SARAH BLEDSOE.
"WE WILL CELEBRATE YOUR HALLOWEEN."
GET UP.
YOU WERE WITH THEM AGAIN, WEREN'T YOU?
THEY'RE GOOD PEOPLE, FATHER! THEY ACTUALLY HEAR ME WHEN I TALK. THEY THINK I HAVE INTERESTING THINGS TO SAY AND THEY TREAT ME LIKE I'M ONE OF THEM.
I KNOW.
YOU... YOU DO?
WILL YOU WALK WITH ME?

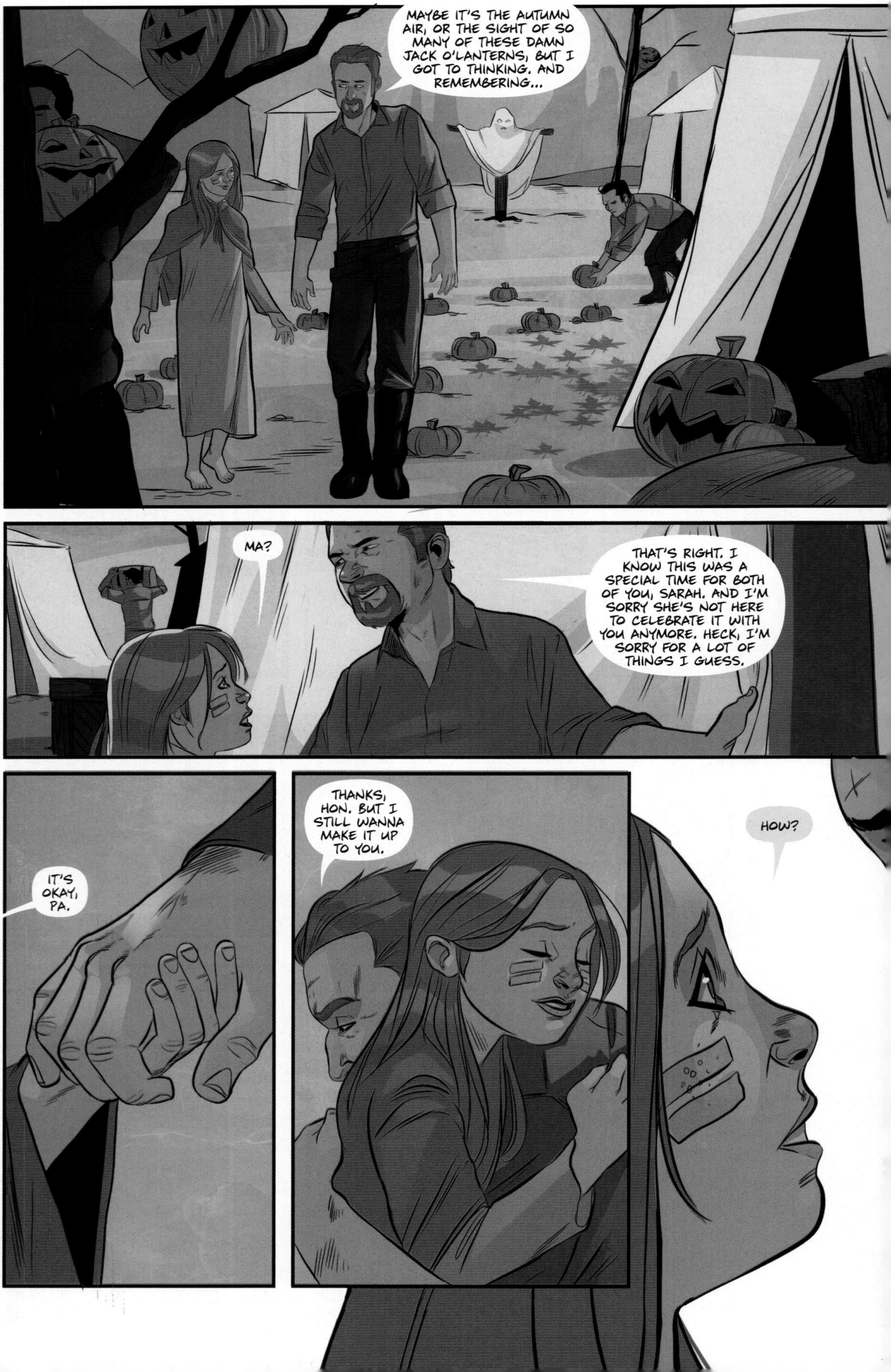
MAYBE IT'S THE AUTUMN AIR, OR THE SIGHT OF SO MANY OF THESE DAMN JACK O'LANTERNS, BUT I GOT TO THINKING. AND REMEMBERING...
MA?
THAT'S RIGHT. I KNOW THIS WAS A SPECIAL TIME FOR BOTH OF YOU, SARAH. AND I'M SORRY SHE'S NOT HERE TO CELEBRATE IT WITH YOU ANYMORE. HECK, I'M SORRY FOR A LOT OF THINGS I GUESS.
IT'S OKAY, PA.
THANKS, HON. BUT I STILL WANNA MAKE IT UP TO YOU.
HOW?

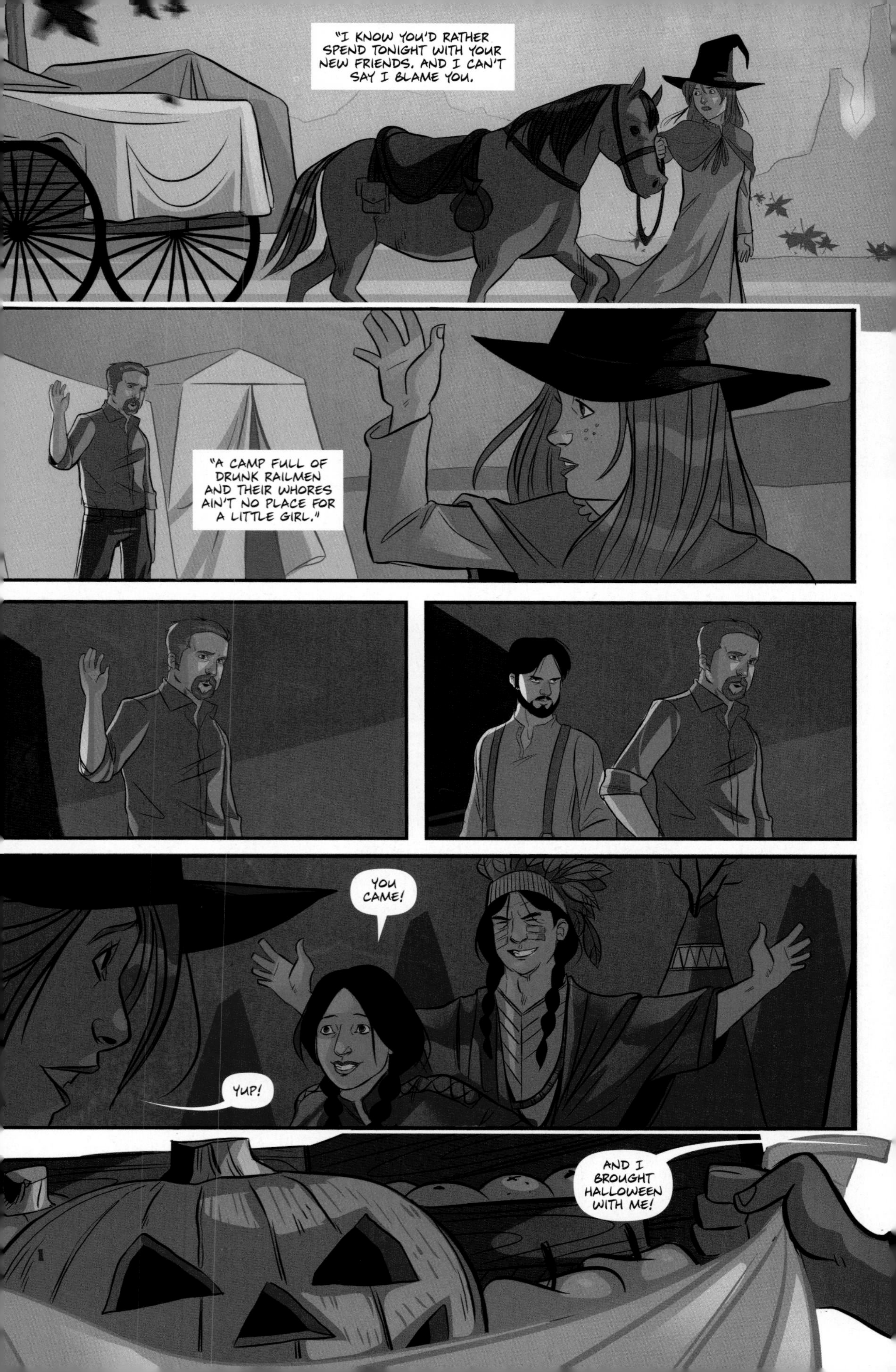

"I KNOW YOU'D RATHER SPEND TONIGHT WITH YOUR NEW FRIENDS. AND I CAN'T SAY I BLAME YOU.
"A CAMP FULL OF DRUNK RAILMEN AND THEIR WHORES AIN'T NO PLACE FOR A LITTLE GIRL."
YOU CAME!
YUP!
AND I BROUGHT HALLOWEEN WITH ME!

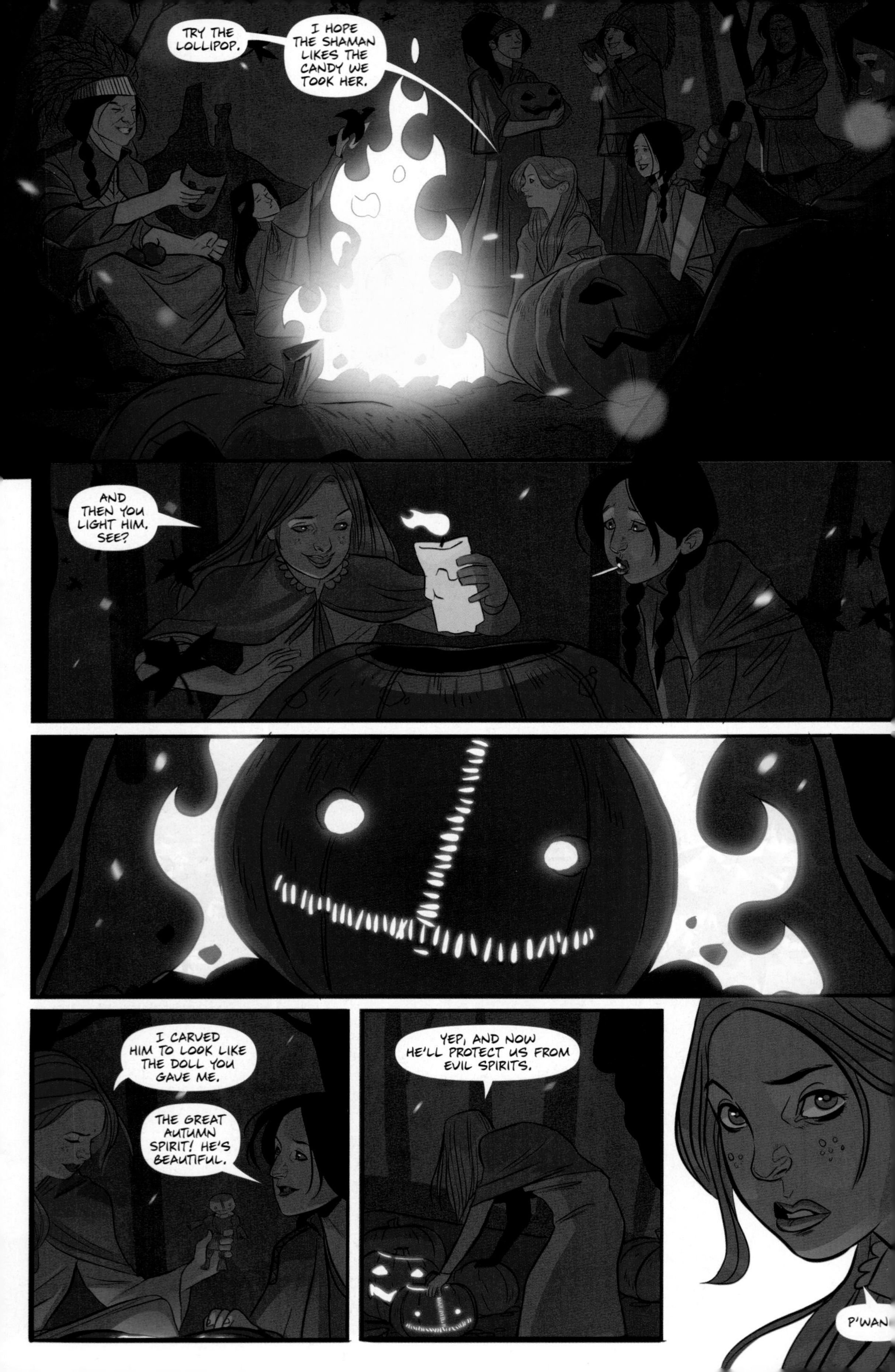

TRY THE LOLLIPOP.
I HOPE THE SHAMAN LIKES THE CANDY WE TOOK HER.
AND THEN YOU LIGHT HIM. SEE?
I CARVED HIM TO LOOK LIKE THE DOLL YOU GAVE ME.
THE GREAT AUTUMN SPIRIT! HE'S BEAUTIFUL.
YEP, AND NOW HE'LL PROTECT US FROM EVIL SPIRITS.
P'WAN

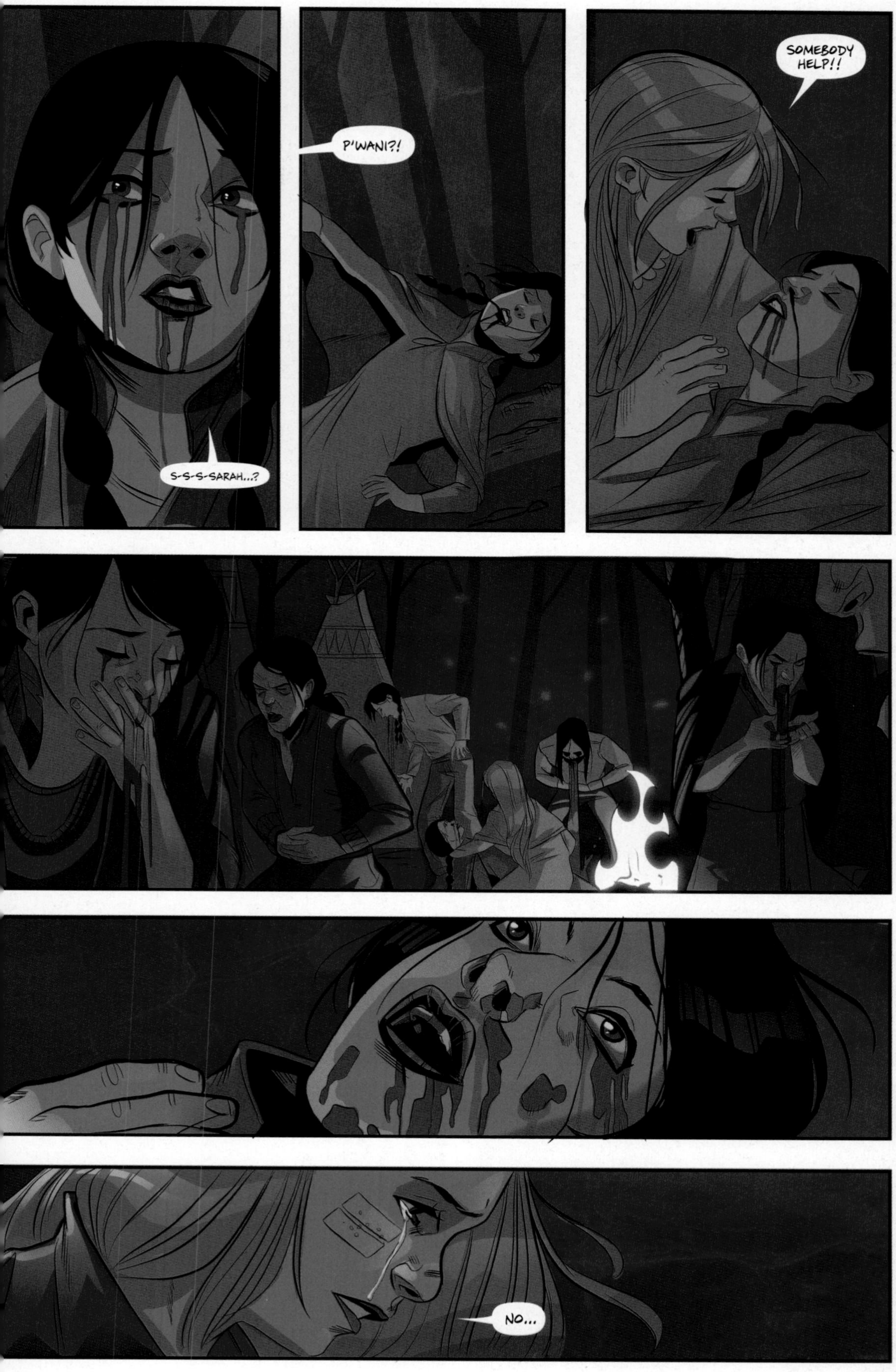
S-S-S-SARAH...?
P'WANI?!
SOMEBODY HELP!!
NO...

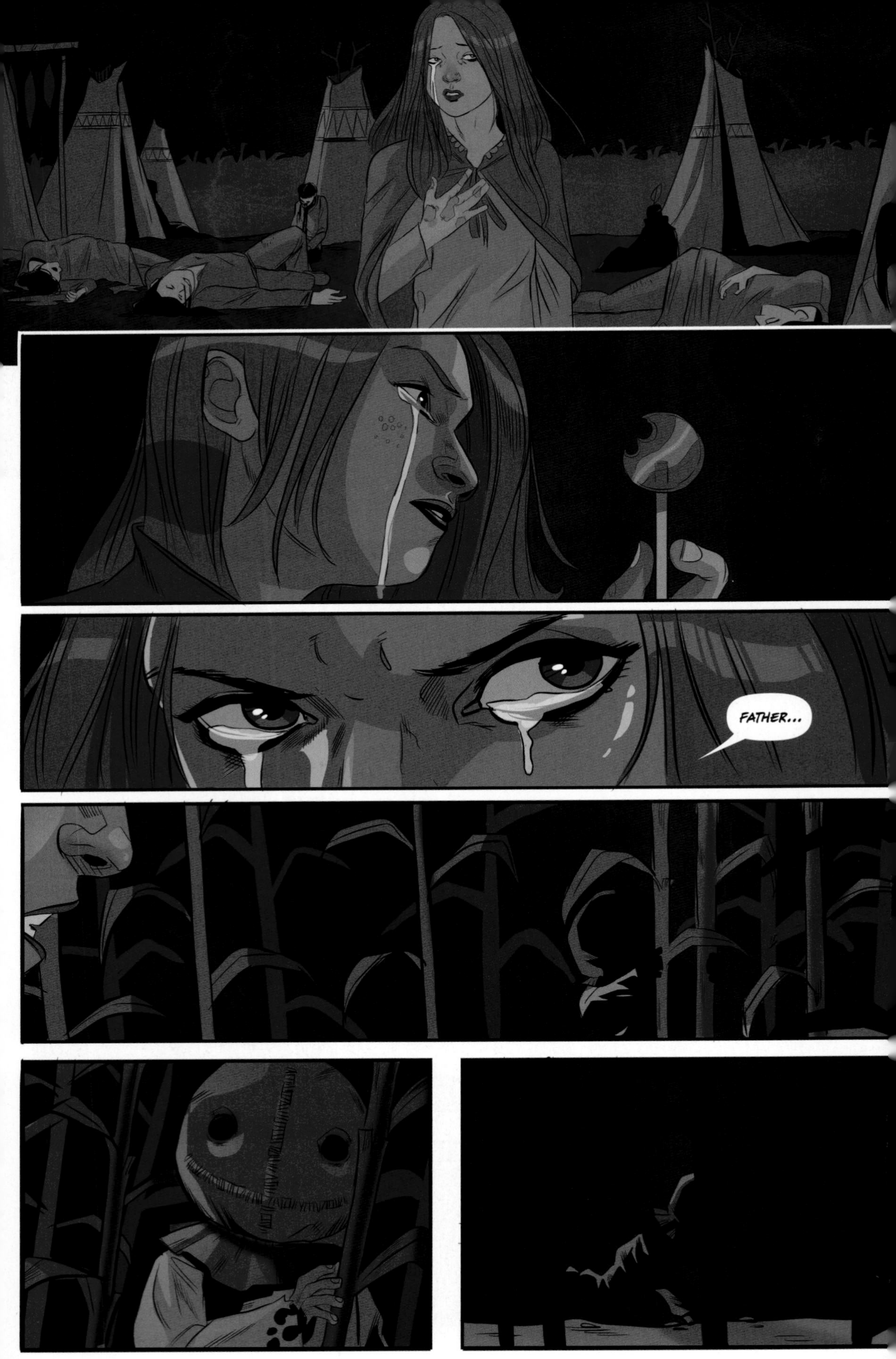
FATHER...

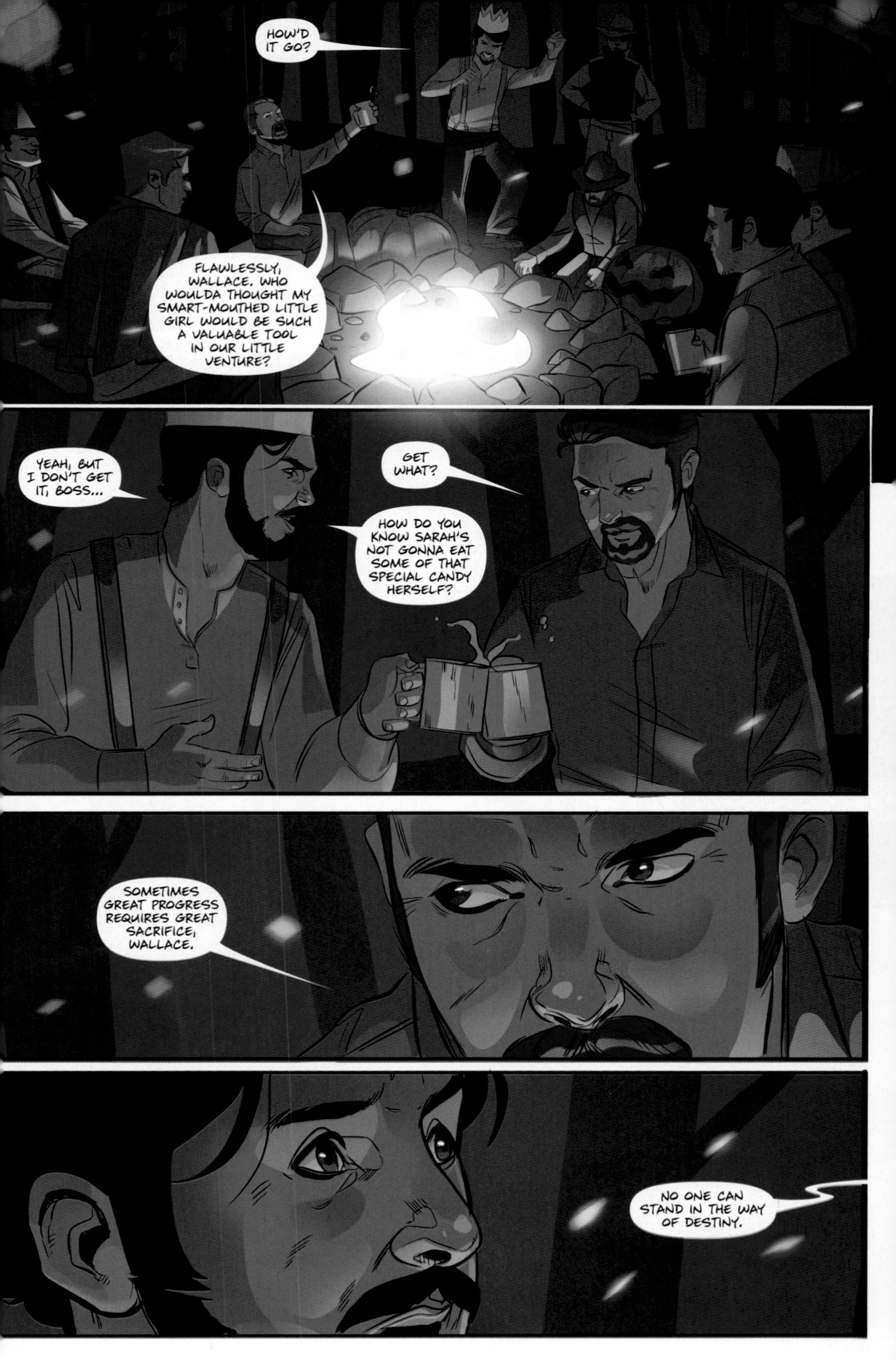
HOW'D IT GO?
FLAWLESSLY, WALLACE. WHO WOULDA THOUGHT MY SMART-MOUTHED LITTLE GIRL WOULD BE SUCH A VALUABLE TOOL IN OUR LITTLE VENTURE?
YEAH, BUT I DON'T GET IT, BOSS...
GET WHAT?
HOW DO YOU KNOW SARAH'S NOT GONNA EAT SOME OF THAT SPECIAL CANDY HERSELF?
SOMETIMES GREAT PROGRESS REQUIRES GREAT SACRIFICE, WALLACE.
NO ONE CAN STAND IN THE WAY OF DESTINY.

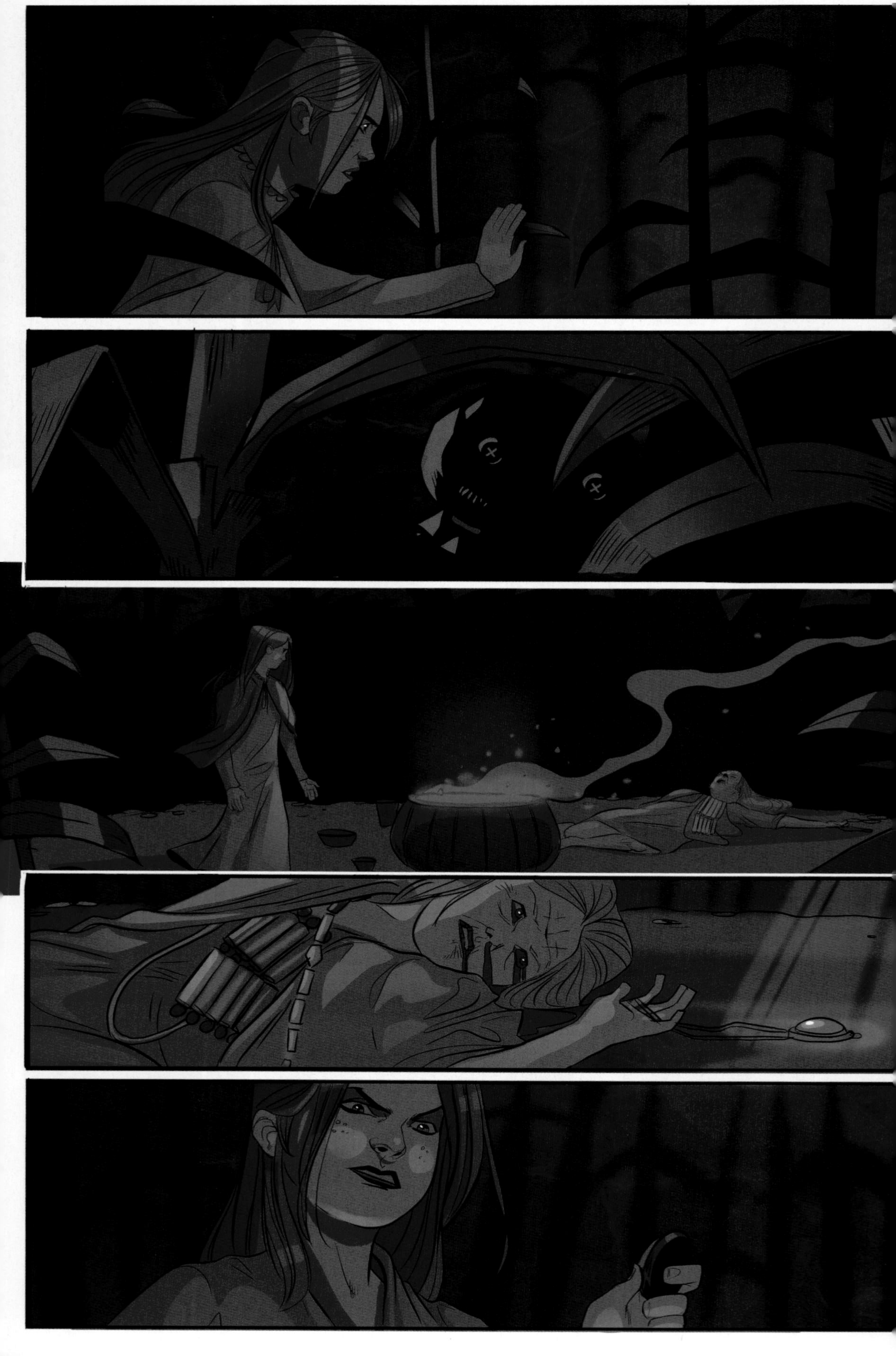

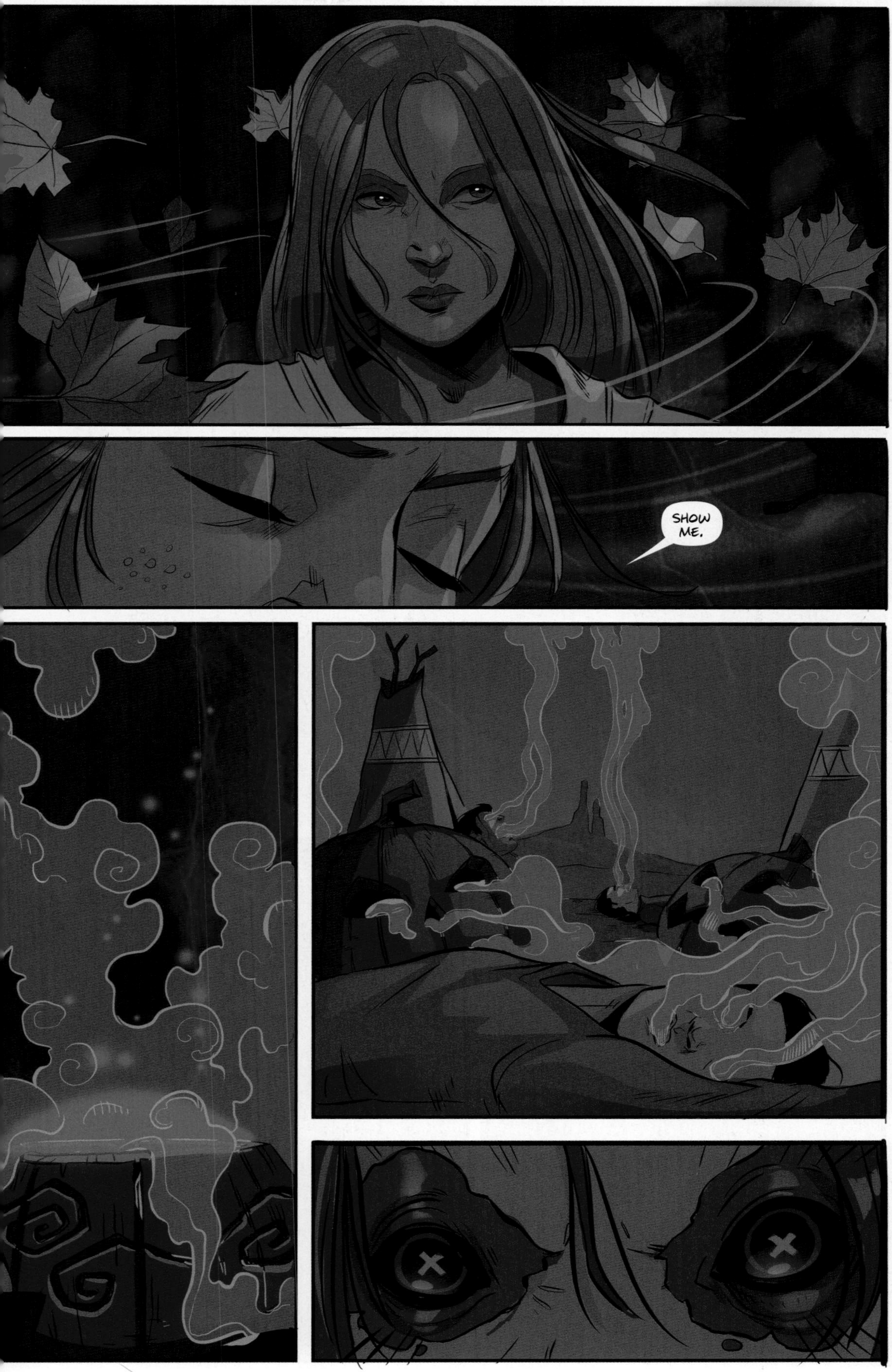
SHOW ME.

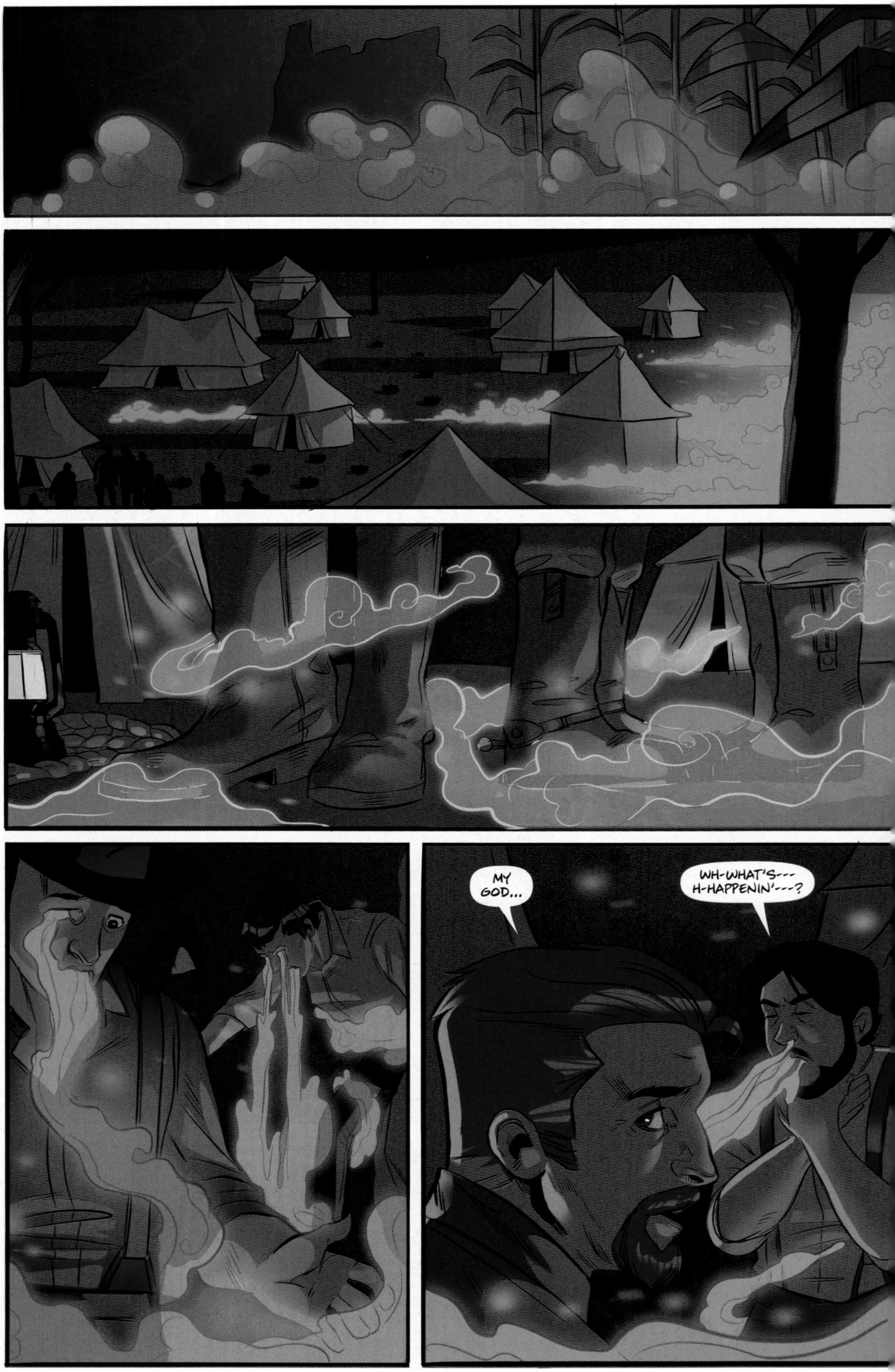
MY GOD...
WH-WHAT'S--- H-HAPPENIN'---?

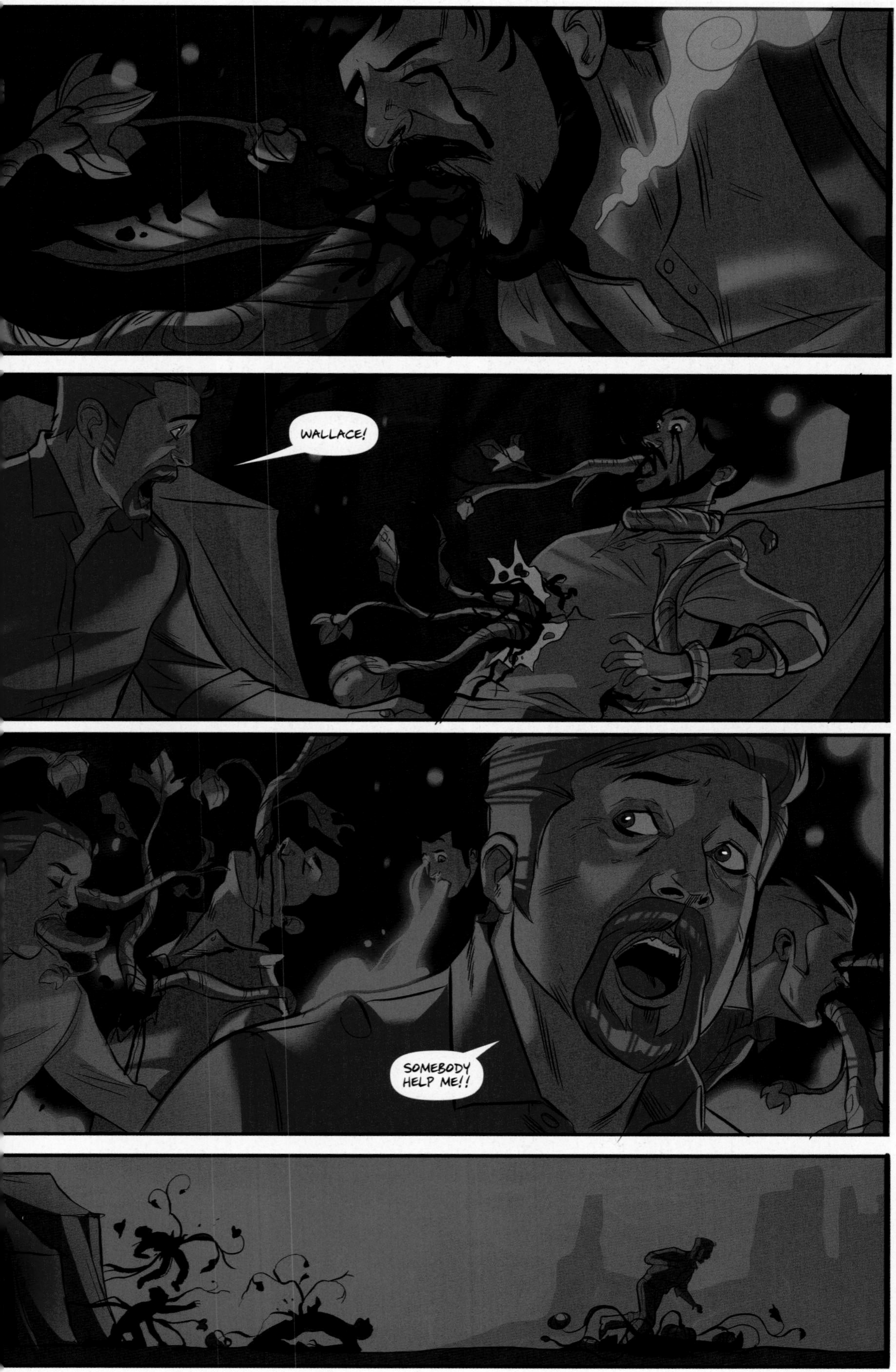
WALLACE!
SOMEBODY HELP ME!!

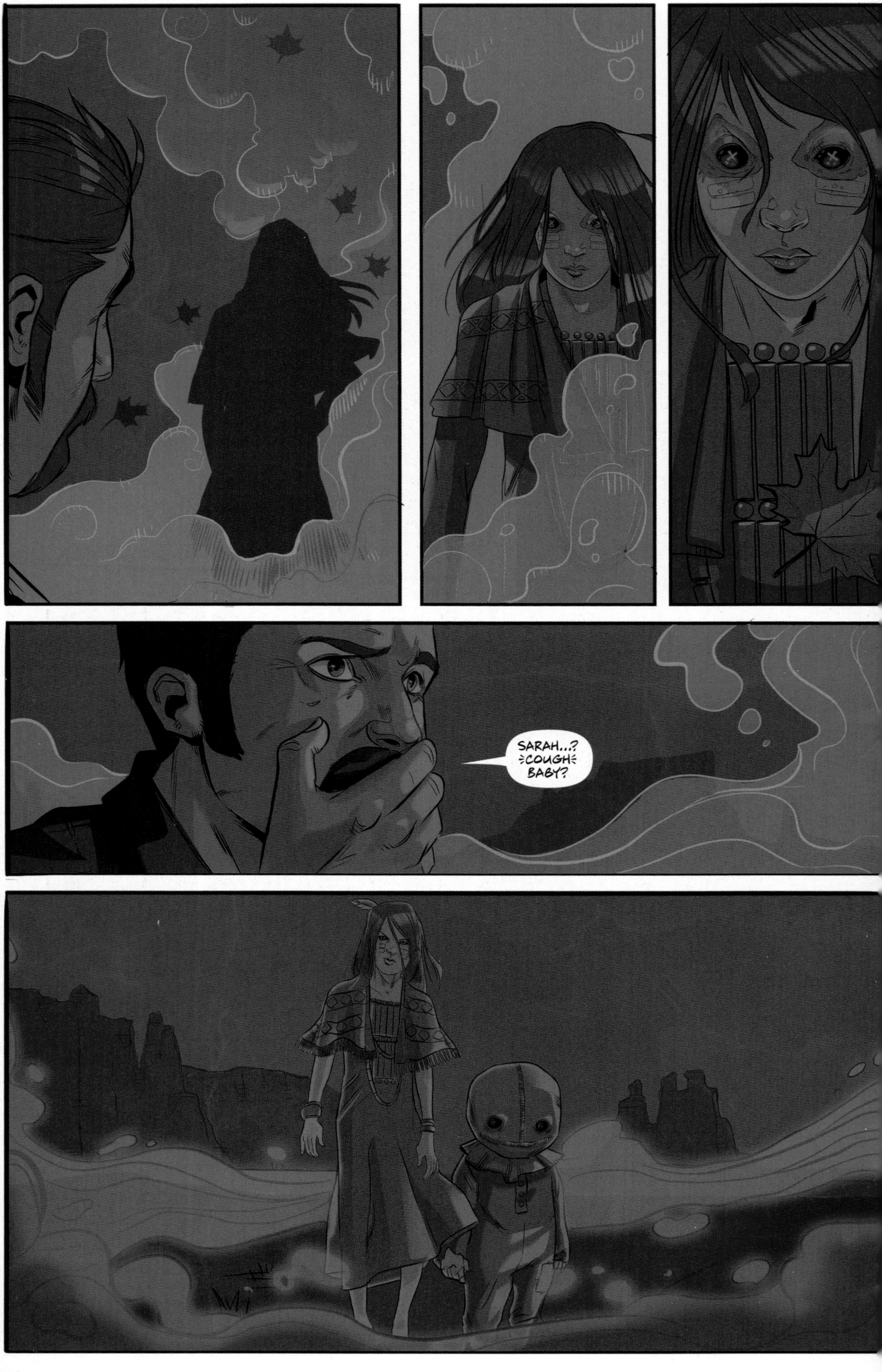
SARAH...? ≈COUGH≈ BABY?

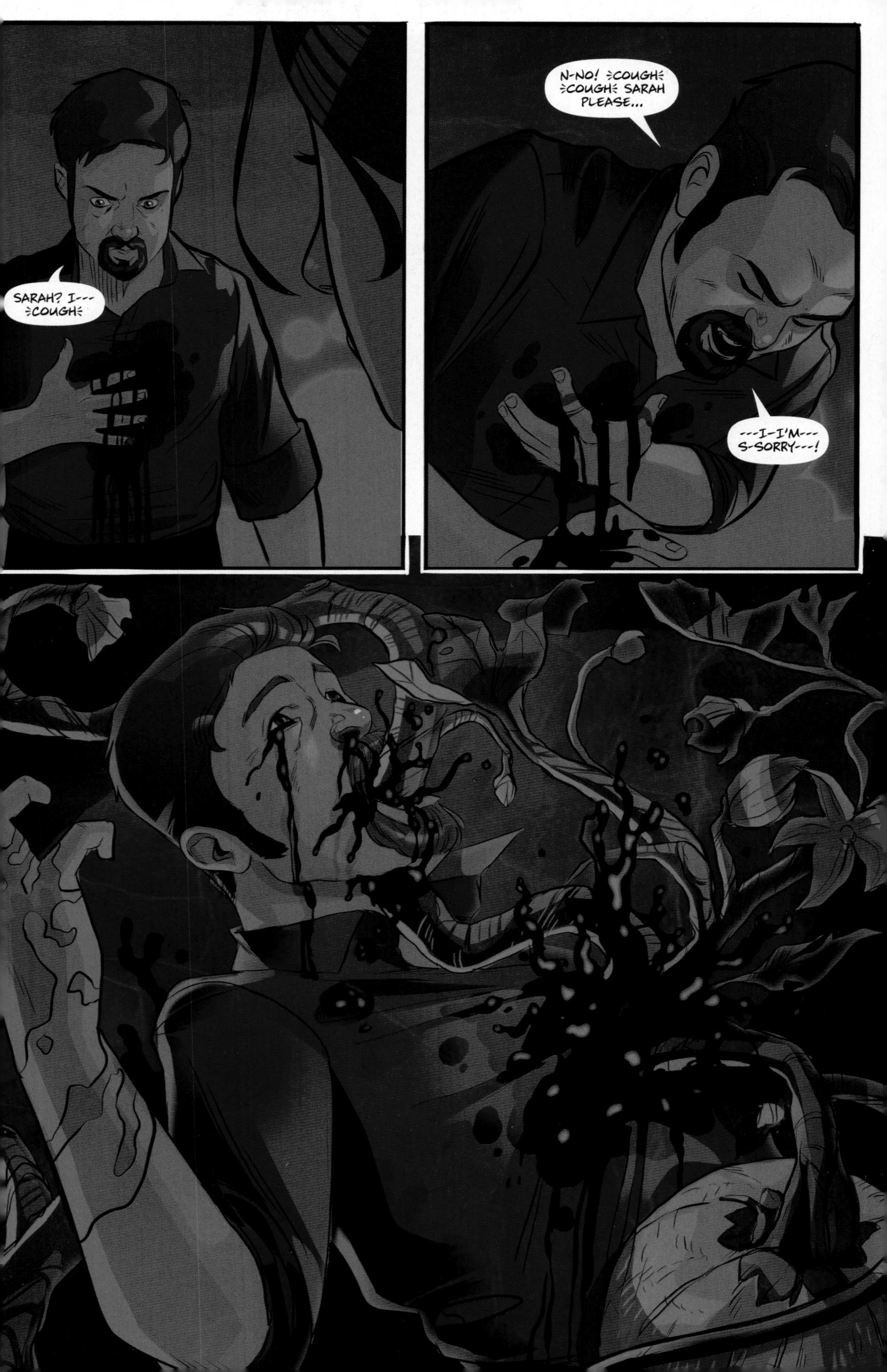
SARAH? I---
≷COUGH≶
N-NO! ≷COUGH≶ ≷COUGH≶ SARAH PLEASE...
---I-I'M--- S-SORRY---!

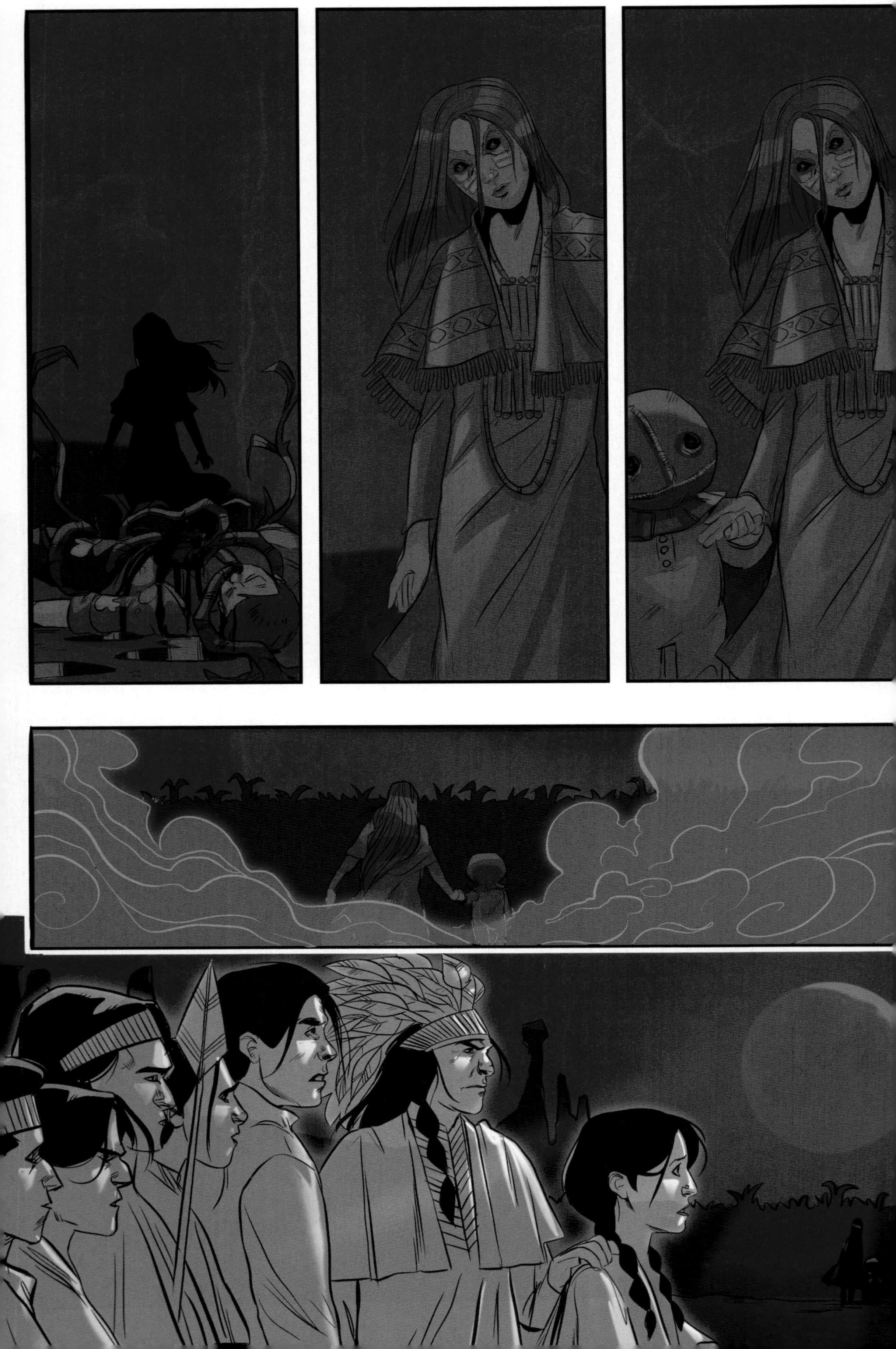

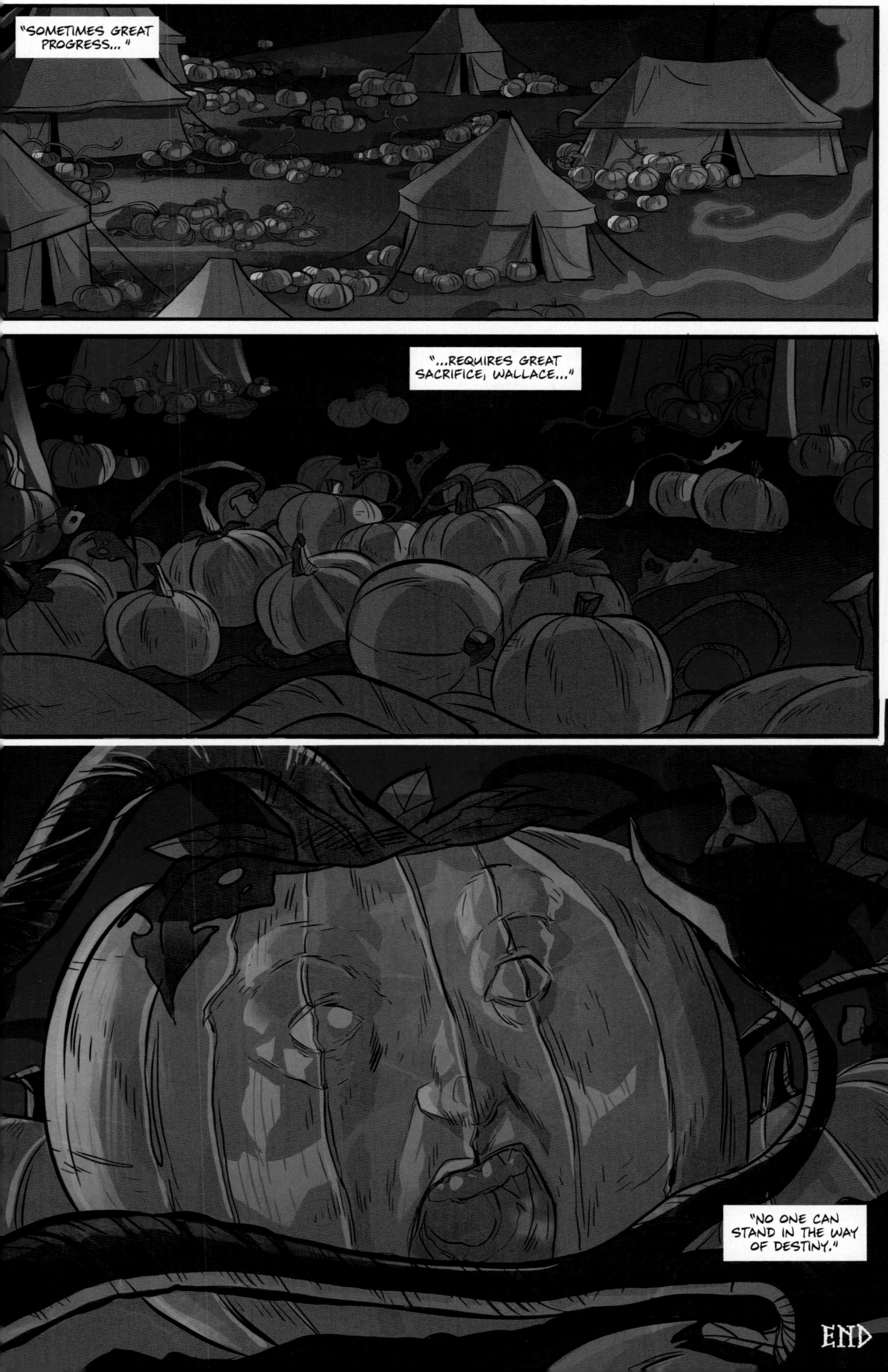
"SOMETIMES GREAT PROGRESS..."
"...REQUIRES GREAT SACRIFICE, WALLACE..."
"NO ONE CAN STAND IN THE WAY OF DESTINY."
END

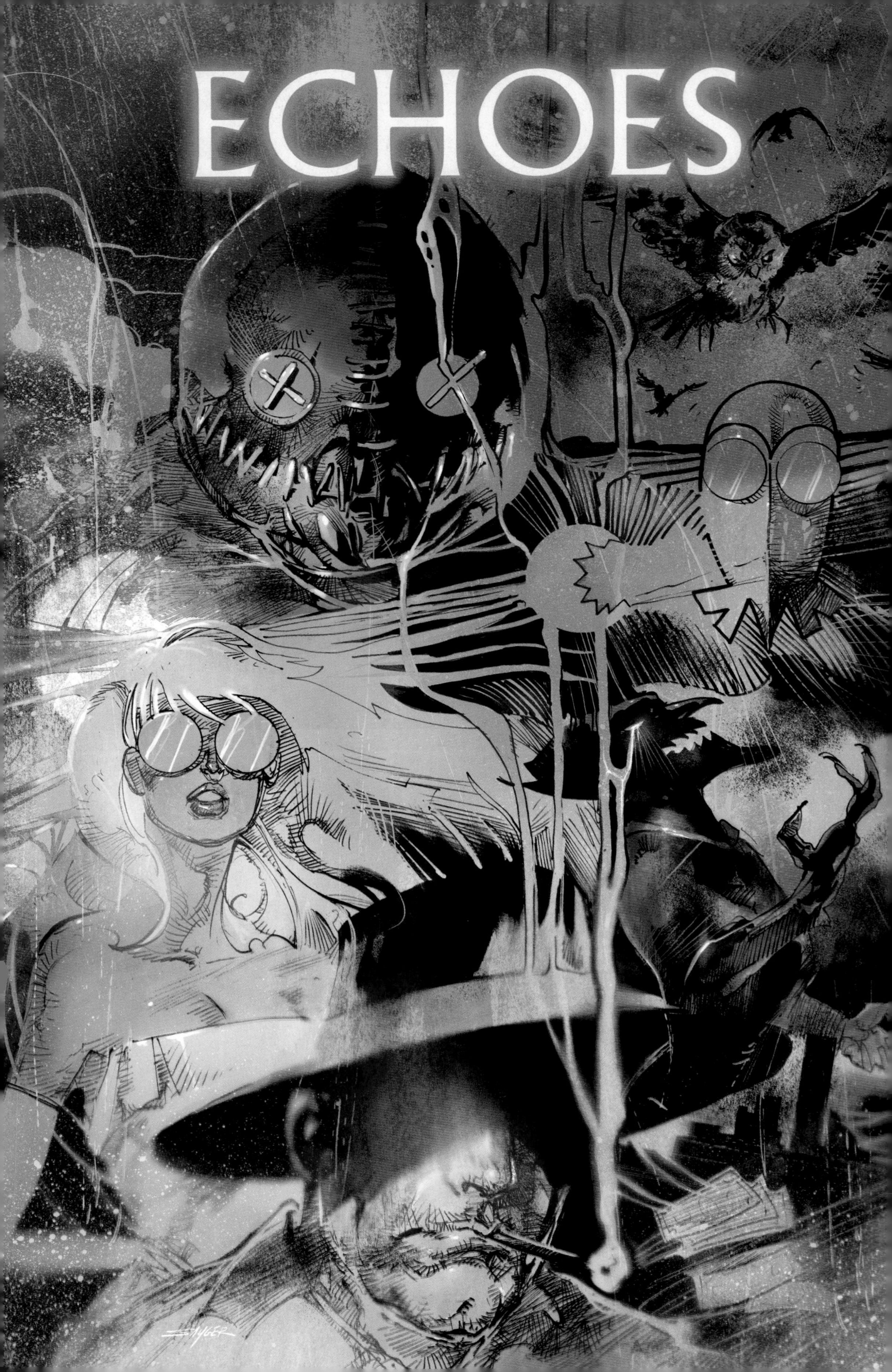
ECHOES

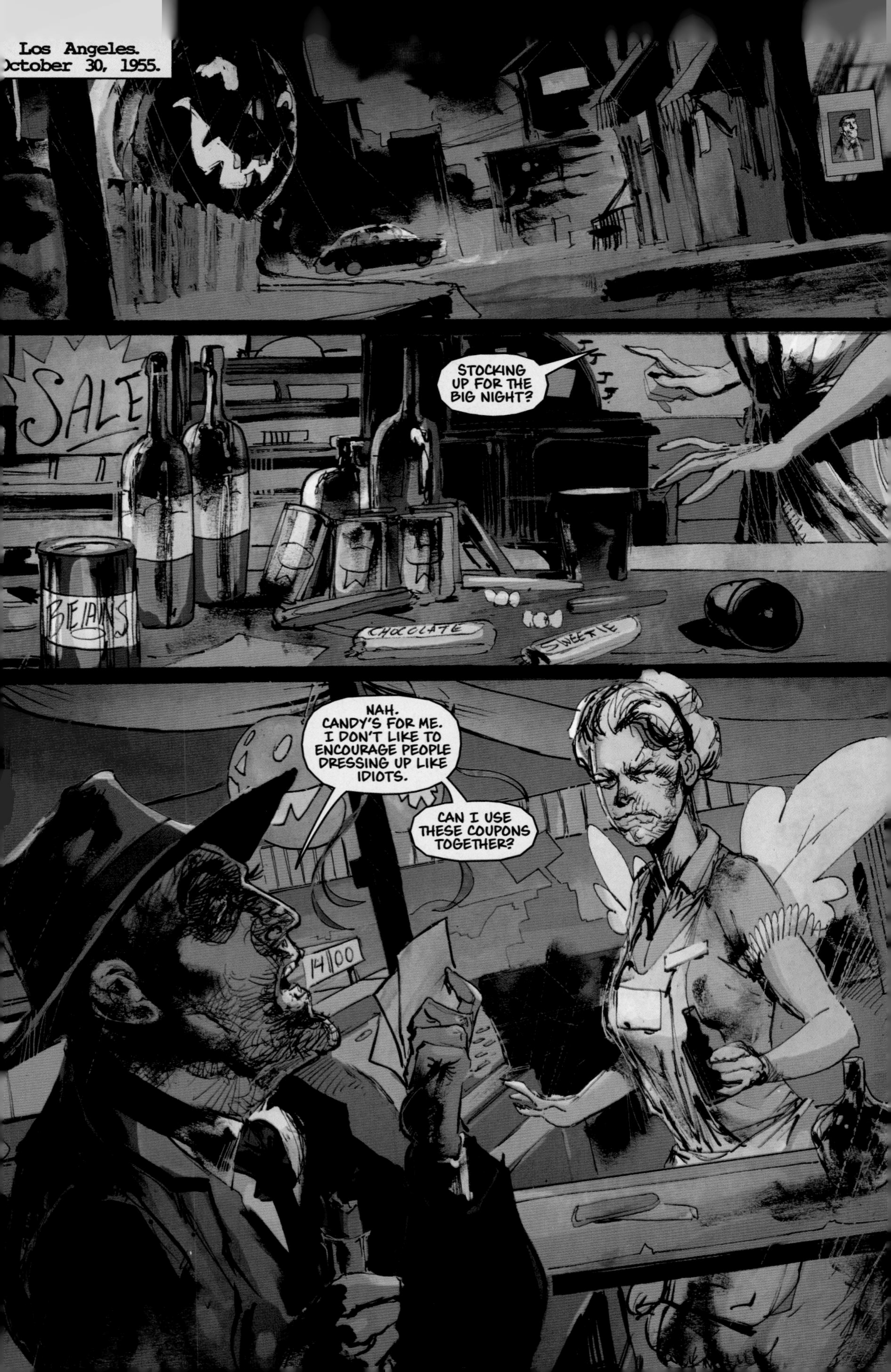
Los Angeles.
October 30, 1955.
SALE
STOCKING UP FOR THE BIG NIGHT?
CHOCOLATE
NAH. CANDY'S FOR ME. I DON'T LIKE TO ENCOURAGE PEOPLE DRESSING UP LIKE IDIOTS.
CAN I USE THESE COUPONS TOGETHER?

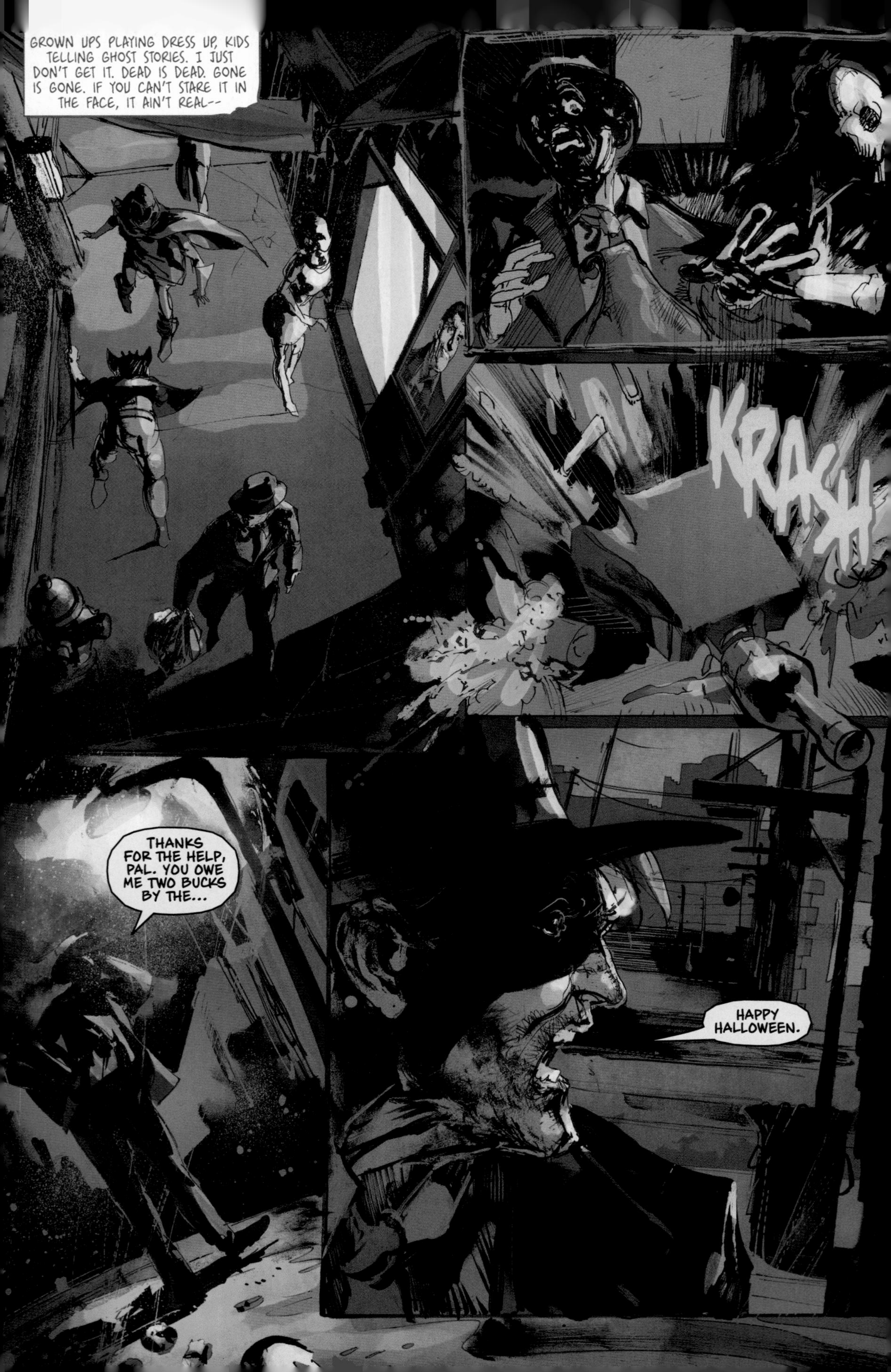
GROWN UPS PLAYING DRESS UP, KIDS TELLING GHOST STORIES. I JUST DON'T GET IT. DEAD IS DEAD. GONE IS GONE. IF YOU CAN'T STARE IT IN THE FACE, IT AIN'T REAL--
KRASH
THANKS FOR THE HELP, PAL. YOU OWE ME TWO BUCKS BY THE...
HAPPY HALLOWEEN.

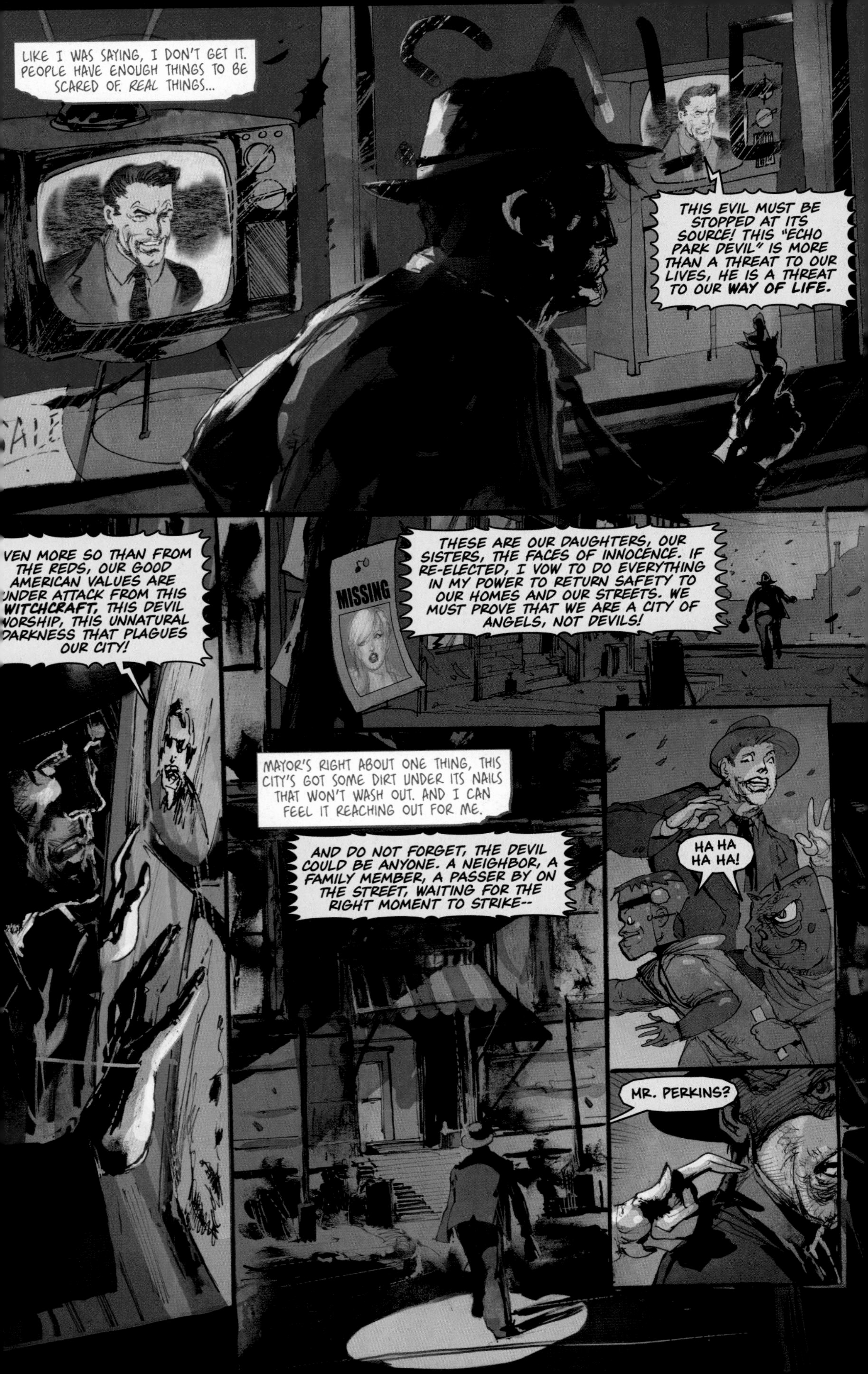

LIKE I WAS SAYING, I DON'T GET IT. PEOPLE HAVE ENOUGH THINGS TO BE SCARED OF. REAL THINGS...
THIS EVIL MUST BE STOPPED AT ITS SOURCE! THIS "ECHO PARK DEVIL" IS MORE THAN A THREAT TO OUR LIVES, HE IS A THREAT TO OUR WAY OF LIFE.
SALE
VEN MORE SO THAN FROM THE REDS, OUR GOOD AMERICAN VALUES ARE UNDER ATTACK FROM THIS WITCHCRAFT, THIS DEVIL WORSHIP, THIS UNNATURAL DARKNESS THAT PLAGUES OUR CITY!
MISSING
THESE ARE OUR DAUGHTERS, OUR SISTERS, THE FACES OF INNOCENCE. IF RE-ELECTED, I VOW TO DO EVERYTHING IN MY POWER TO RETURN SAFETY TO OUR HOMES AND OUR STREETS. WE MUST PROVE THAT WE ARE A CITY OF ANGELS, NOT DEVILS!
MAYOR'S RIGHT ABOUT ONE THING, THIS CITY'S GOT SOME DIRT UNDER ITS NAILS THAT WON'T WASH OUT. AND I CAN FEEL IT REACHING OUT FOR ME.
AND DO NOT FORGET, THE DEVIL COULD BE ANYONE. A NEIGHBOR, A FAMILY MEMBER, A PASSER BY ON THE STREET, WAITING FOR THE RIGHT MOMENT TO STRIKE--
HA HA HA HA!
MR. PERKINS?

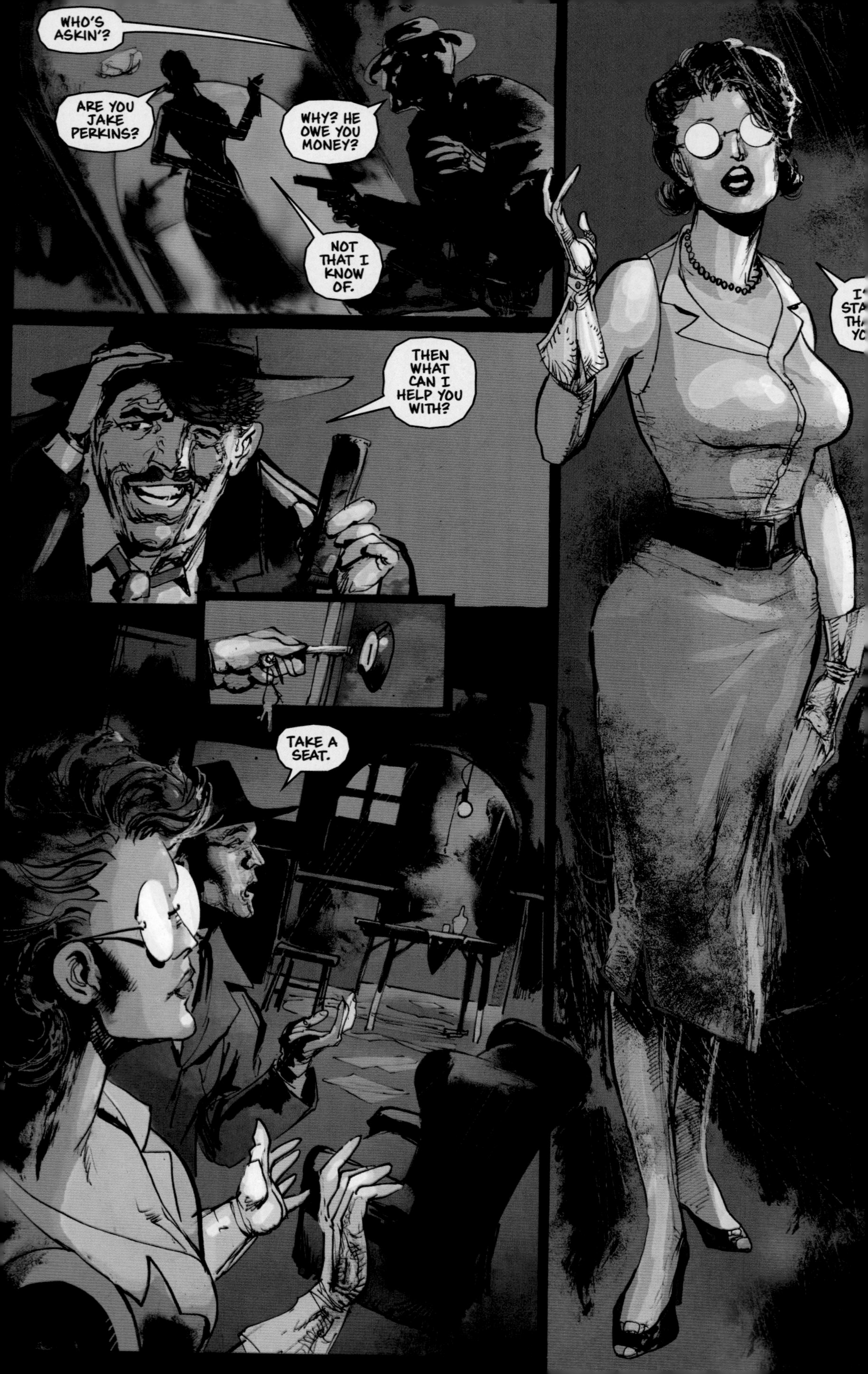
WHO'S ASKIN'?
ARE YOU JAKE PERKINS?
WHY? HE OWE YOU MONEY?
NOT THAT I KNOW OF.
THEN WHAT CAN I HELP YOU WITH?
TAKE A SEAT.

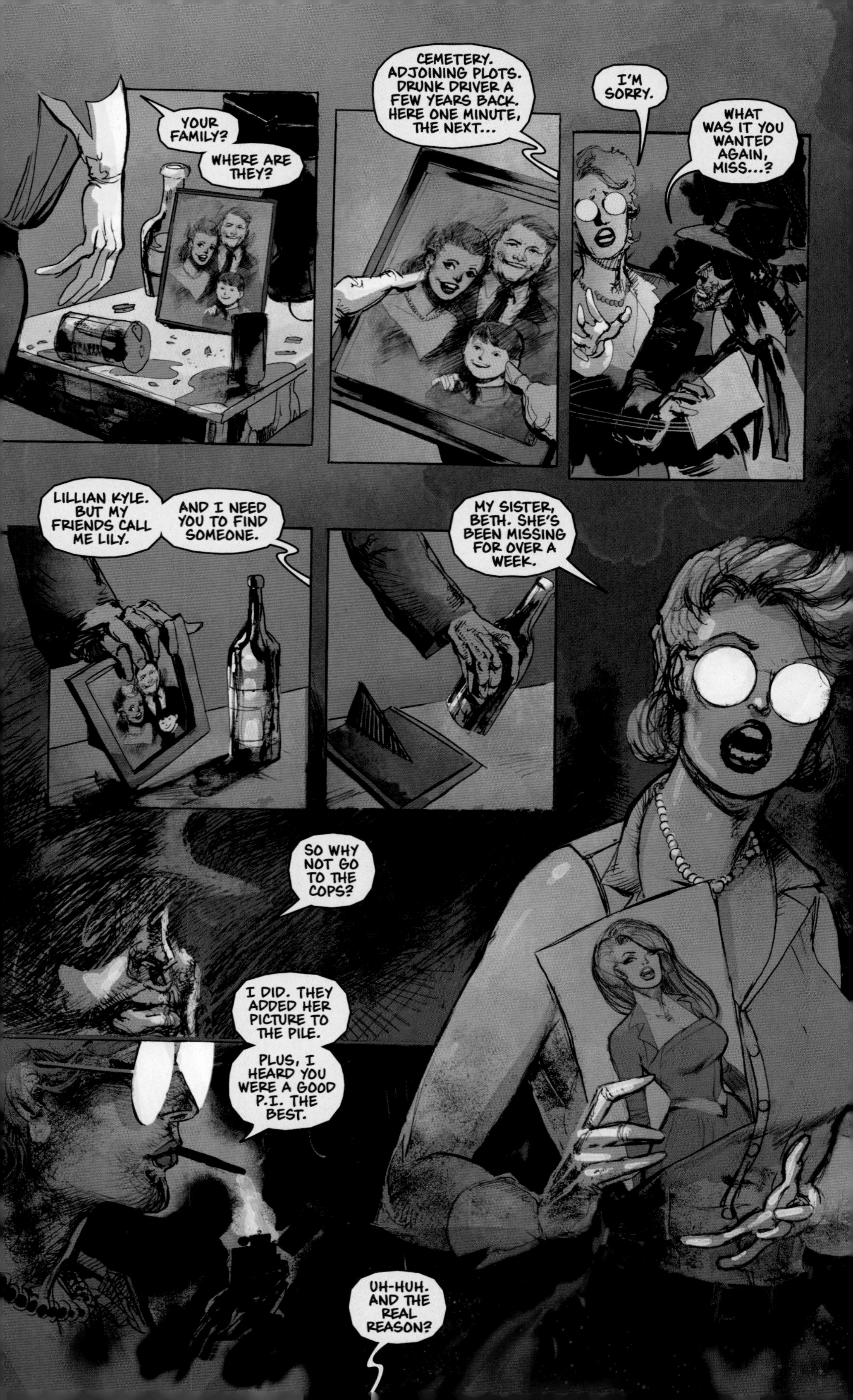
YOUR FAMILY?
WHERE ARE THEY?
CEMETERY. ADJOINING PLOTS. DRUNK DRIVER A FEW YEARS BACK. HERE ONE MINUTE, THE NEXT...
I'M SORRY.
WHAT WAS IT YOU WANTED AGAIN, MISS...?
LILLIAN KYLE. BUT MY FRIENDS CALL ME LILY.
AND I NEED YOU TO FIND SOMEONE.
MY SISTER, BETH. SHE'S BEEN MISSING FOR OVER A WEEK.
SO WHY NOT GO TO THE COPS?
I DID. THEY ADDED HER PICTURE TO THE PILE.
PLUS, I HEARD YOU WERE A GOOD P.I. THE BEST.
UH-HUH. AND THE REAL REASON?

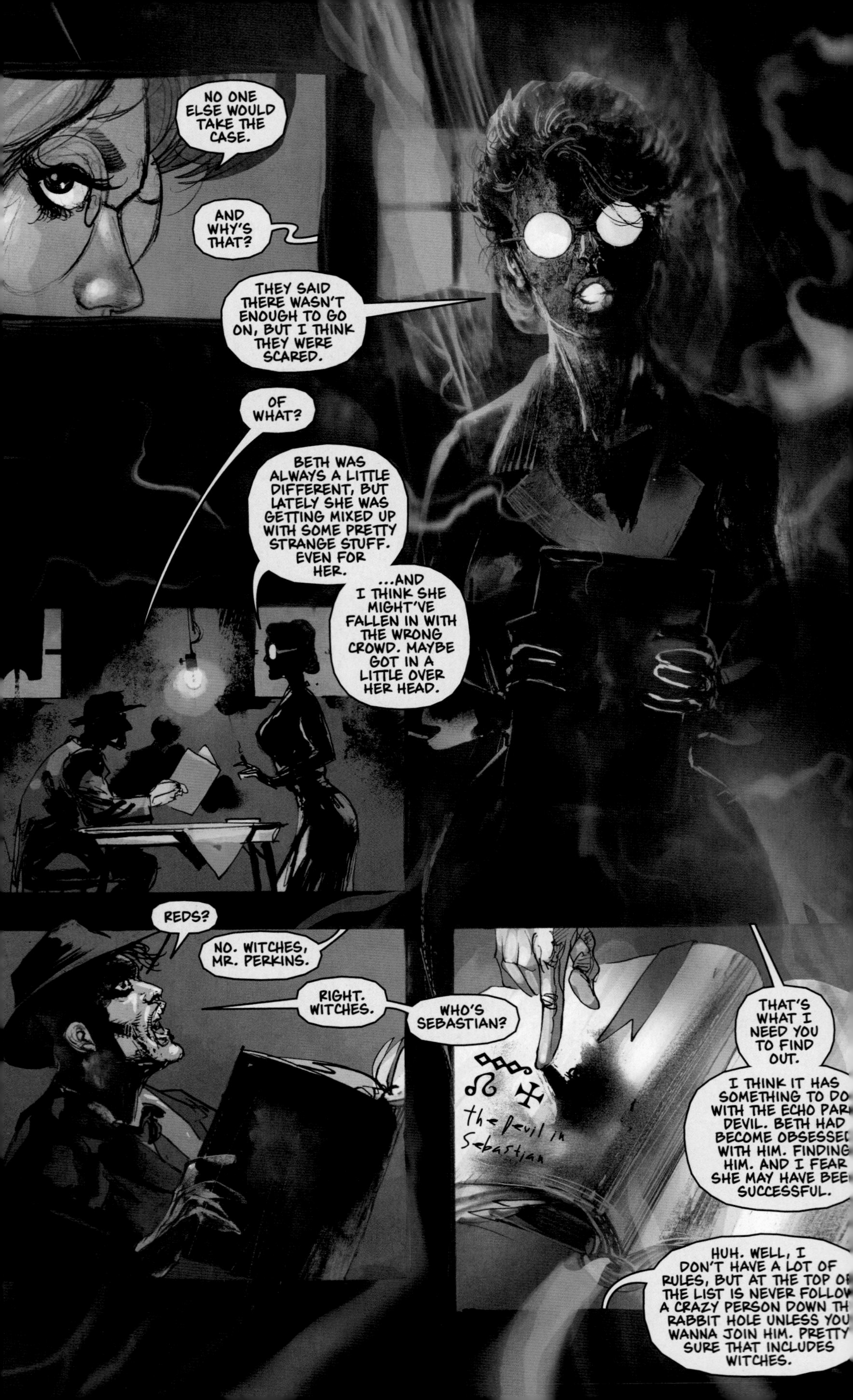
NO ONE ELSE WOULD TAKE THE CASE.
AND WHY'S THAT?
THEY SAID THERE WASN'T ENOUGH TO GO ON, BUT I THINK THEY WERE SCARED.
OF WHAT?
BETH WAS ALWAYS A LITTLE DIFFERENT, BUT LATELY SHE WAS GETTING MIXED UP WITH SOME PRETTY STRANGE STUFF. EVEN FOR HER.
...AND I THINK SHE MIGHT'VE FALLEN IN WITH THE WRONG CROWD. MAYBE GOT IN A LITTLE OVER HER HEAD.
REDS?
NO. WITCHES, MR. PERKINS.
RIGHT. WITCHES.
WHO'S SEBASTIAN?
The Devil in Sebastian
THAT'S WHAT I NEED YOU TO FIND OUT.
I THINK IT HAS SOMETHING TO DO WITH THE ECHO PAR DEVIL. BETH HAD BECOME OBSESSE WITH HIM. FINDING HIM. AND I FEAR SHE MAY HAVE BEE SUCCESSFUL.
HUH. WELL, I DON'T HAVE A LOT OF RULES, BUT AT THE TOP O THE LIST IS NEVER FOLLOW A CRAZY PERSON DOWN TH RABBIT HOLE UNLESS YOU WANNA JOIN HIM. PRETTY SURE THAT INCLUDES WITCHES.

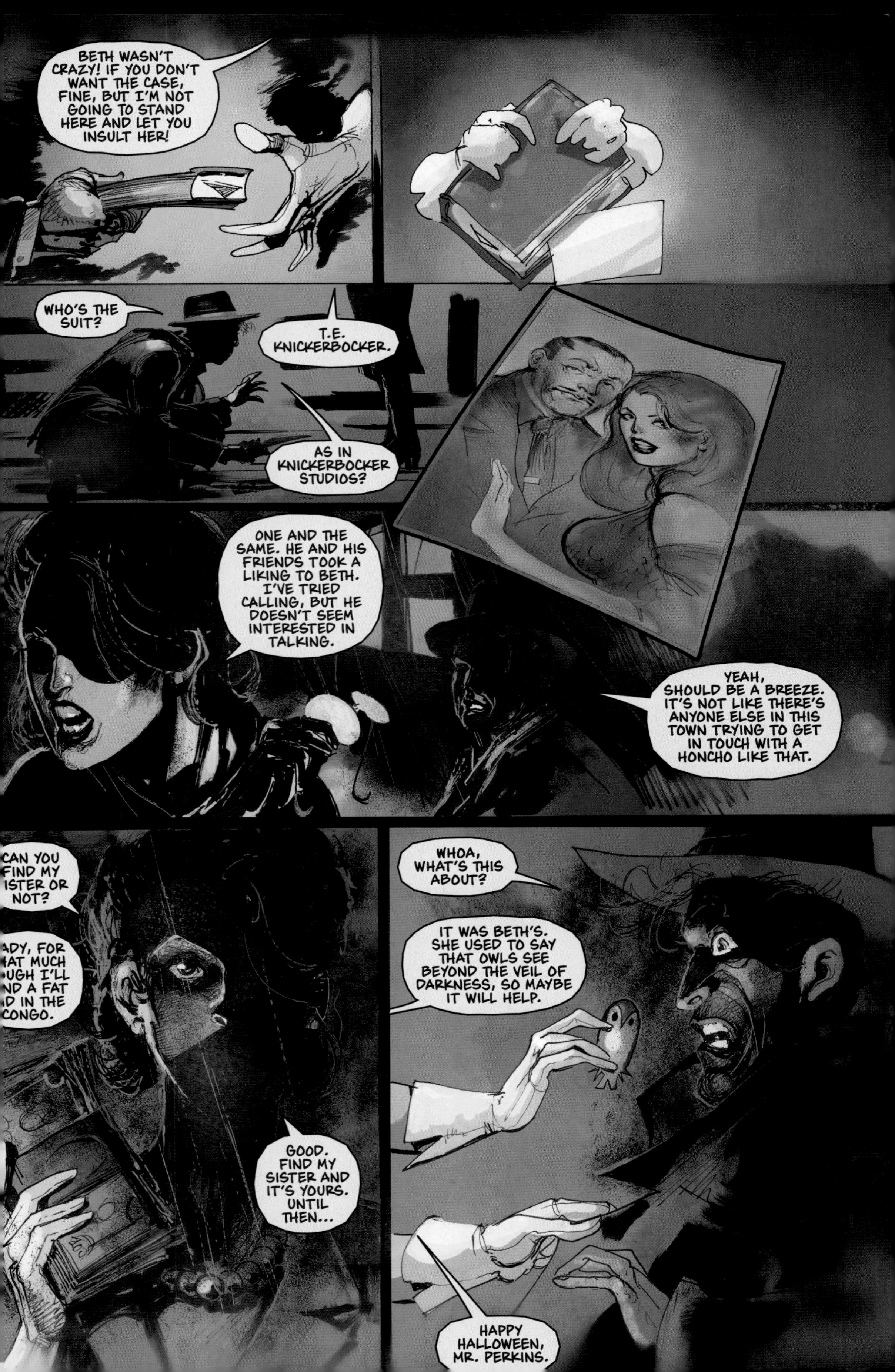
BETH WASN'T CRAZY! IF YOU DON'T WANT THE CASE, FINE, BUT I'M NOT GOING TO STAND HERE AND LET YOU INSULT HER!
WHO'S THE SUIT?
T.E. KNICKERBOCKER.
AS IN KNICKERBOCKER STUDIOS?
ONE AND THE SAME. HE AND HIS FRIENDS TOOK A LIKING TO BETH. I'VE TRIED CALLING, BUT HE DOESN'T SEEM INTERESTED IN TALKING.
YEAH, SHOULD BE A BREEZE. IT'S NOT LIKE THERE'S ANYONE ELSE IN THIS TOWN TRYING TO GET IN TOUCH WITH A HONCHO LIKE THAT.
CAN YOU FIND MY ISTER OR NOT?
ADY, FOR HAT MUCH OUGH I'LL ND A FAT D IN THE CONGO.
GOOD. FIND MY SISTER AND IT'S YOURS. UNTIL THEN...
WHOA, WHAT'S THIS ABOUT?
IT WAS BETH'S. SHE USED TO SAY THAT OWLS SEE BEYOND THE VEIL OF DARKNESS, SO MAYBE IT WILL HELP.
HAPPY HALLOWEEN, MR. PERKINS.

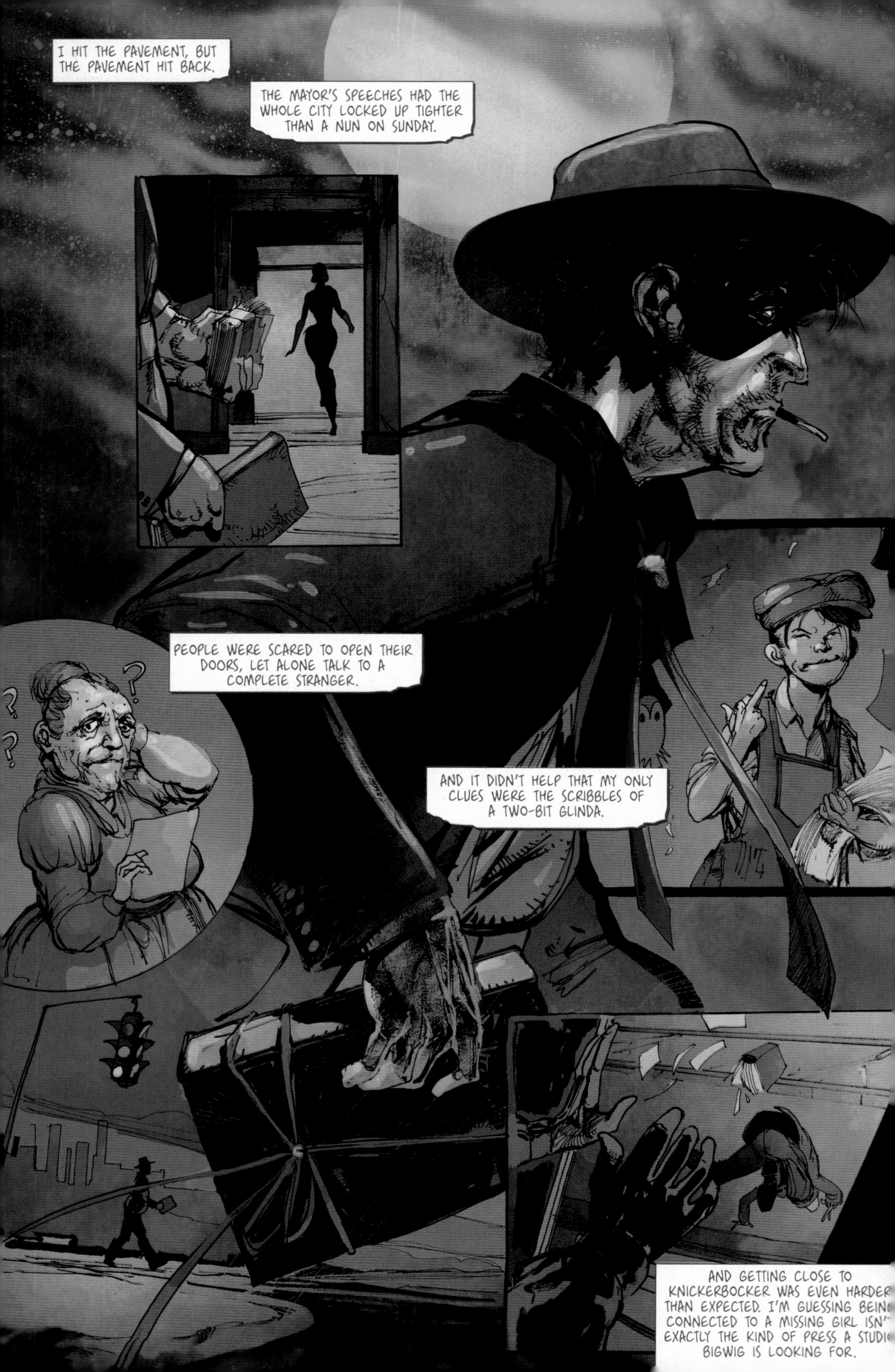
I HIT THE PAVEMENT, BUT THE PAVEMENT HIT BACK.
THE MAYOR'S SPEECHES HAD THE WHOLE CITY LOCKED UP TIGHTER THAN A NUN ON SUNDAY.
PEOPLE WERE SCARED TO OPEN THEIR DOORS, LET ALONE TALK TO A COMPLETE STRANGER.
AND IT DIDN'T HELP THAT MY ONLY CLUES WERE THE SCRIBBLES OF A TWO-BIT GLINDA.
AND GETTING CLOSE TO KNICKERBOCKER WAS EVEN HARDER THAN EXPECTED. I'M GUESSING BEING CONNECTED TO A MISSING GIRL ISN'T EXACTLY THE KIND OF PRESS A STUDIO BIGWIG IS LOOKING FOR.

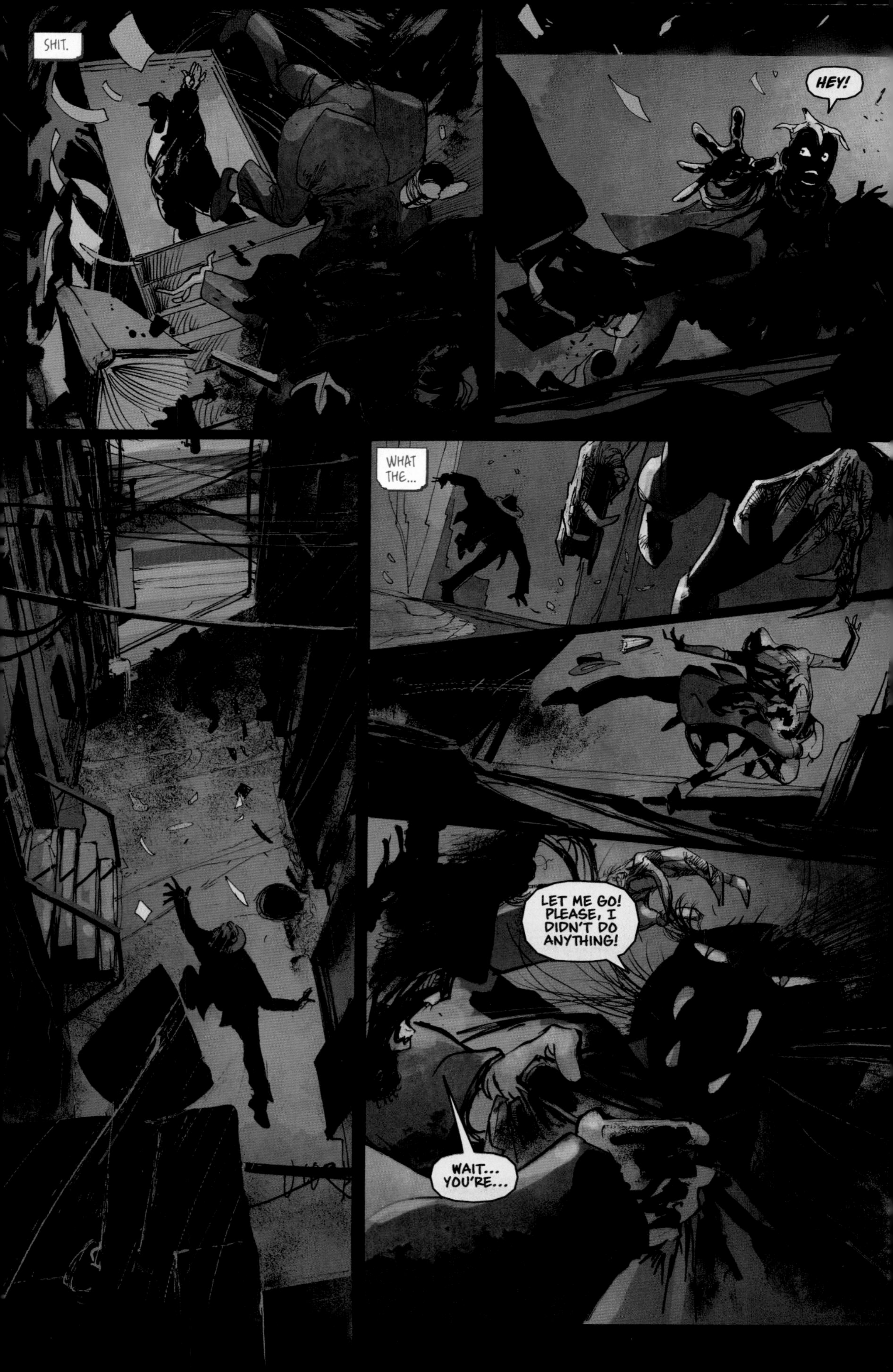
SHIT.
HEY!
WHAT THE...
LET ME GO! PLEASE, I DIDN'T DO ANYTHING!
WAIT... YOU'RE...

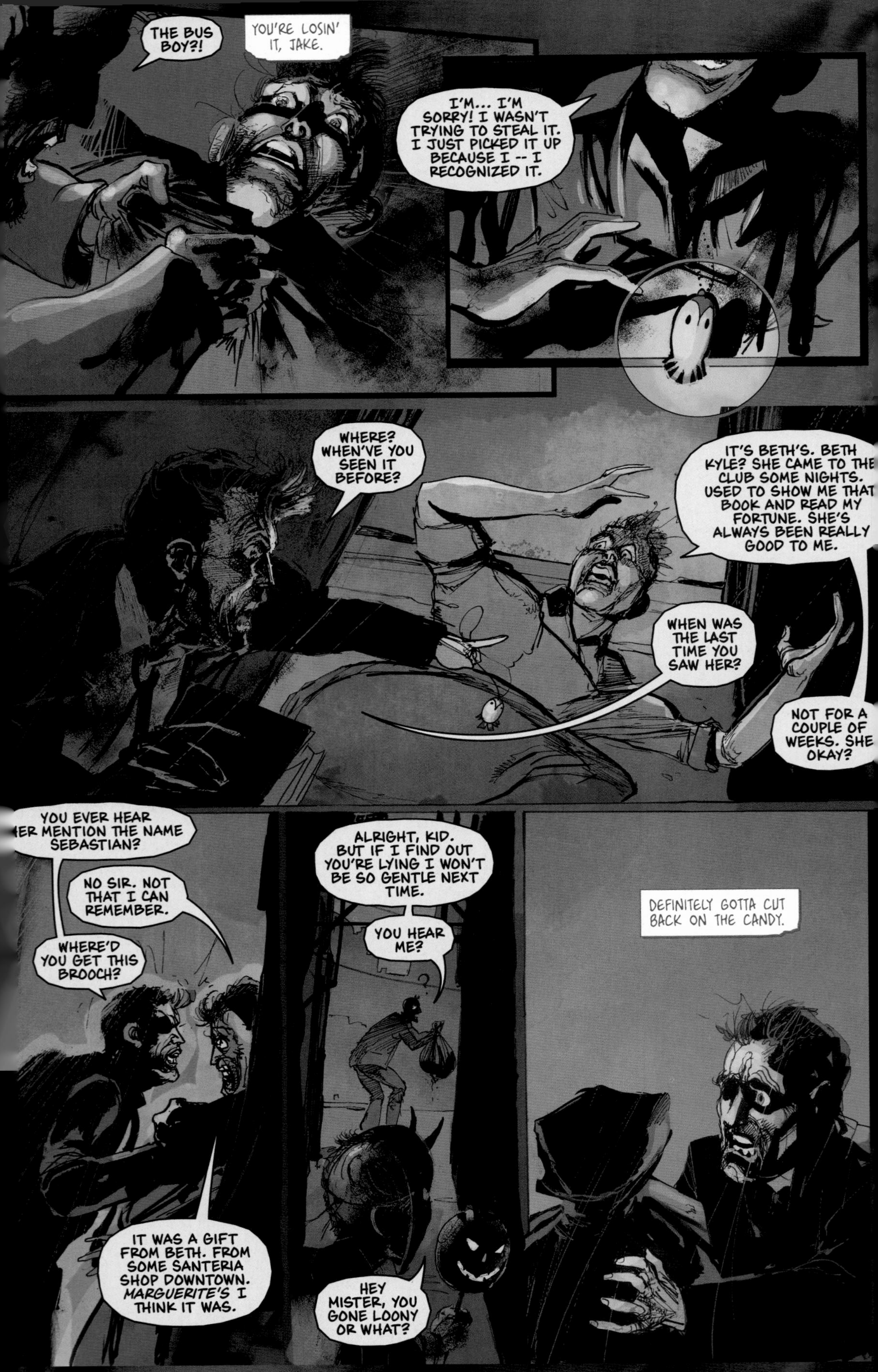
THE BUS BOY?!
YOU'RE LOSIN' IT, JAKE.
I'M... I'M SORRY! I WASN'T TRYING TO STEAL IT. I JUST PICKED IT UP BECAUSE I -- I RECOGNIZED IT.
WHERE? WHEN'VE YOU SEEN IT BEFORE?
IT'S BETH'S. BETH KYLE? SHE CAME TO THE CLUB SOME NIGHTS. USED TO SHOW ME THAT BOOK AND READ MY FORTUNE. SHE'S ALWAYS BEEN REALLY GOOD TO ME.
WHEN WAS THE LAST TIME YOU SAW HER?
NOT FOR A COUPLE OF WEEKS. SHE OKAY?
YOU EVER HEAR HER MENTION THE NAME SEBASTIAN?
NO SIR. NOT THAT I CAN REMEMBER.
WHERE'D YOU GET THIS BROOCH?
IT WAS A GIFT FROM BETH. FROM SOME SANTERIA SHOP DOWNTOWN. MARGUERITE'S I THINK IT WAS.
ALRIGHT, KID. BUT IF I FIND OUT YOU'RE LYING I WON'T BE SO GENTLE NEXT TIME.
YOU HEAR ME?
HEY MISTER, YOU GONE LOONY OR WHAT?
DEFINITELY GOTTA CUT BACK ON THE CANDY.

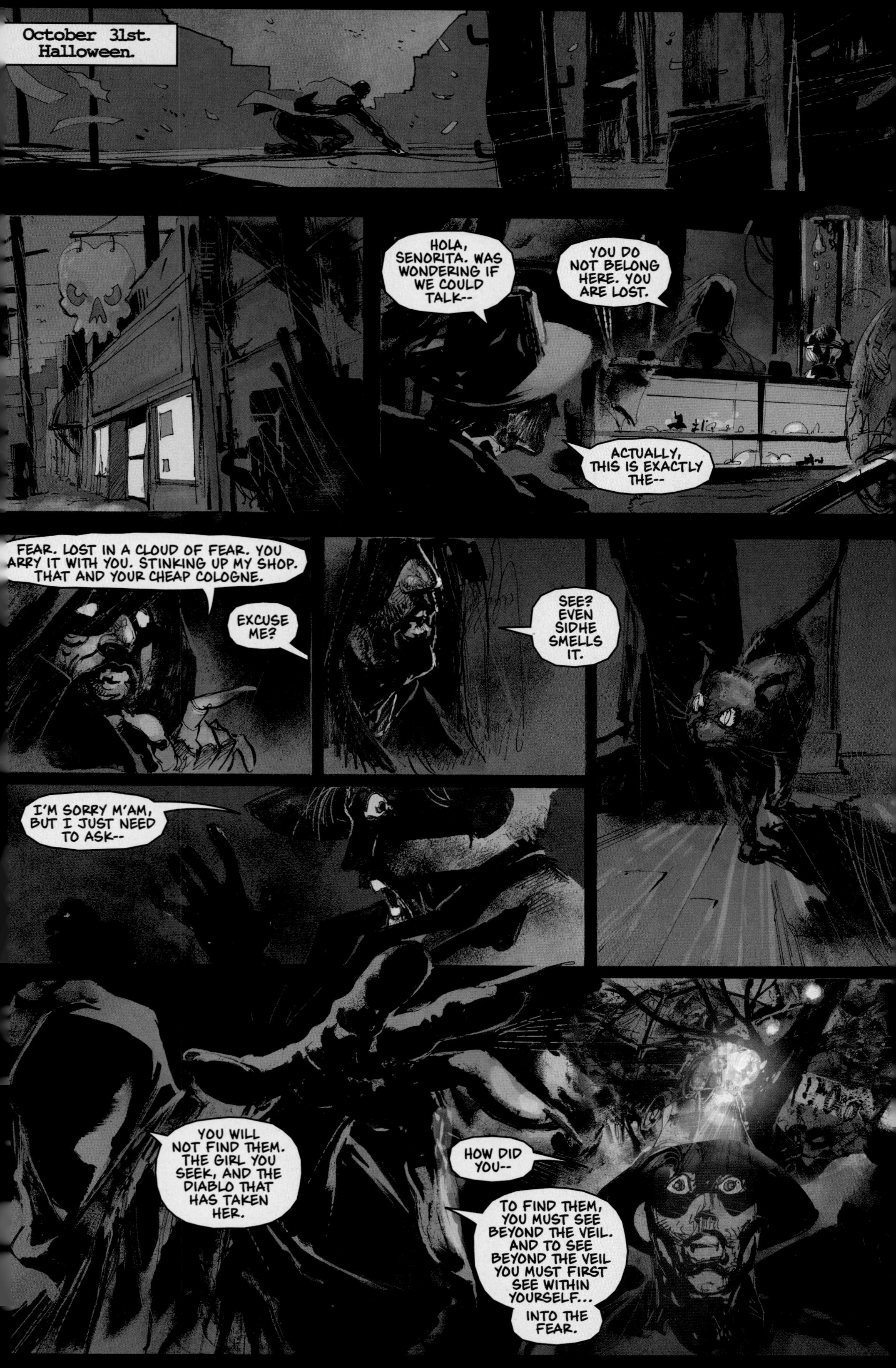
October 31st.
Halloween.
HOLA, SENORITA. WAS WONDERING IF WE COULD TALK--
YOU DO NOT BELONG HERE. YOU ARE LOST.
ACTUALLY, THIS IS EXACTLY THE--
FEAR. LOST IN A CLOUD OF FEAR. YOU ARRY IT WITH YOU. STINKING UP MY SHOP. THAT AND YOUR CHEAP COLOGNE.
EXCUSE ME?
SEE? EVEN SIDHE SMELLS IT.
I'M SORRY M'AM, BUT I JUST NEED TO ASK--
YOU WILL NOT FIND THEM. THE GIRL YOU SEEK, AND THE DIABLO THAT HAS TAKEN HER.
HOW DID YOU--
TO FIND THEM, YOU MUST SEE BEYOND THE VEIL. AND TO SEE BEYOND THE VEIL YOU MUST FIRST SEE WITHIN YOURSELF...
INTO THE FEAR.

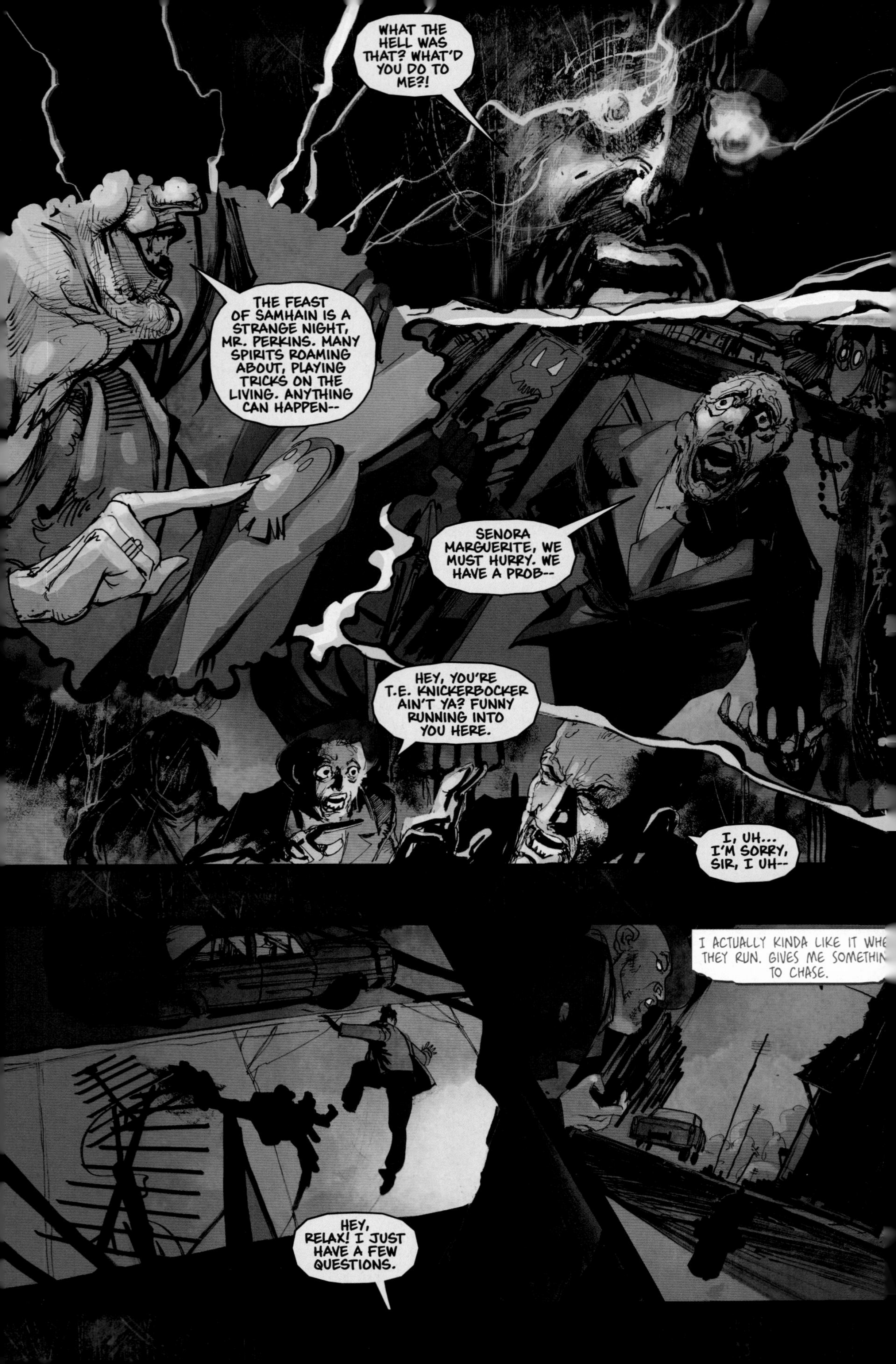
WHAT THE HELL WAS THAT? WHAT'D YOU DO TO ME?!
THE FEAST OF SAMHAIN IS A STRANGE NIGHT, MR. PERKINS. MANY SPIRITS ROAMING ABOUT, PLAYING TRICKS ON THE LIVING. ANYTHING CAN HAPPEN--
SENORA MARGUERITE, WE MUST HURRY. WE HAVE A PROB--
HEY, YOU'RE T.E. KNICKERBOCKER AIN'T YA? FUNNY RUNNING INTO YOU HERE.
I, UH... I'M SORRY, SIR, I UH--
I ACTUALLY KINDA LIKE IT WHE THEY RUN. GIVES ME SOMETHIN TO CHASE.
HEY, RELAX! I JUST HAVE A FEW QUESTIONS.

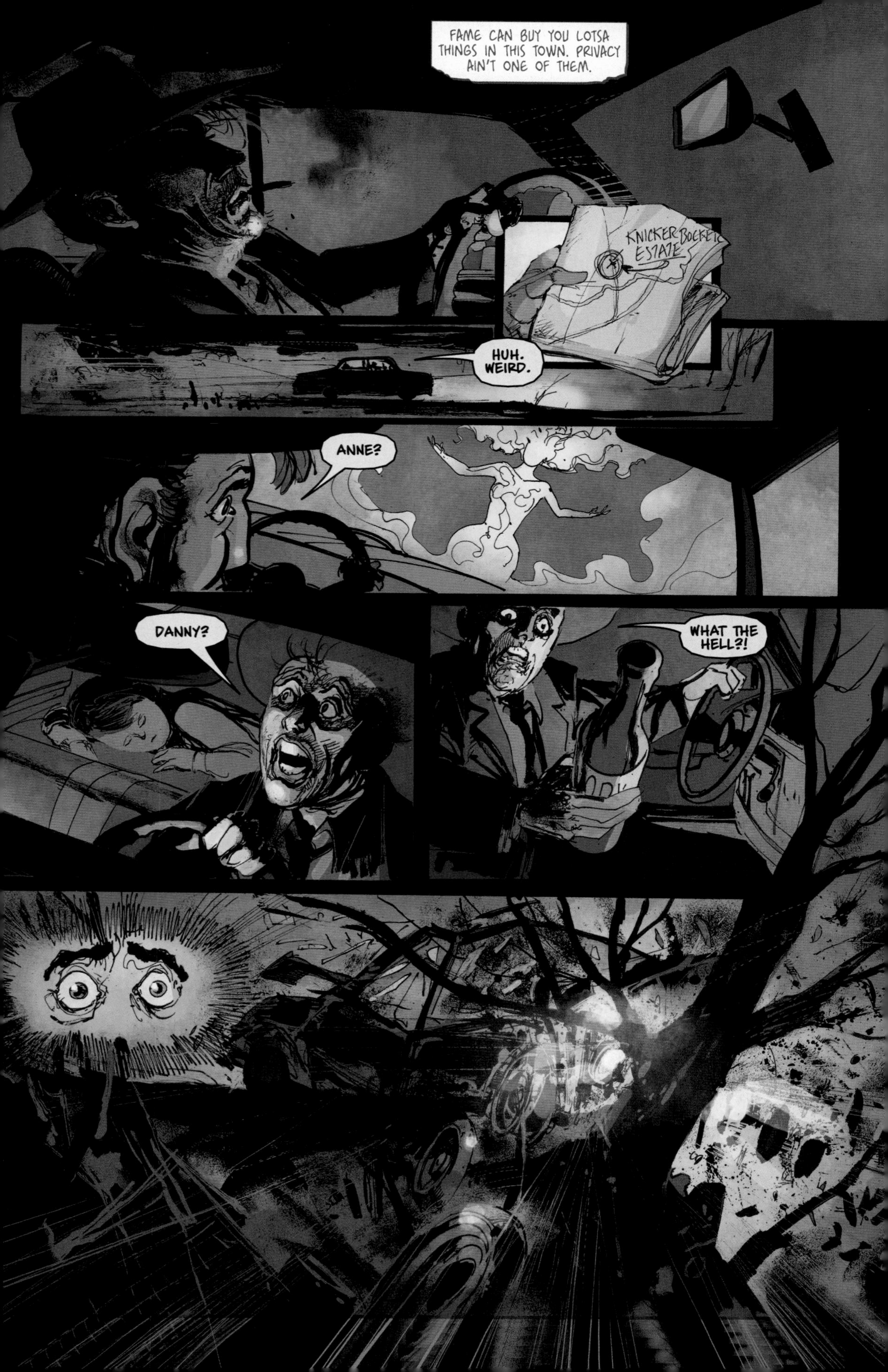
FAME CAN BUY YOU LOTSA THINGS IN THIS TOWN. PRIVACY AIN'T ONE OF THEM.
KNICKERBOCKER ESTATE
HUH. WEIRD.
ANNE?
DANNY?
WHAT THE HELL?!

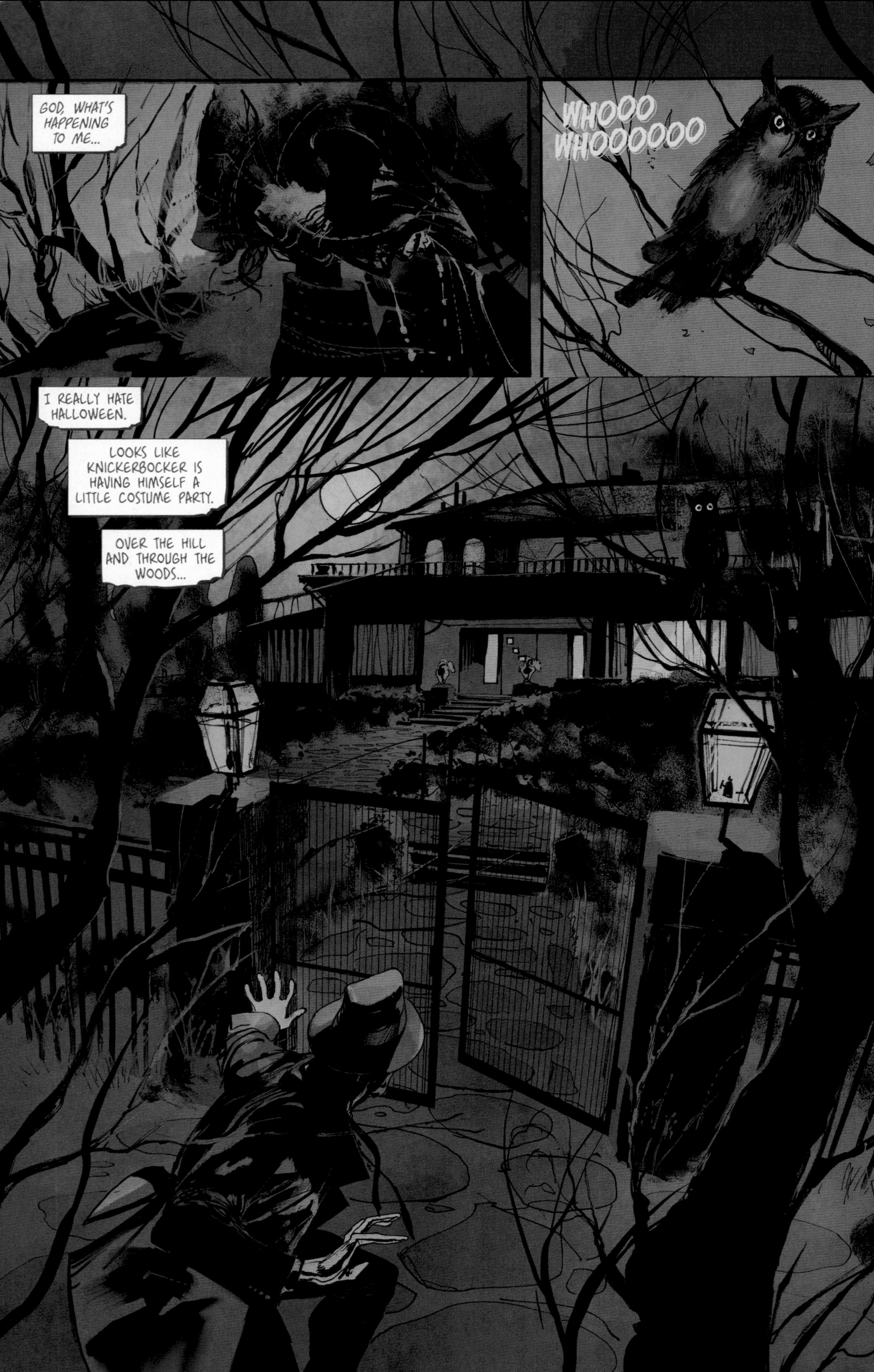
GOD, WHAT'S HAPPENING TO ME...
WHOOO WHOOOOOO
I REALLY HATE HALLOWEEN.
LOOKS LIKE KNICKERBOCKER IS HAVING HIMSELF A LITTLE COSTUME PARTY.
OVER THE HILL AND THROUGH THE WOODS...

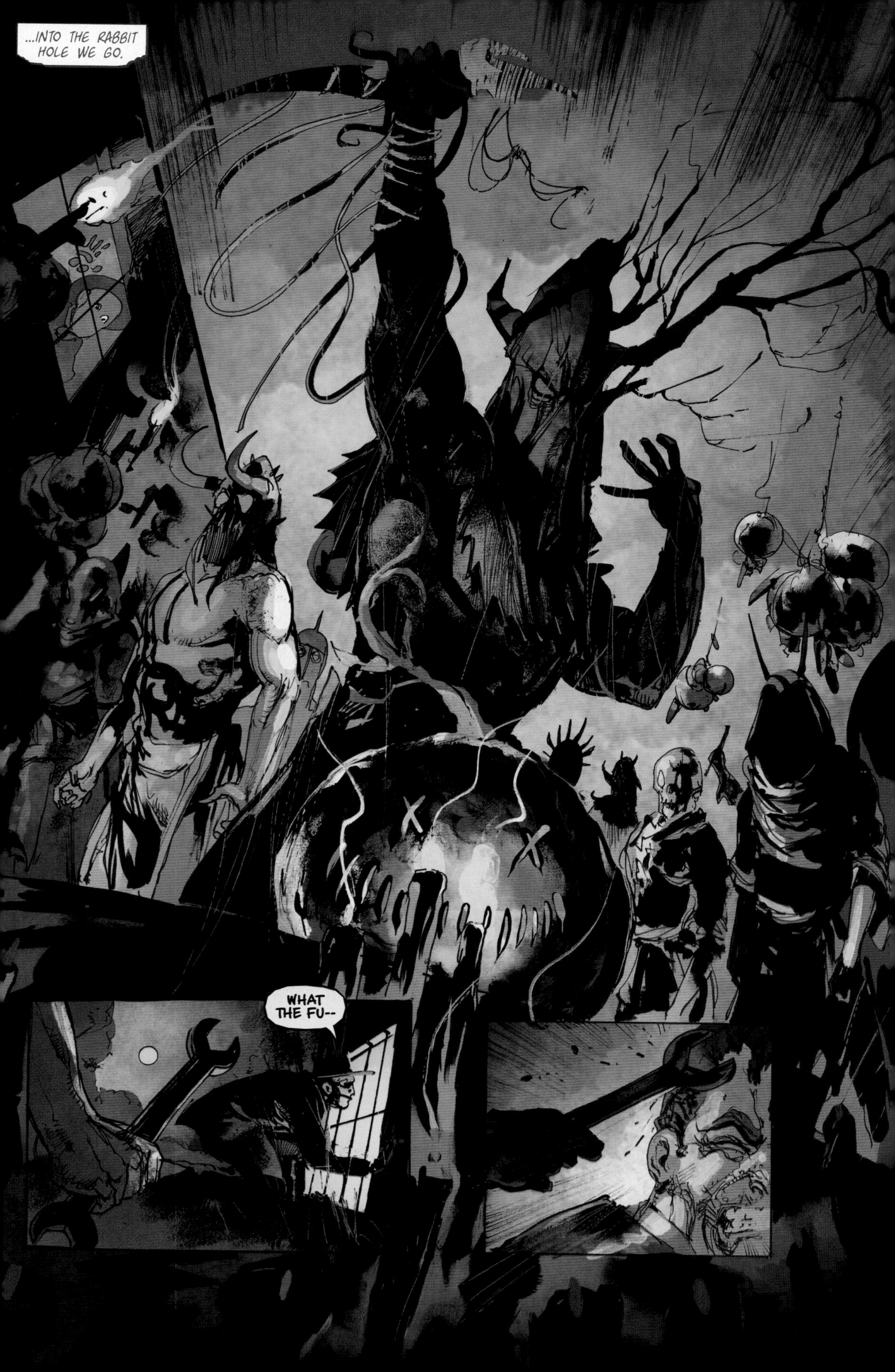

...INTO THE RABBIT HOLE WE GO.
WHAT THE FU--

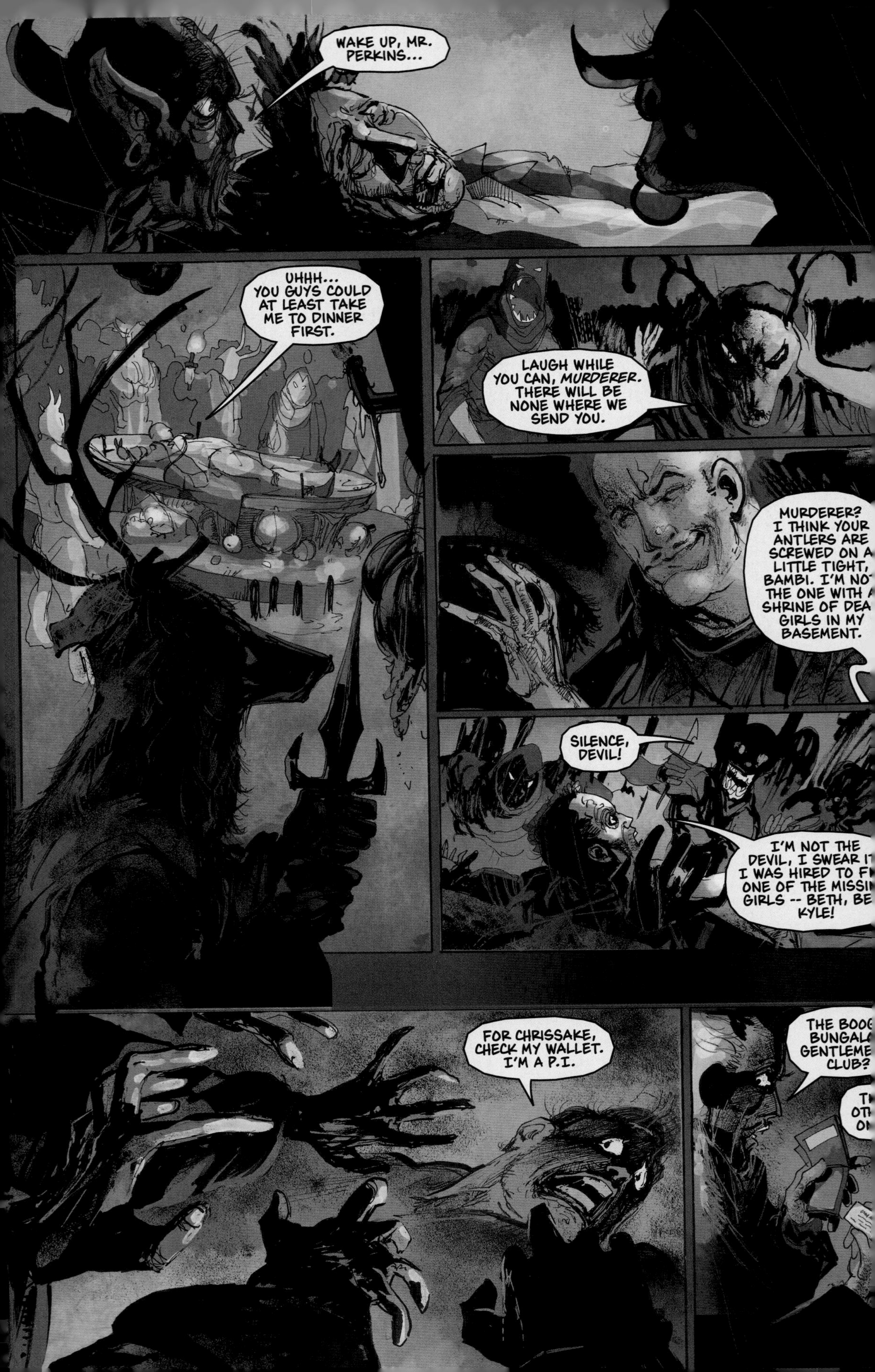
WAKE UP, MR. PERKINS...
UHHH... YOU GUYS COULD AT LEAST TAKE ME TO DINNER FIRST.
LAUGH WHILE YOU CAN, MURDERER. THERE WILL BE NONE WHERE WE SEND YOU.
MURDERER? I THINK YOUR ANTLERS ARE SCREWED ON A LITTLE TIGHT, BAMBI. I'M NOT THE ONE WITH A SHRINE OF DEA GIRLS IN MY BASEMENT.
SILENCE, DEVIL!
I'M NOT THE DEVIL, I SWEAR IT I WAS HIRED TO F ONE OF THE MISSIN GIRLS -- BETH, BE KYLE!
FOR CHRISSAKE, CHECK MY WALLET. I'M A P.I.
THE BOOG BUNGALO GENTLEME CLUB?

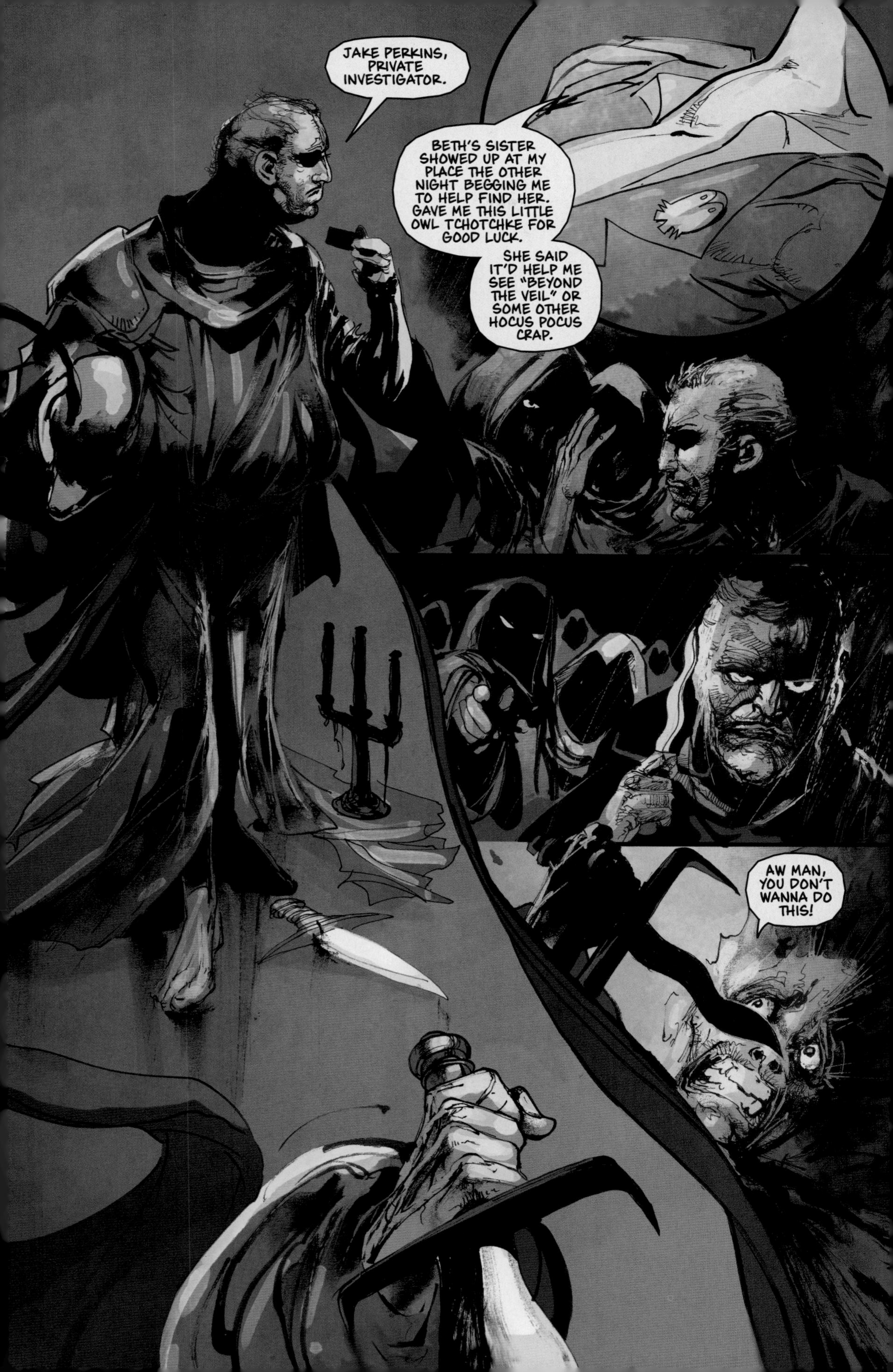
JAKE PERKINS, PRIVATE INVESTIGATOR.
BETH'S SISTER SHOWED UP AT MY PLACE THE OTHER NIGHT BEGGING ME TO HELP FIND HER. GAVE ME THIS LITTLE OWL TCHOTCHKE FOR GOOD LUCK.
SHE SAID IT'D HELP ME SEE "BEYOND THE VEIL" OR SOME OTHER HOCUS POCUS CRAP.
AW MAN, YOU DON'T WANNA DO THIS!

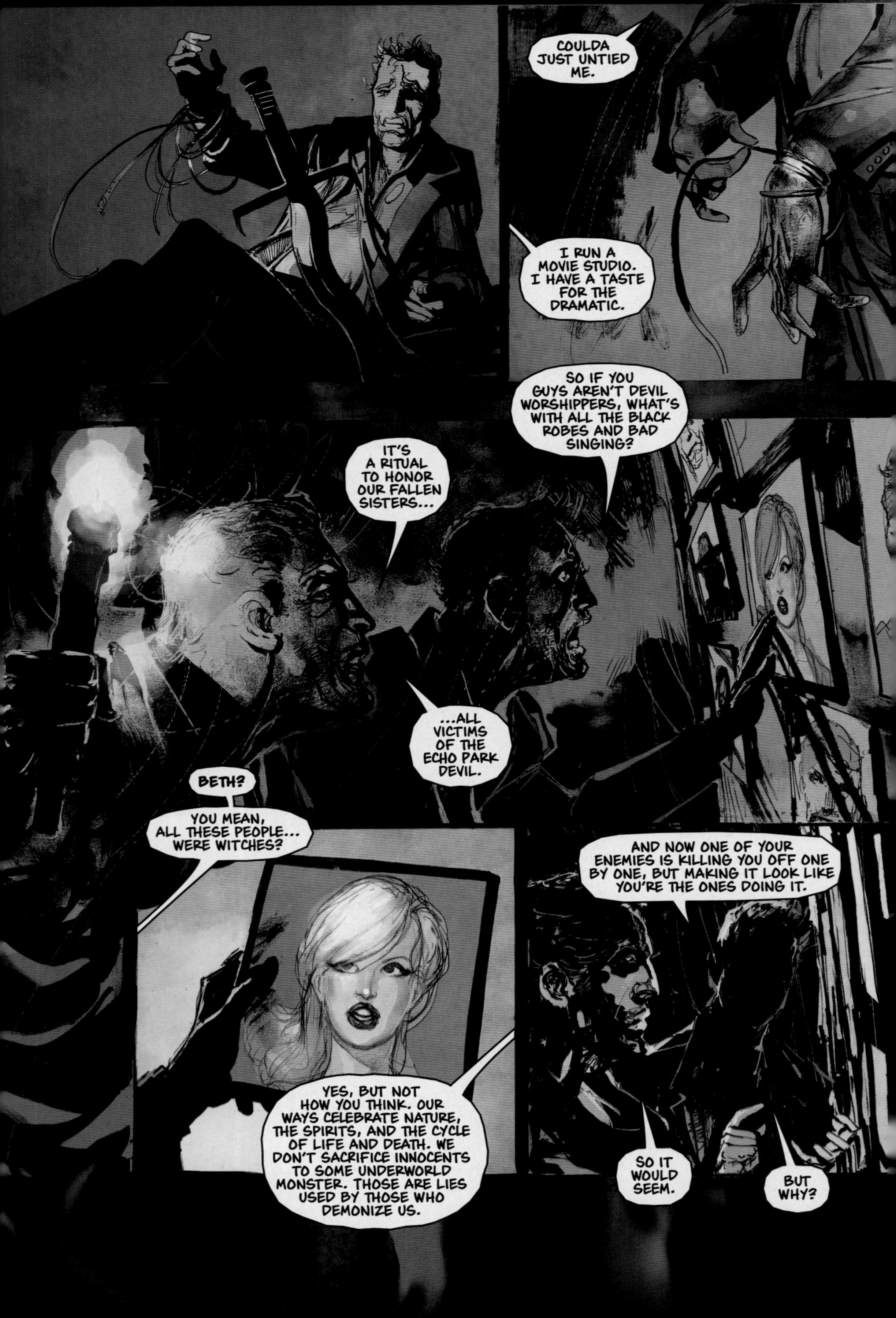
COULDA JUST UNTIED ME.
I RUN A MOVIE STUDIO. I HAVE A TASTE FOR THE DRAMATIC.
SO IF YOU GUYS AREN'T DEVIL WORSHIPPERS, WHAT'S WITH ALL THE BLACK ROBES AND BAD SINGING?
IT'S A RITUAL TO HONOR OUR FALLEN SISTERS...
...ALL VICTIMS OF THE ECHO PARK DEVIL.
BETH?
YOU MEAN, ALL THESE PEOPLE... WERE WITCHES?
YES, BUT NOT HOW YOU THINK. OUR WAYS CELEBRATE NATURE, THE SPIRITS, AND THE CYCLE OF LIFE AND DEATH. WE DON'T SACRIFICE INNOCENTS TO SOME UNDERWORLD MONSTER. THOSE ARE LIES USED BY THOSE WHO DEMONIZE US.
AND NOW ONE OF YOUR ENEMIES IS KILLING YOU OFF ONE BY ONE, BUT MAKING IT LOOK LIKE YOU'RE THE ONES DOING IT.
SO IT WOULD SEEM.
BUT WHY?

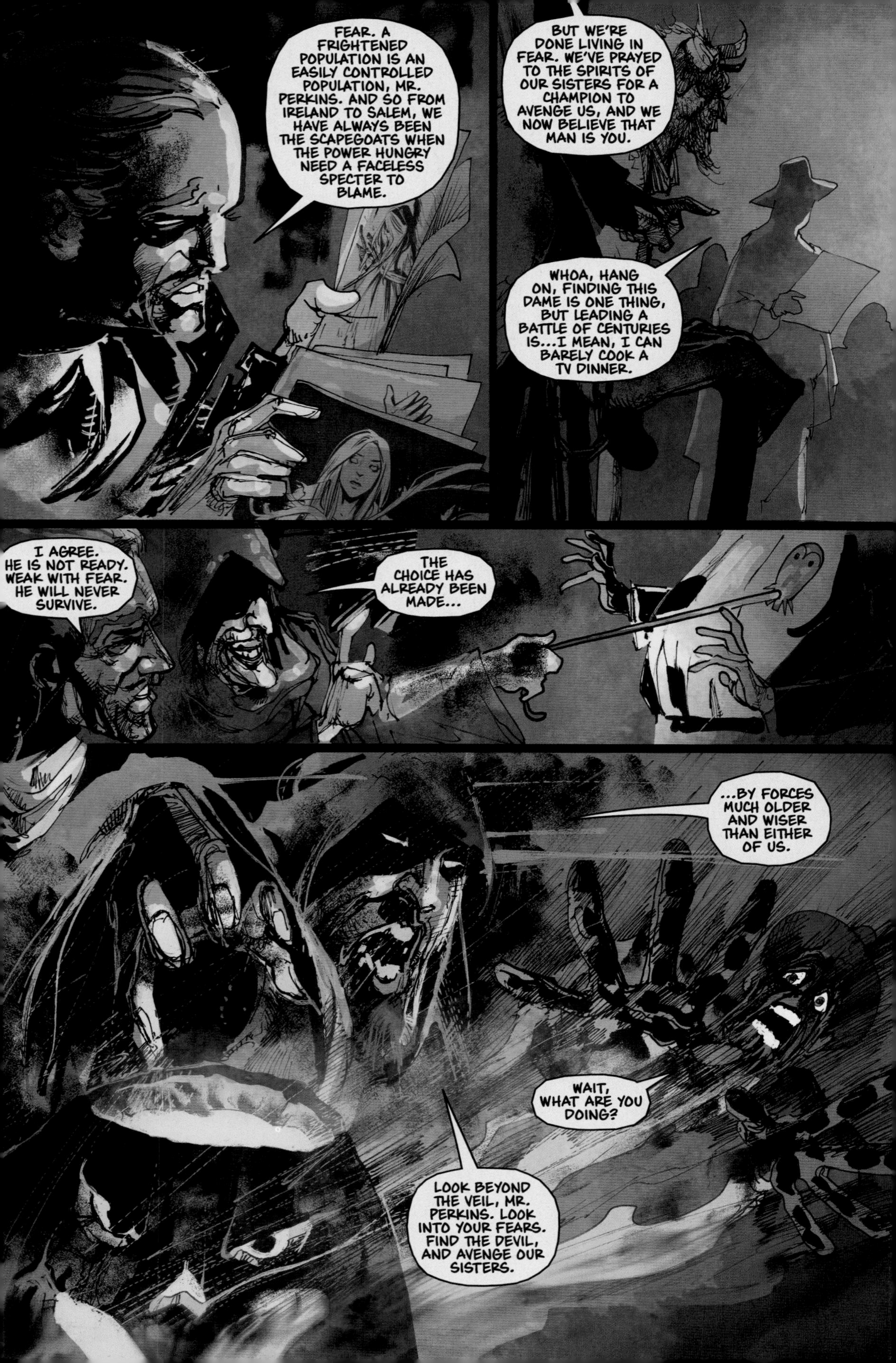

FEAR. A FRIGHTENED POPULATION IS AN EASILY CONTROLLED POPULATION, MR. PERKINS. AND SO FROM IRELAND TO SALEM, WE HAVE ALWAYS BEEN THE SCAPEGOATS WHEN THE POWER HUNGRY NEED A FACELESS SPECTER TO BLAME.
BUT WE'RE DONE LIVING IN FEAR. WE'VE PRAYED TO THE SPIRITS OF OUR SISTERS FOR A CHAMPION TO AVENGE US, AND WE NOW BELIEVE THAT MAN IS YOU.
WHOA, HANG ON, FINDING THIS DAME IS ONE THING, BUT LEADING A BATTLE OF CENTURIES IS...I MEAN, I CAN BARELY COOK A TV DINNER.
I AGREE. HE IS NOT READY. WEAK WITH FEAR. HE WILL NEVER SURVIVE.
THE CHOICE HAS ALREADY BEEN MADE...
...BY FORCES MUCH OLDER AND WISER THAN EITHER OF US.
WAIT, WHAT ARE YOU DOING?
LOOK BEYOND THE VEIL, MR. PERKINS. LOOK INTO YOUR FEARS. FIND THE DEVIL, AND AVENGE OUR SISTERS.

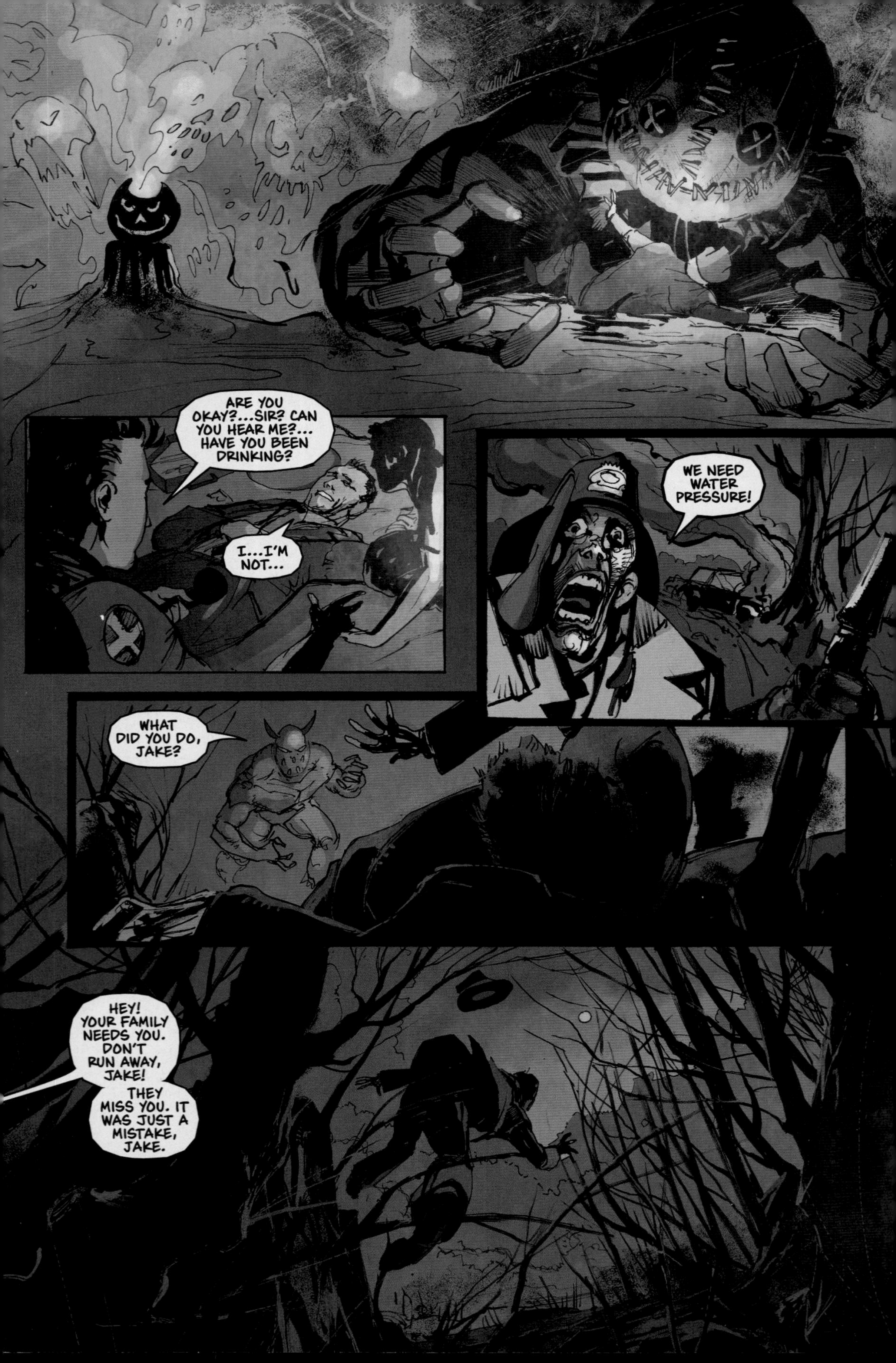
ARE YOU OKAY?...SIR? CAN YOU HEAR ME?... HAVE YOU BEEN DRINKING?
I...I'M NOT...
WE NEED WATER PRESSURE!
WHAT DID YOU DO, JAKE?
HEY! YOUR FAMILY NEEDS YOU. DON'T RUN AWAY, JAKE!
THEY MISS YOU. IT WAS JUST A MISTAKE, JAKE.

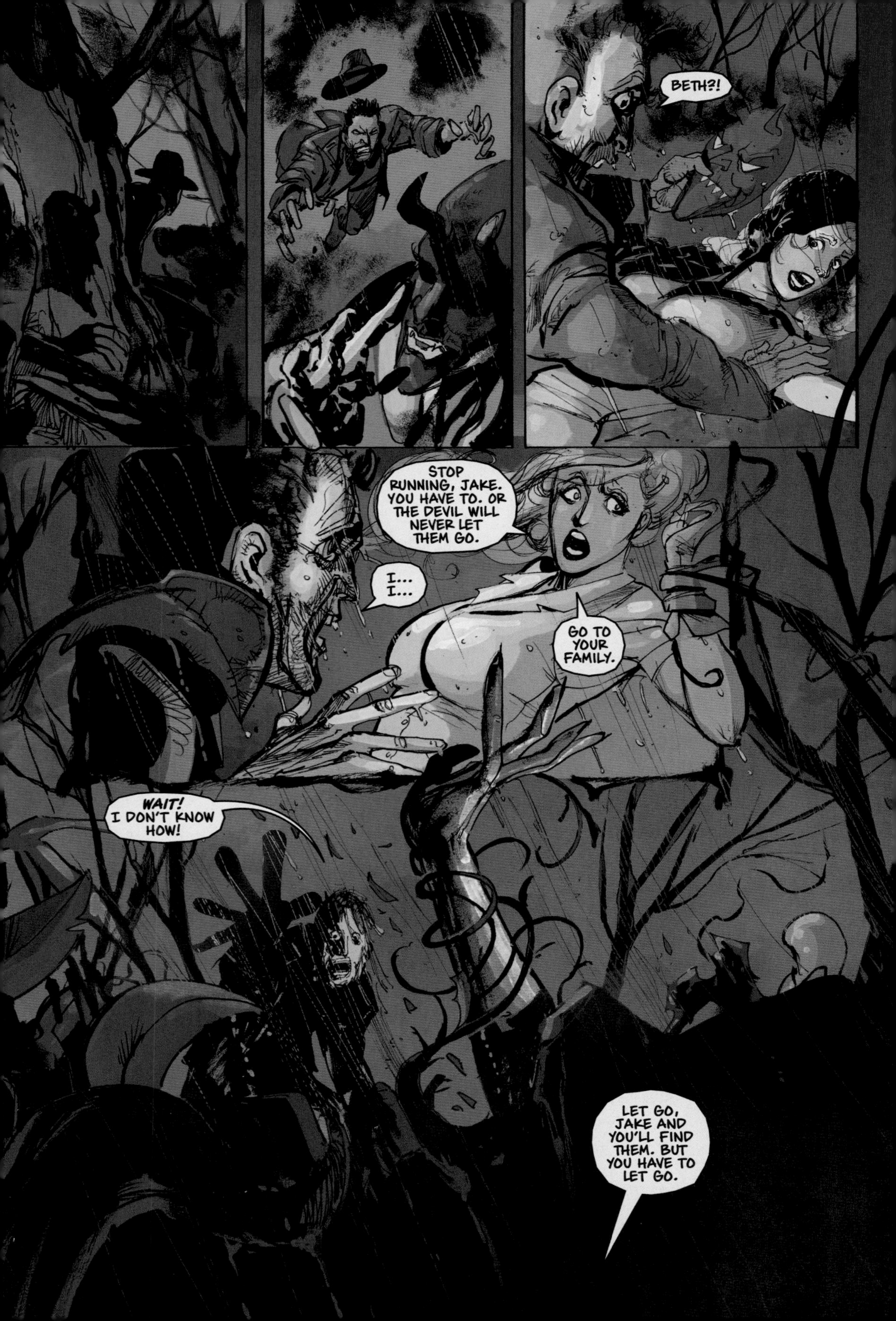
BETH?!
STOP RUNNING, JAKE. YOU HAVE TO. OR THE DEVIL WILL NEVER LET THEM GO.
I... I...
GO TO YOUR FAMILY.
WAIT! I DON'T KNOW HOW!
LET GO, JAKE AND YOU'LL FIND THEM. BUT YOU HAVE TO LET GO.

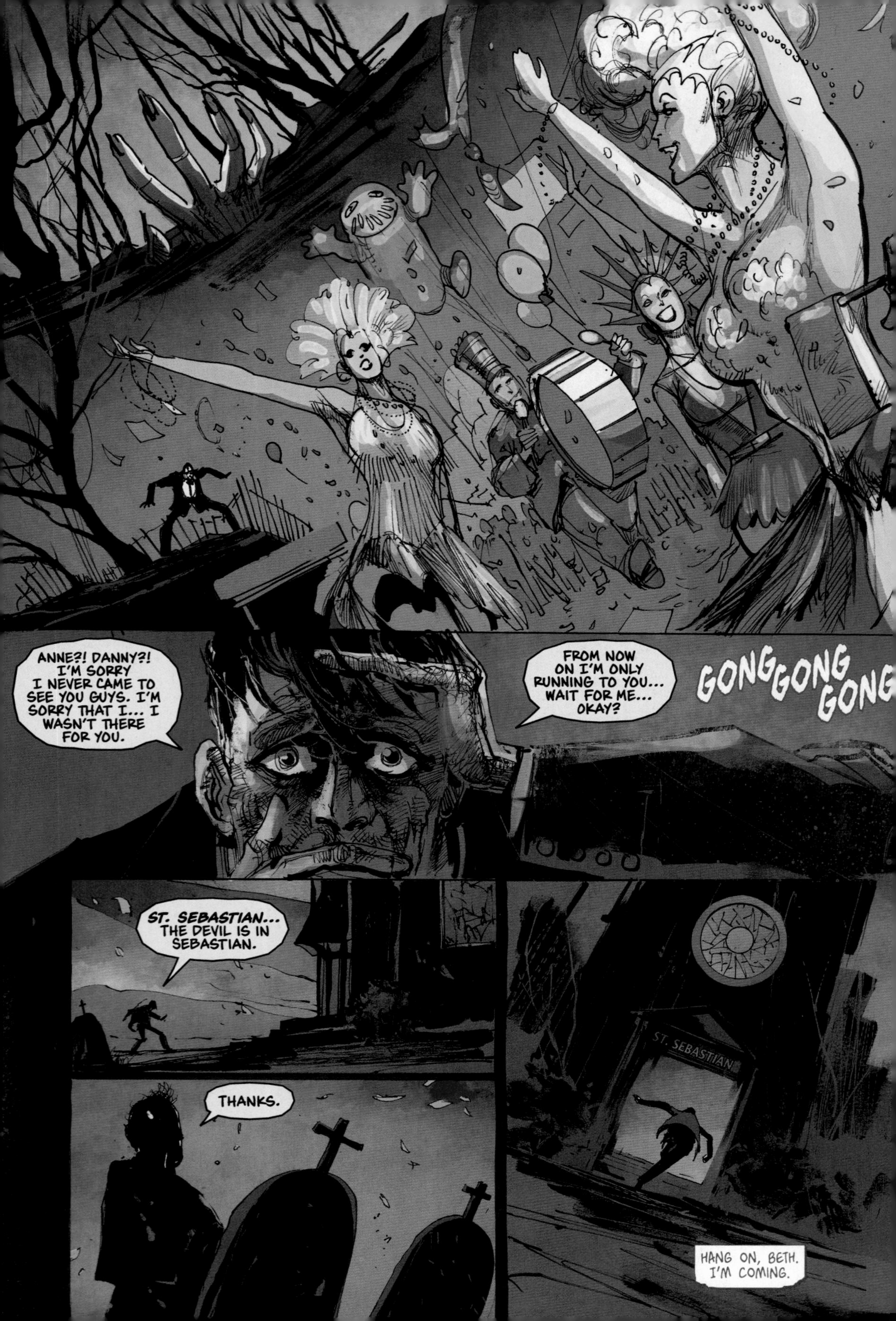
ANNE?! DANNY?! I'M SORRY I NEVER CAME TO SEE YOU GUYS. I'M SORRY THAT I... I WASN'T THERE FOR YOU.
FROM NOW ON I'M ONLY RUNNING TO YOU... WAIT FOR ME... OKAY?
GONG GONG GONG
ST. SEBASTIAN... THE DEVIL IS IN SEBASTIAN.
THANKS.
ST. SEBASTIAN
HANG ON, BETH. I'M COMING.

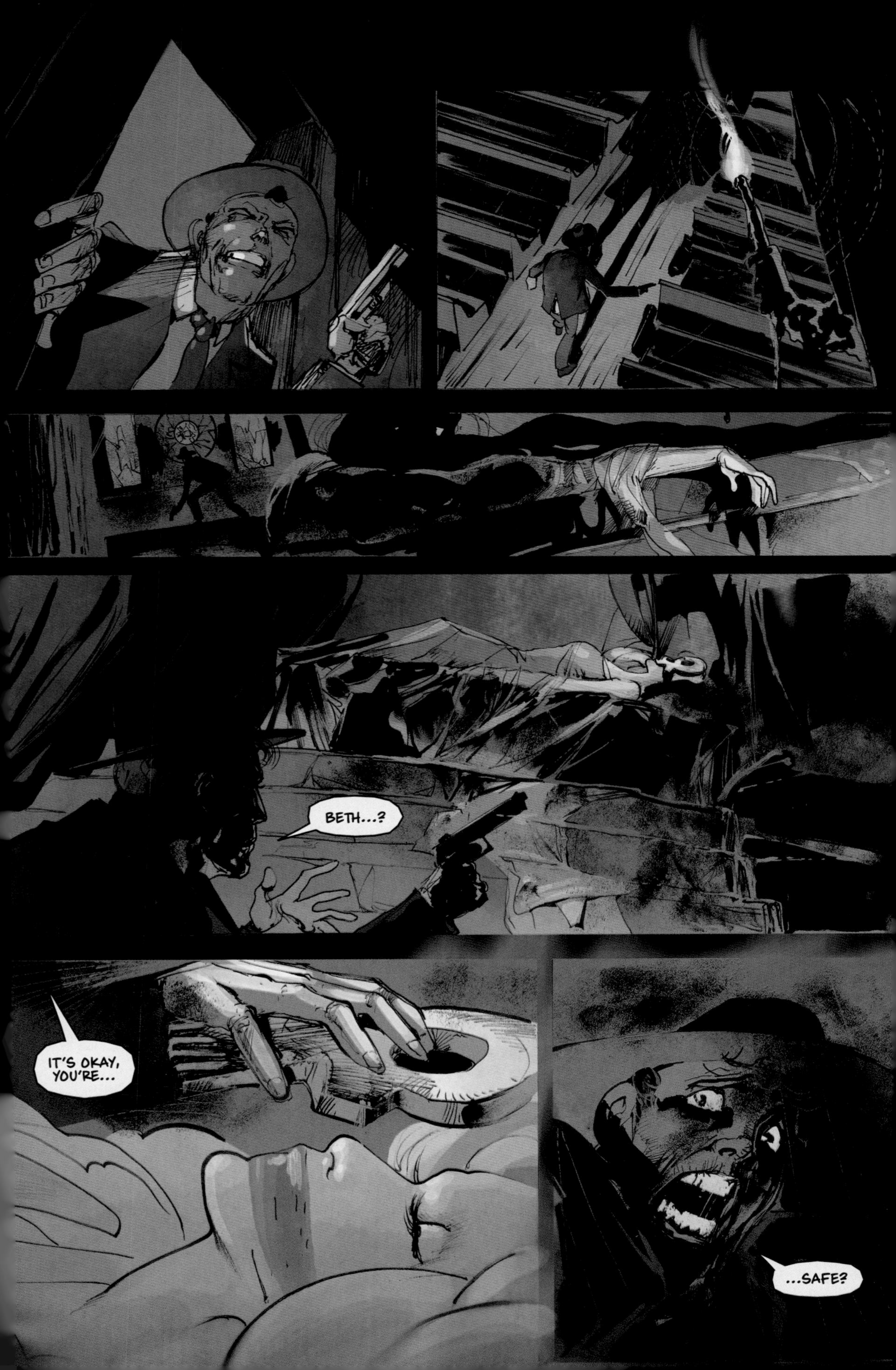
BETH...?
IT'S OKAY, YOU'RE...
...SAFE?

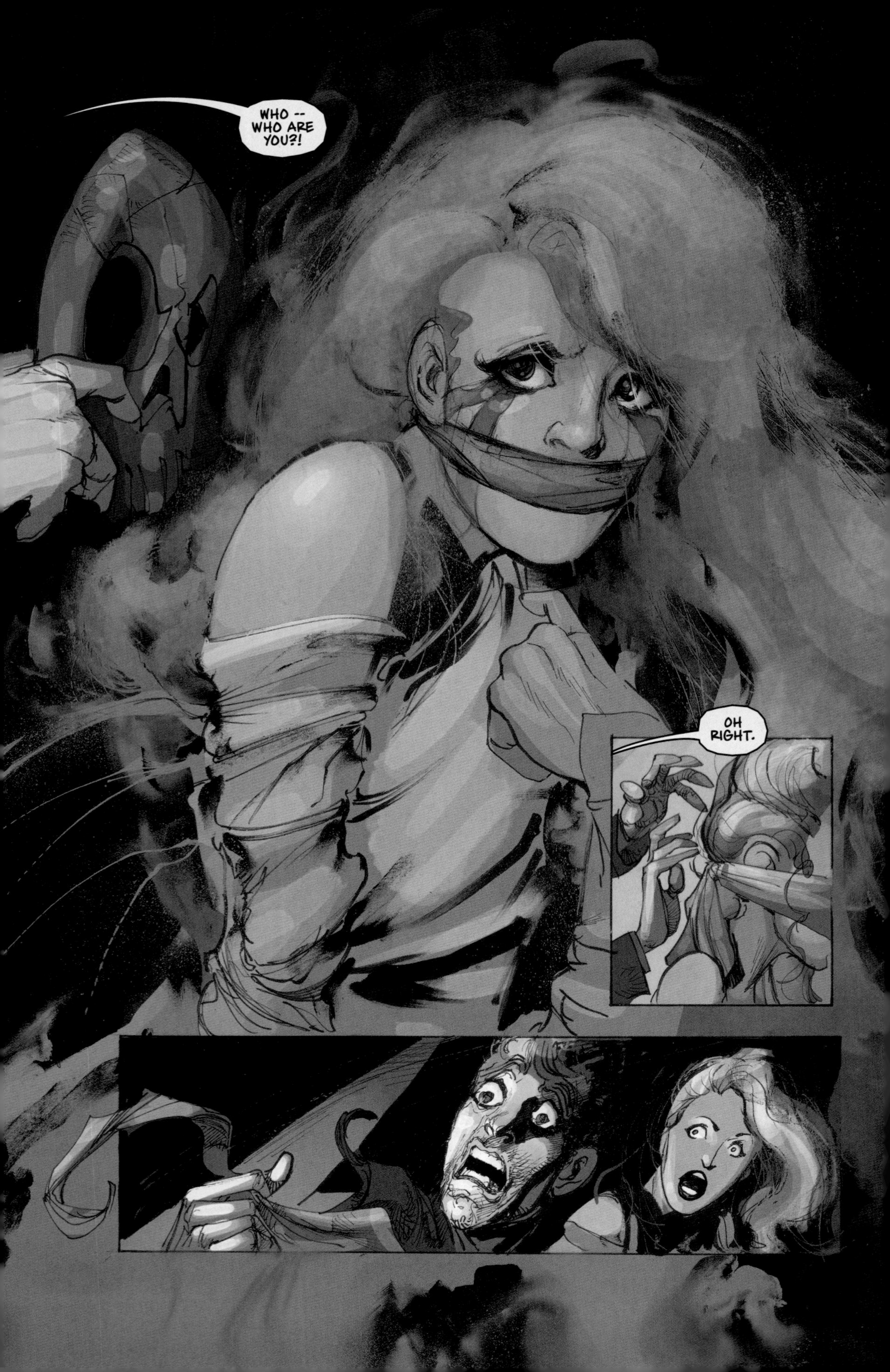
WHO -- WHO ARE YOU?!
OH RIGHT.

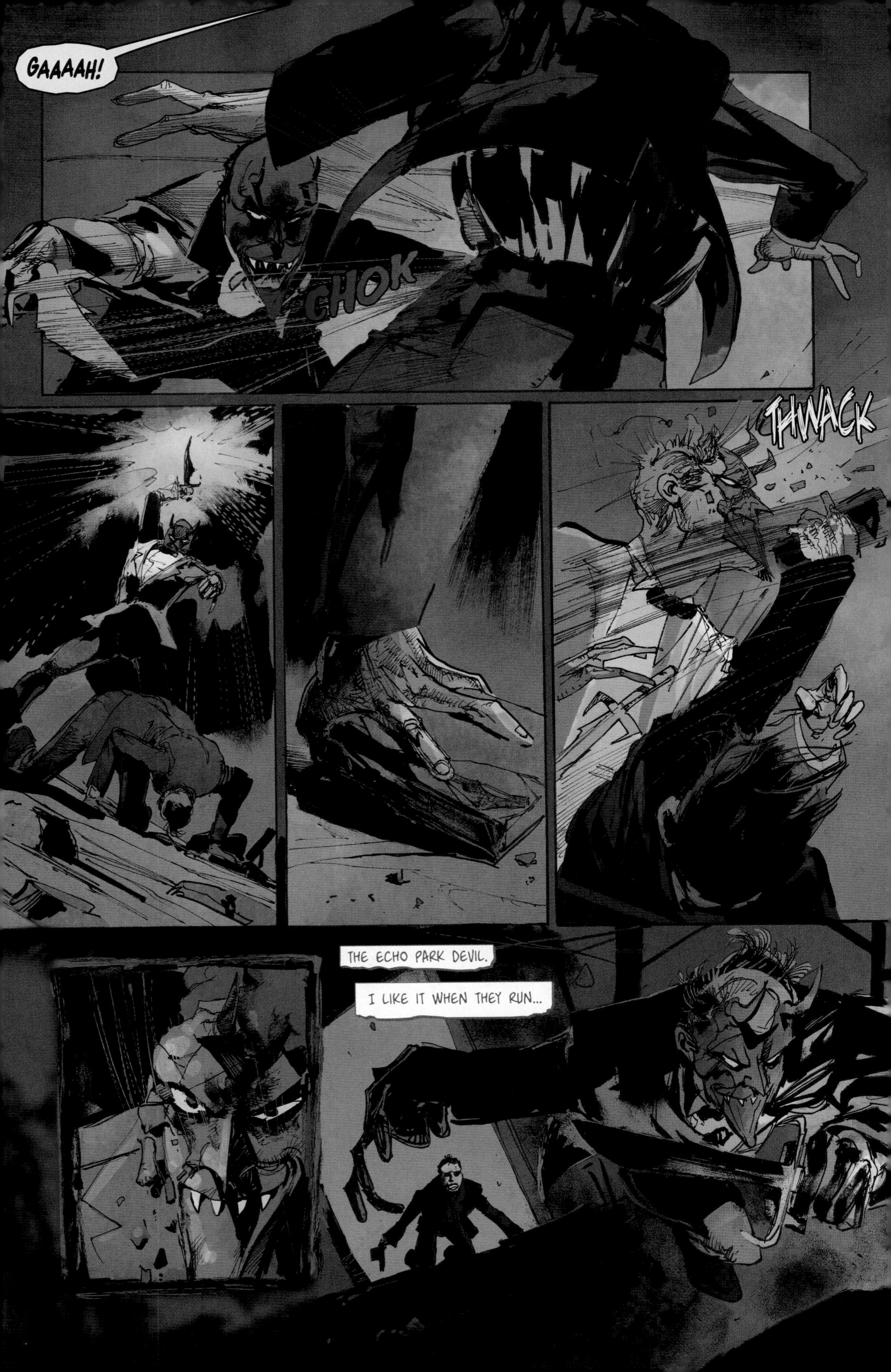
GAAAAH!
CHOK
THWACK
THE ECHO PARK DEVIL.
I LIKE IT WHEN THEY RUN...

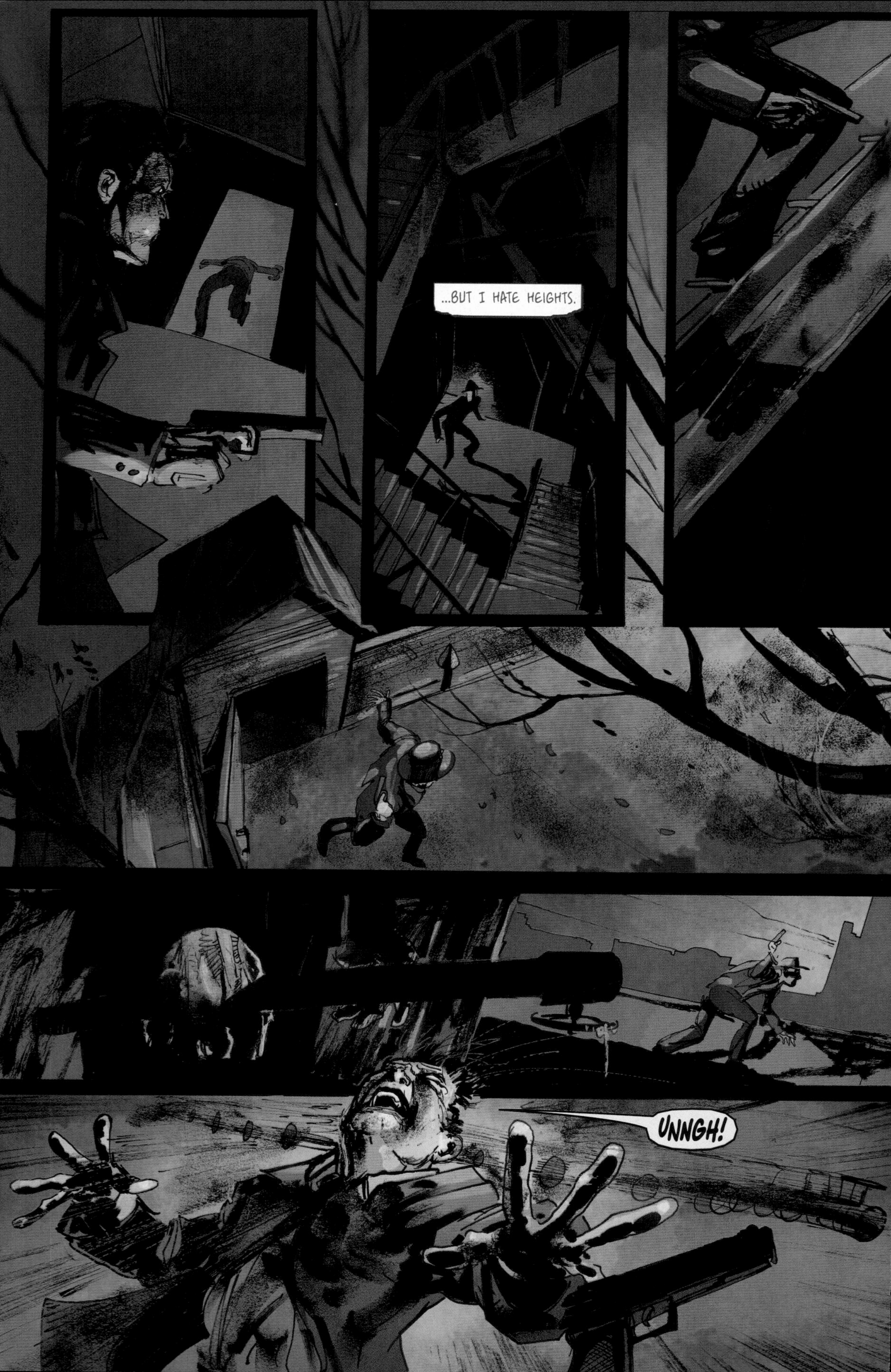
...BUT I HATE HEIGHTS.
UNNGH!

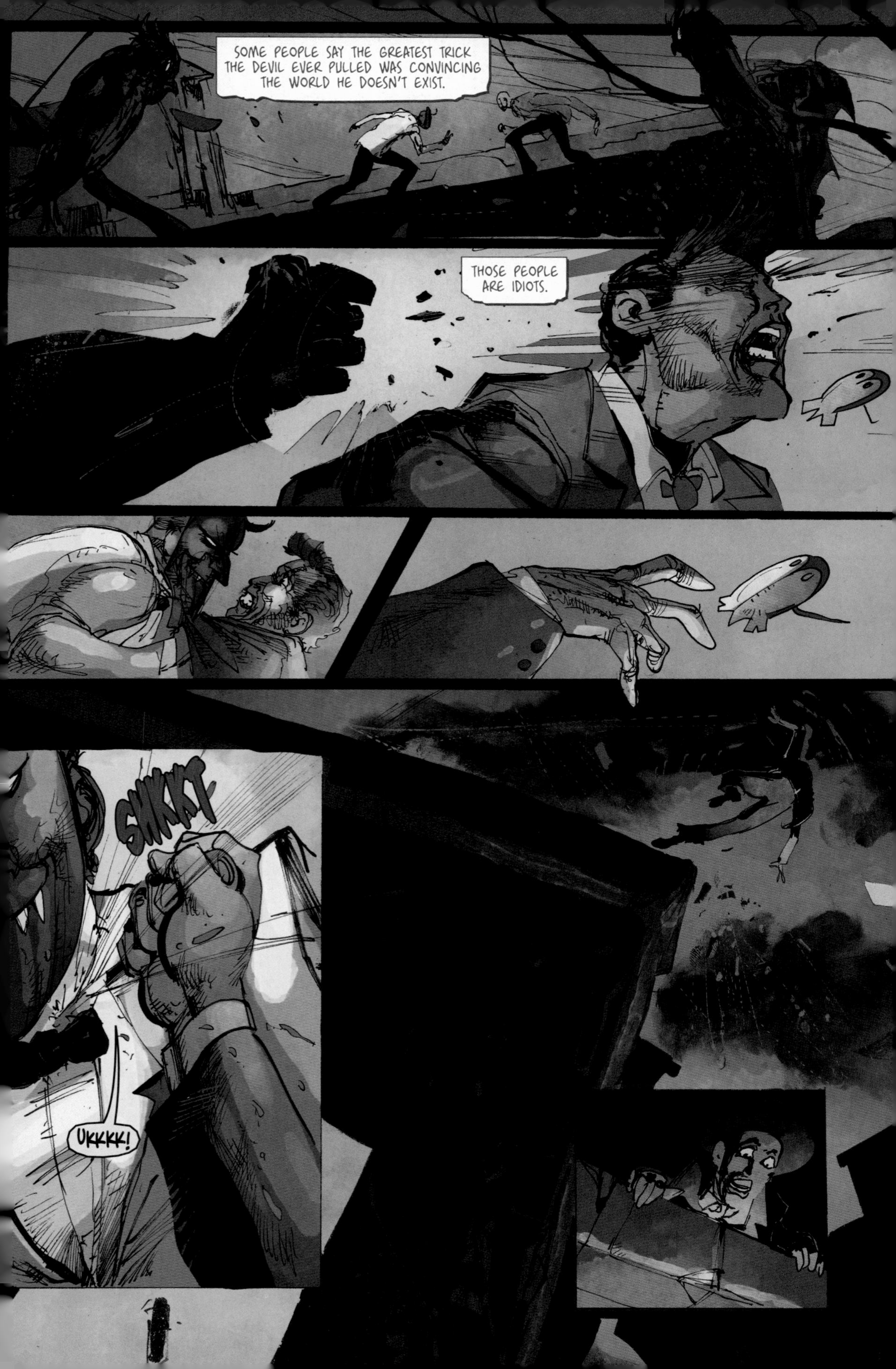
SOME PEOPLE SAY THE GREATEST TRICK THE DEVIL EVER PULLED WAS CONVINCING THE WORLD HE DOESN'T EXIST.
THOSE PEOPLE ARE IDIOTS.
SHKKT
UKKKK!

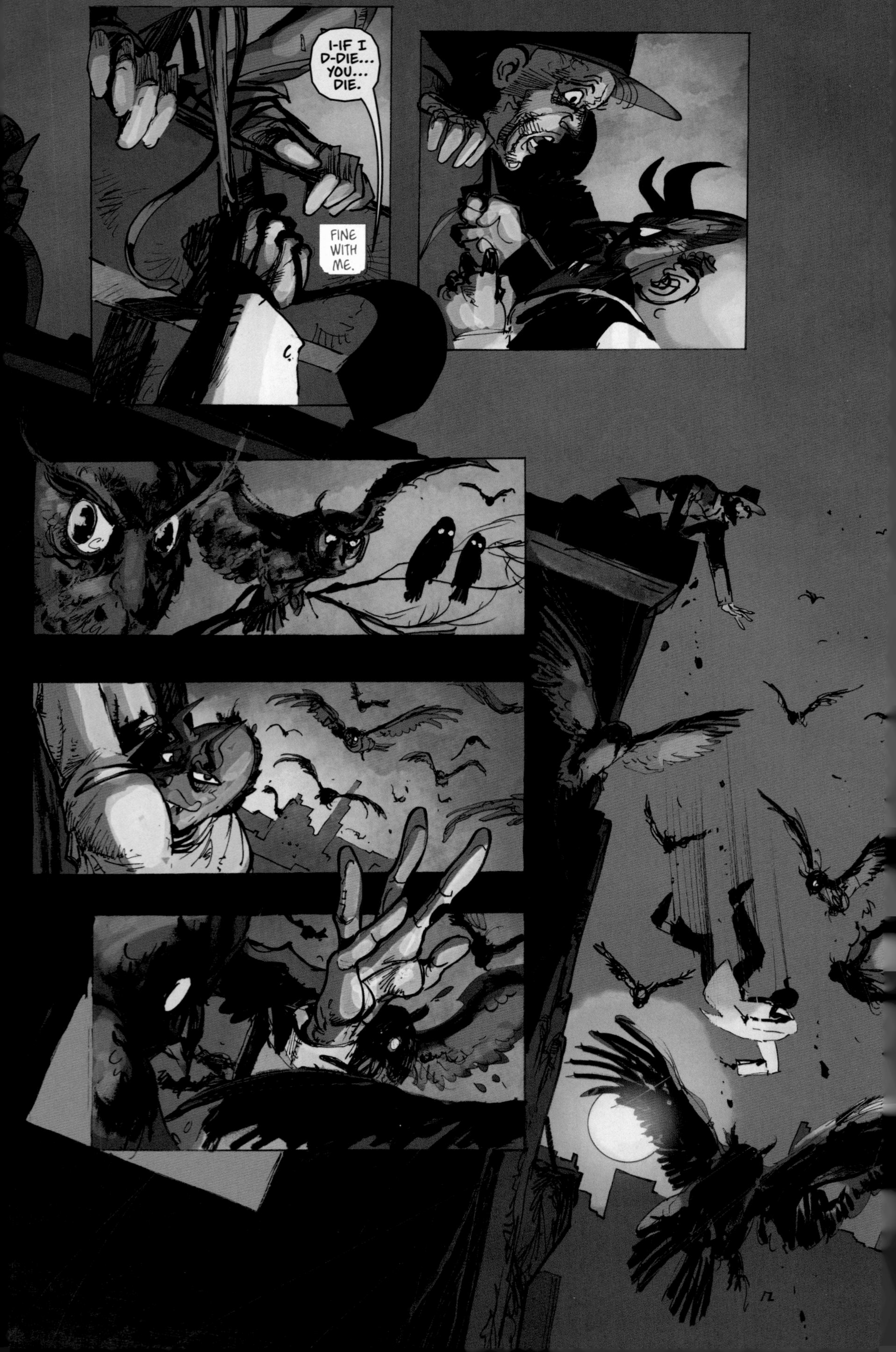
I-IF I D-DIE... YOU... DIE.
FINE WITH ME.

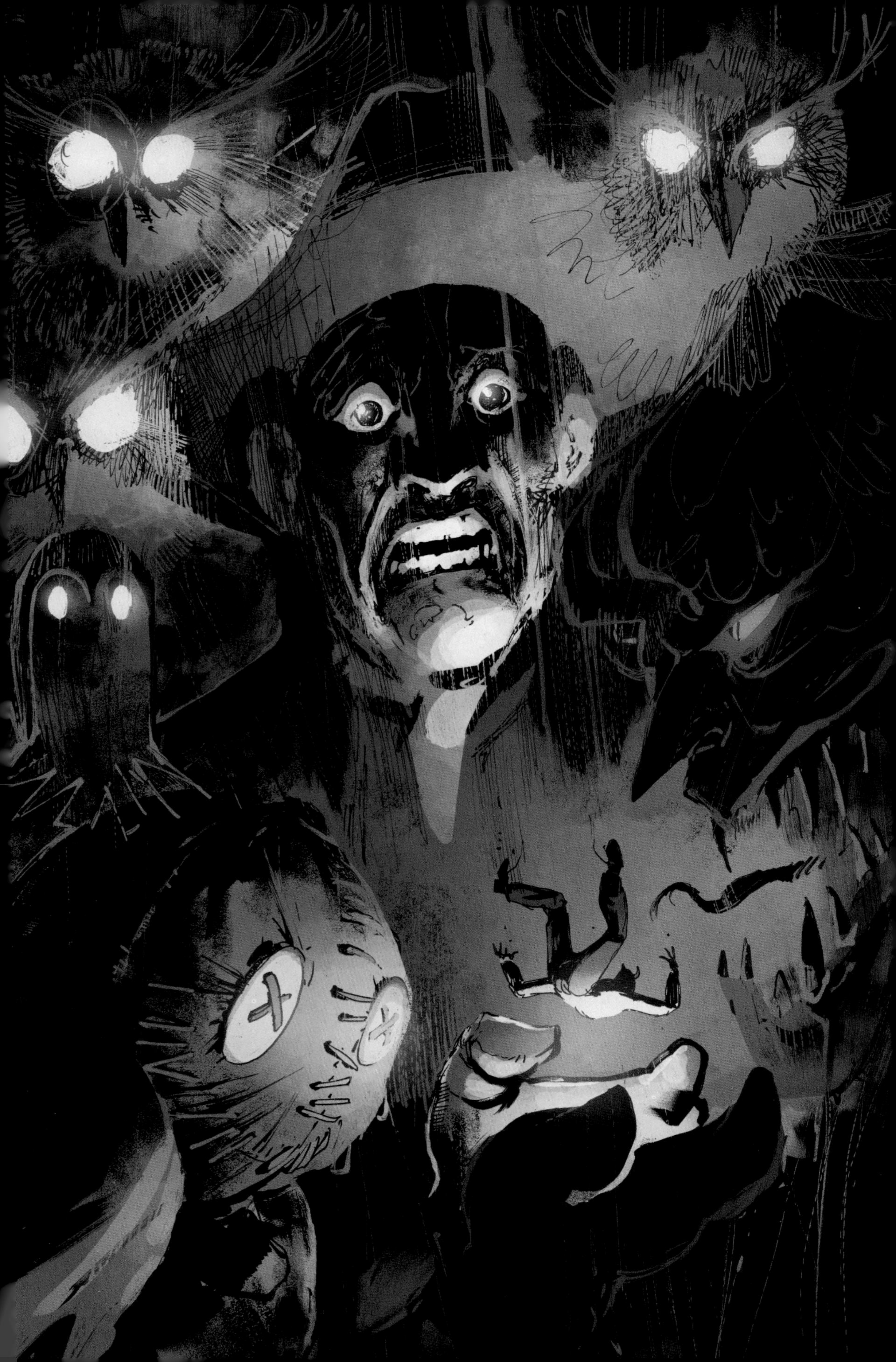

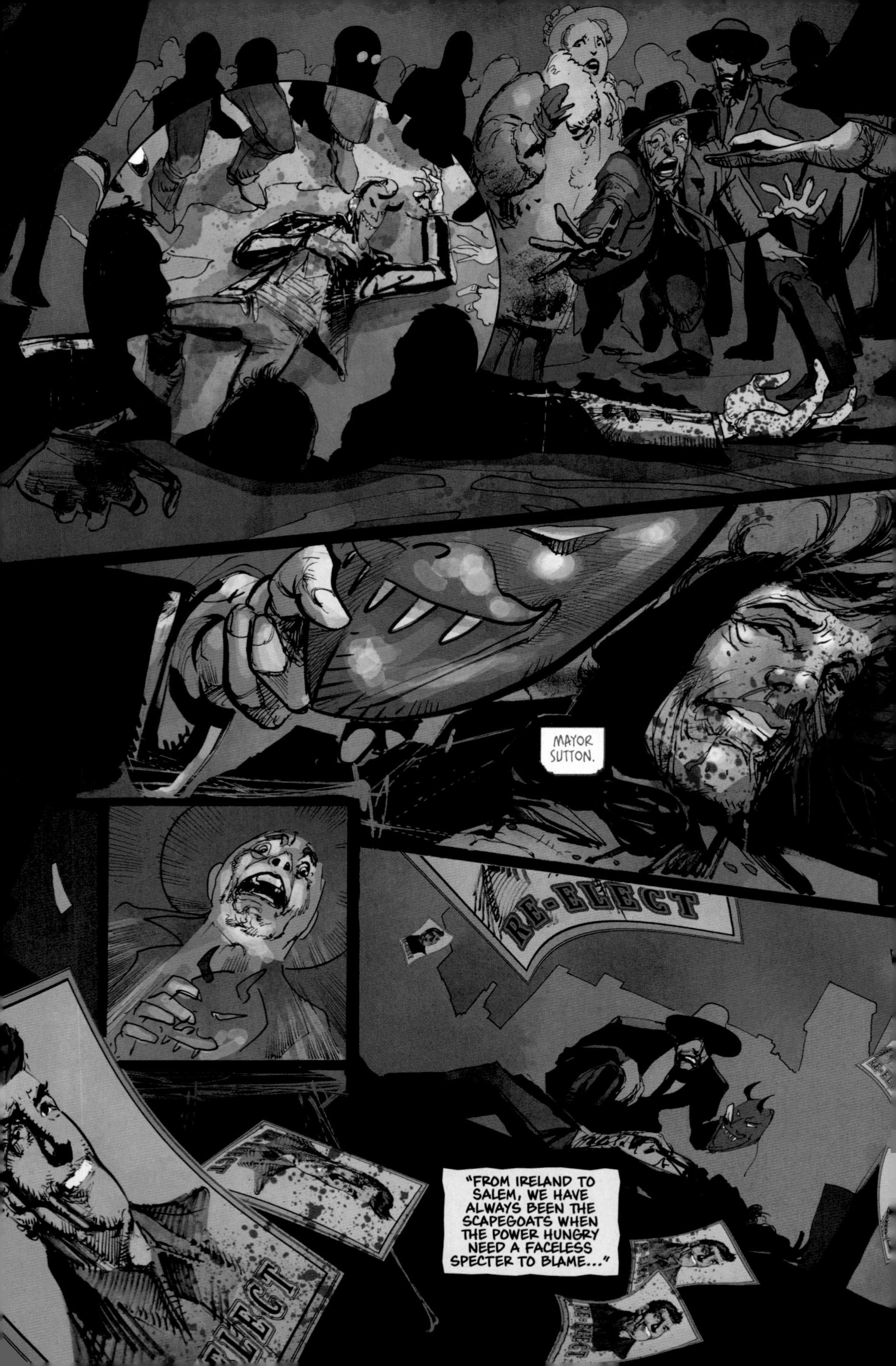

MAYOR SUTTON.
RE-ELECT
"FROM IRELAND TO SALEM, WE HAVE ALWAYS BEEN THE SCAPEGOATS WHEN THE POWER HUNGRY NEED A FACELESS SPECTER TO BLAME..."

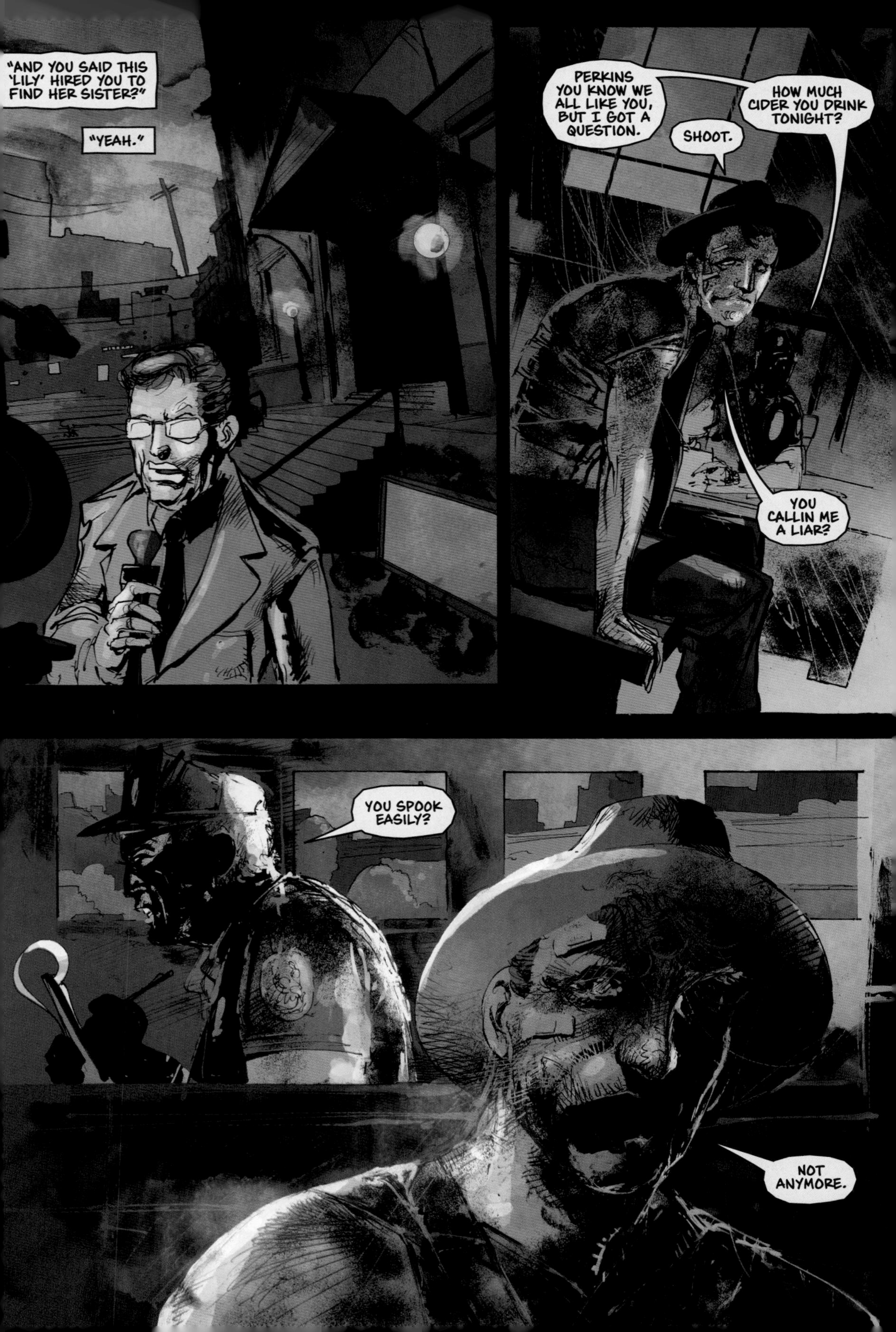
"AND YOU SAID THIS 'LILY' HIRED YOU TO FIND HER SISTER?"
"YEAH."
PERKINS YOU KNOW WE ALL LIKE YOU, BUT I GOT A QUESTION.
SHOOT.
HOW MUCH CIDER YOU DRINK TONIGHT?
YOU CALLIN ME A LIAR?
YOU SPOOK EASILY?
NOT ANYMORE.

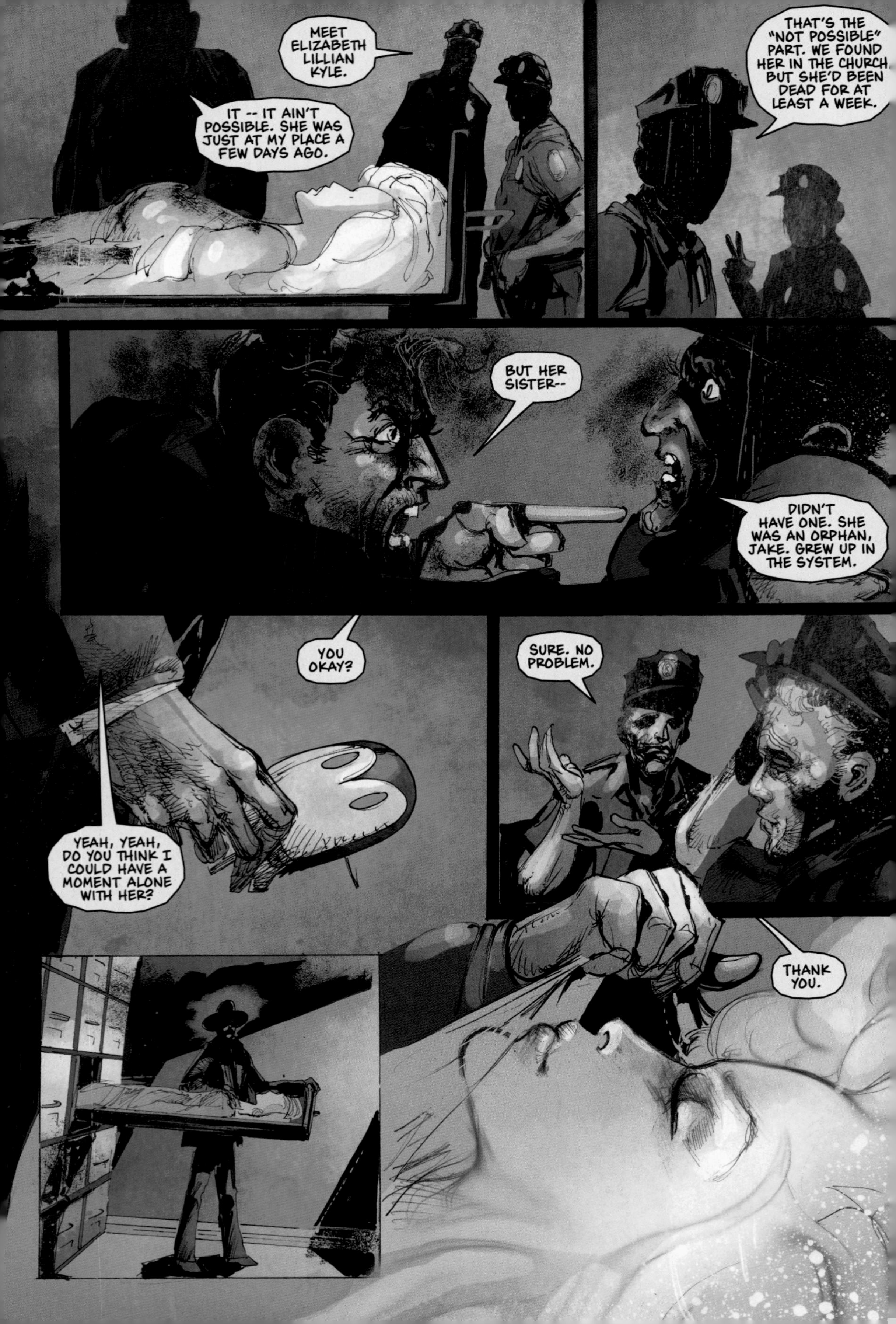
MEET ELIZABETH LILLIAN KYLE.
IT -- IT AIN'T POSSIBLE. SHE WAS JUST AT MY PLACE A FEW DAYS AGO.
THAT'S THE "NOT POSSIBLE" PART. WE FOUND HER IN THE CHURCH, BUT SHE'D BEEN DEAD FOR AT LEAST A WEEK.
BUT HER SISTER--
DIDN'T HAVE ONE. SHE WAS AN ORPHAN, JAKE. GREW UP IN THE SYSTEM.
YOU OKAY?
YEAH, YEAH, DO YOU THINK I COULD HAVE A MOMENT ALONE WITH HER?
SURE. NO PROBLEM.
THANK YOU.

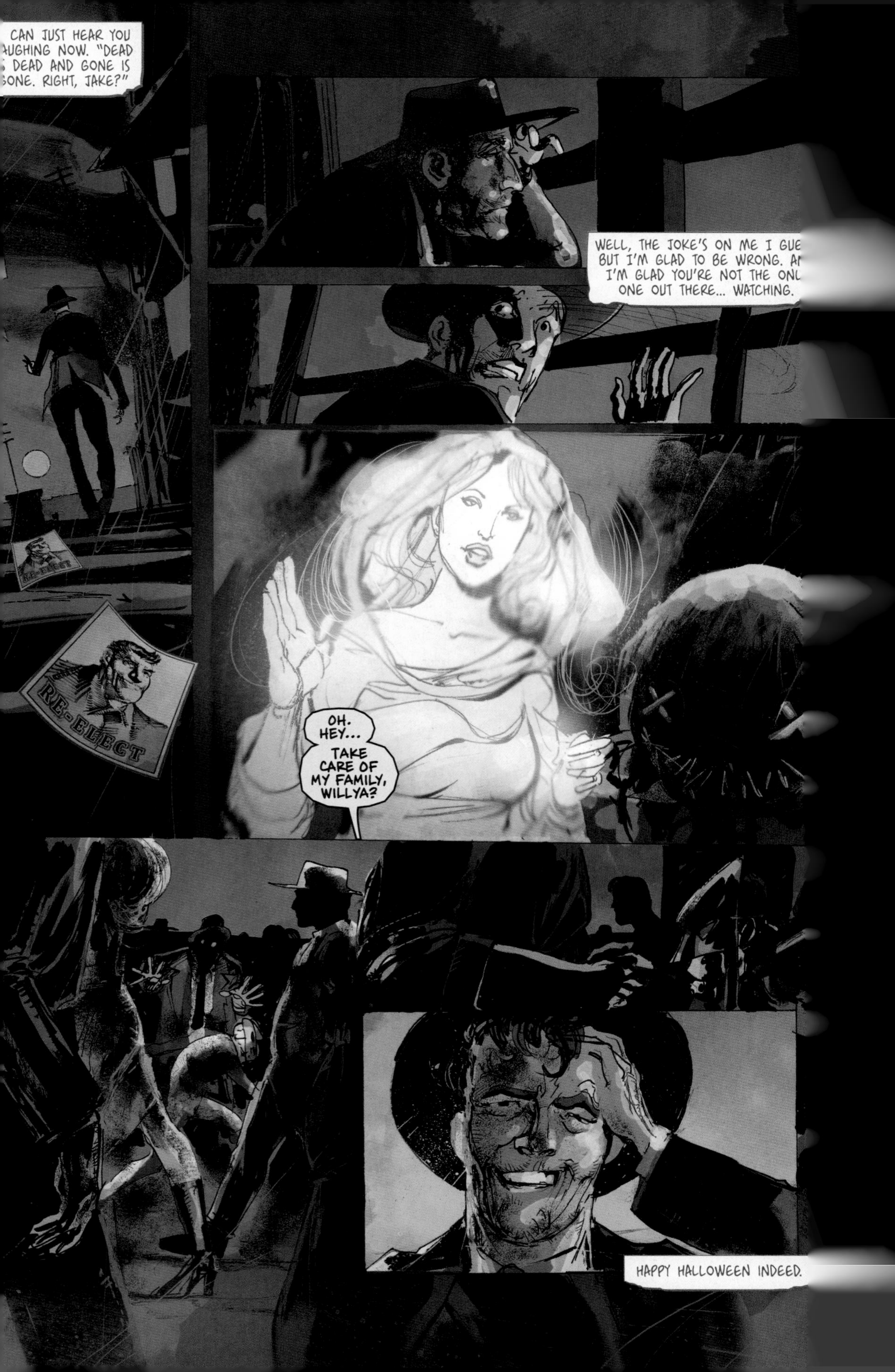

CAN JUST HEAR YOU AUGHING NOW. "DEAD S DEAD AND GONE IS SONE. RIGHT, JAKE?"
WELL, THE JOKE'S ON ME I GUE BUT I'M GLAD TO BE WRONG. AI I'M GLAD YOU'RE NOT THE ONL ONE OUT THERE... WATCHING.
RE-ELECT
RE-ELECT
OH. HEY...
TAKE CARE OF MY FAMILY, WILLYA?
HAPPY HALLOWEEN INDEED.

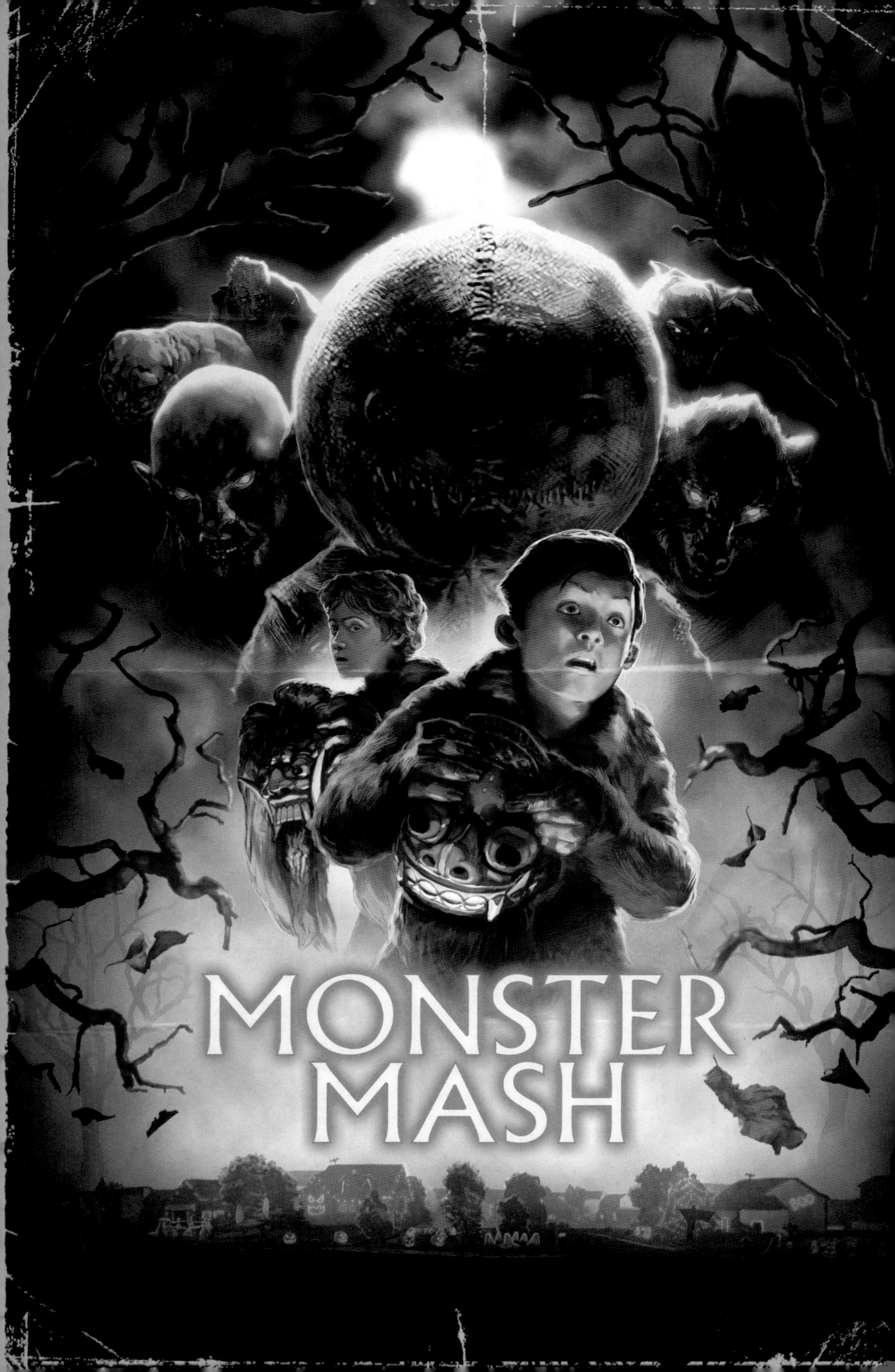
MONSTER
MASH

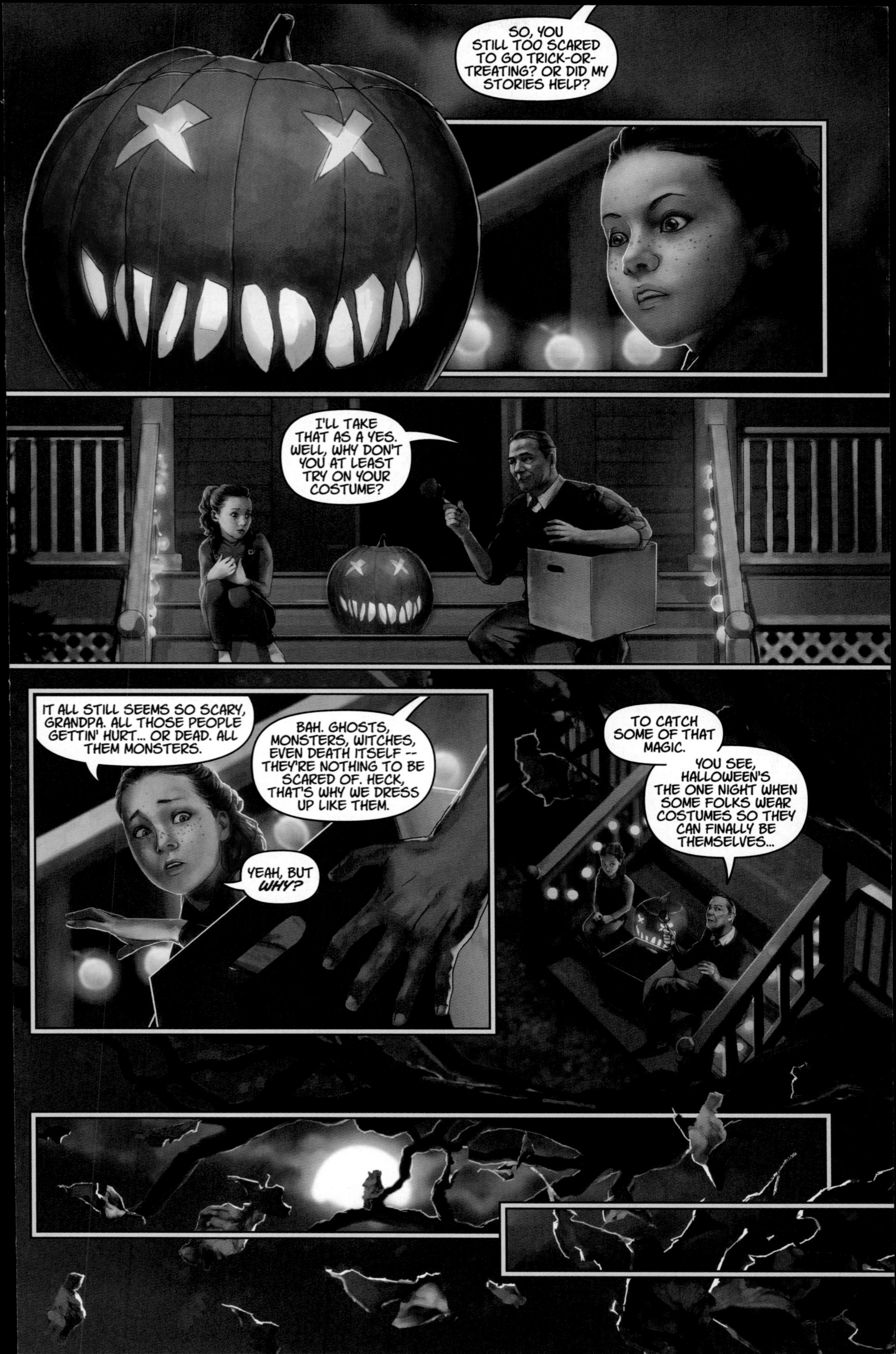
SO, YOU STILL TOO SCARED TO GO TRICK-OR-TREATING? OR DID MY STORIES HELP?
I'LL TAKE THAT AS A YES. WELL, WHY DON'T YOU AT LEAST TRY ON YOUR COSTUME?
IT ALL STILL SEEMS SO SCARY, GRANDPA. ALL THOSE PEOPLE GETTIN' HURT... OR DEAD. ALL THEM MONSTERS.
BAH. GHOSTS, MONSTERS, WITCHES, EVEN DEATH ITSELF -- THEY'RE NOTHING TO BE SCARED OF. HECK, THAT'S WHY WE DRESS UP LIKE THEM.
YEAH, BUT *WHY?*
TO CATCH SOME OF THAT MAGIC.
YOU SEE, HALLOWEEN'S THE ONE NIGHT WHEN SOME FOLKS WEAR COSTUMES SO THEY CAN FINALLY BE THEMSELVES...

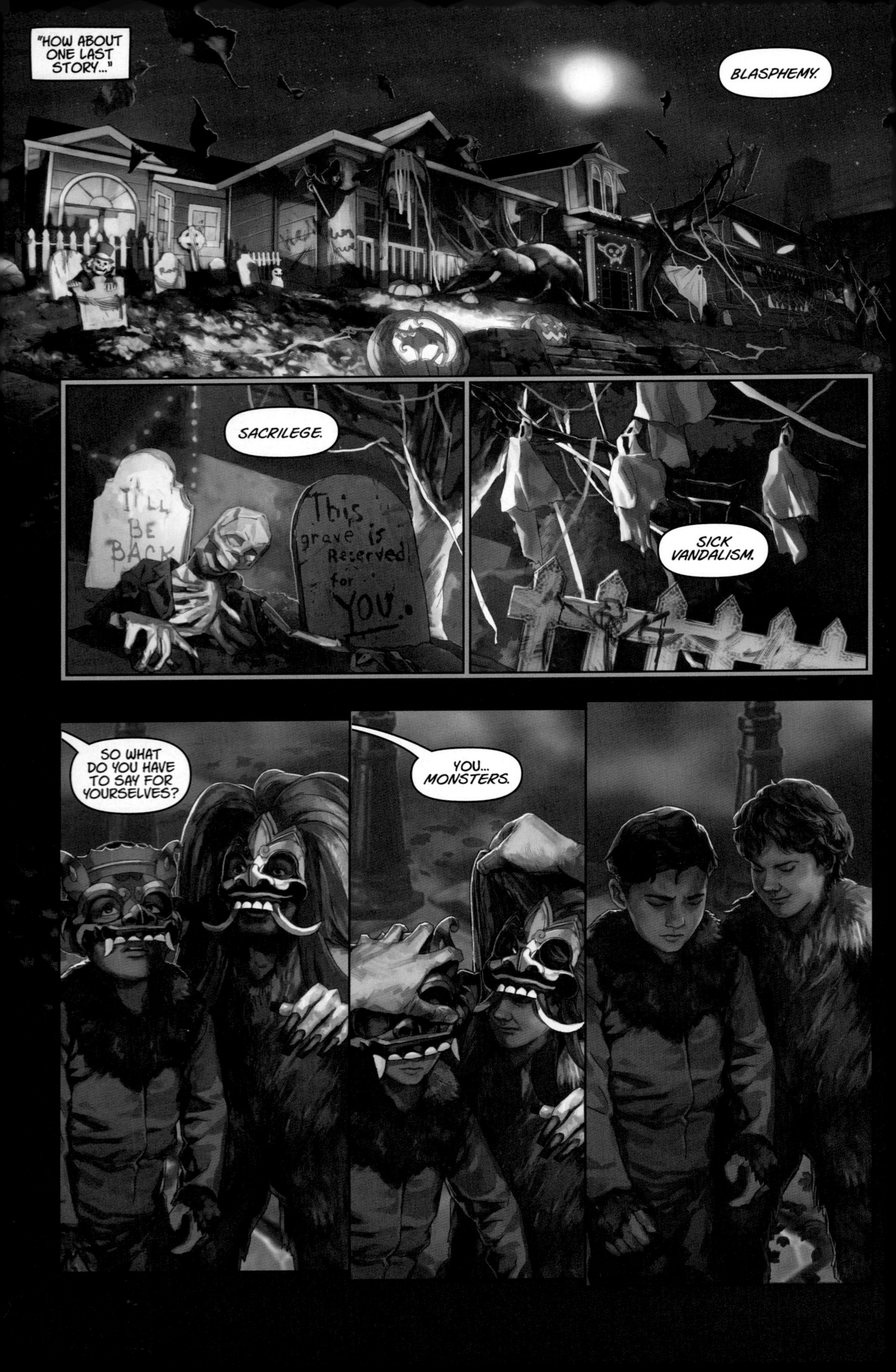
"HOW ABOUT ONE LAST STORY..."
BLASPHEMY.
SACRILEGE.
I'LL BE BACK
This grave is Reserved for YOU.
SICK VANDALISM.
SO WHAT DO YOU HAVE TO SAY FOR YOURSELVES?
YOU... MONSTERS.

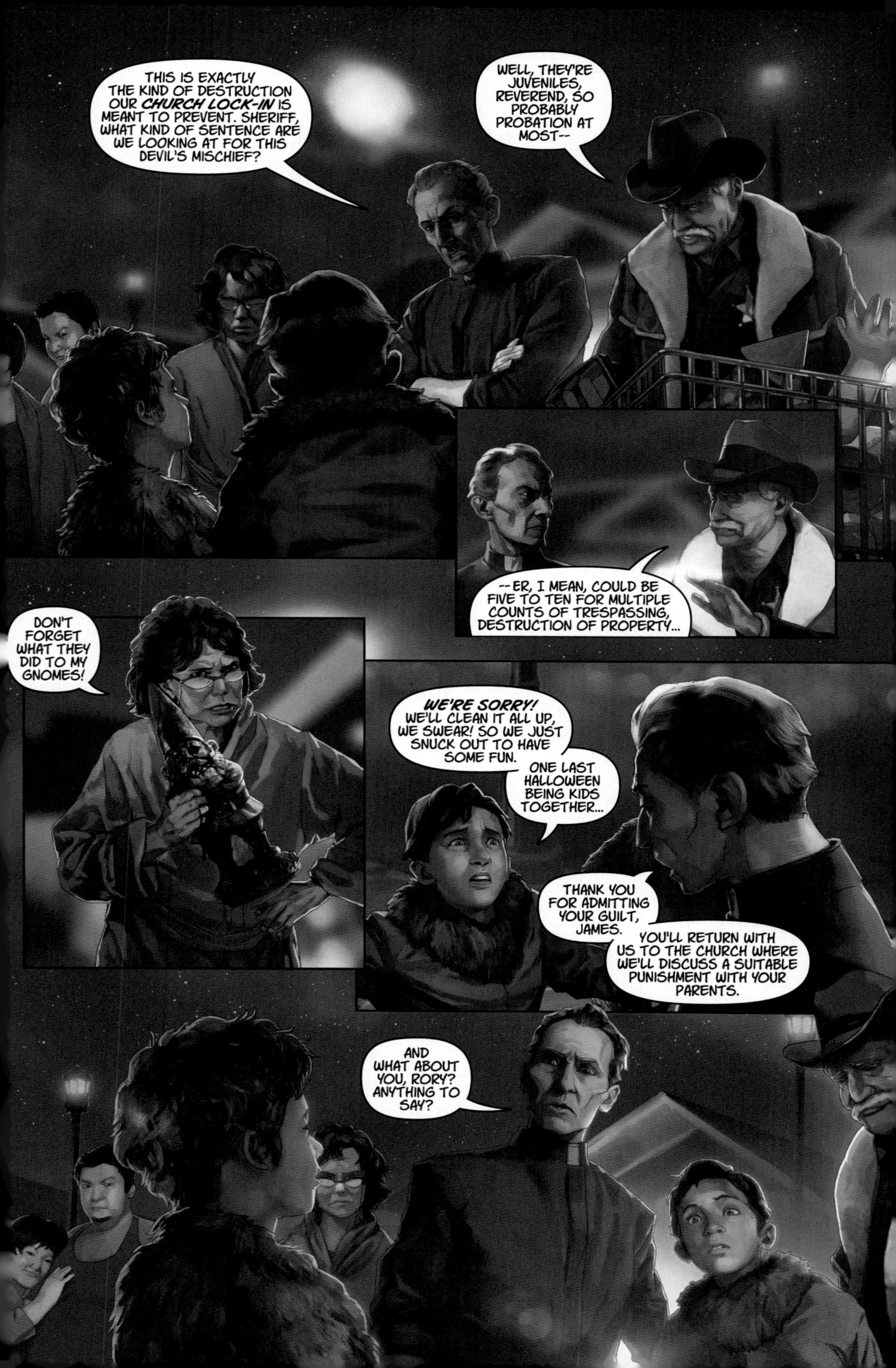
THIS IS EXACTLY THE KIND OF DESTRUCTION OUR CHURCH LOCK-IN IS MEANT TO PREVENT. SHERIFF, WHAT KIND OF SENTENCE ARE WE LOOKING AT FOR THIS DEVIL'S MISCHIEF?
WELL, THEY'RE JUVENILES, REVEREND, SO PROBABLY PROBATION AT MOST--
--ER, I MEAN, COULD BE FIVE TO TEN FOR MULTIPLE COUNTS OF TRESPASSING, DESTRUCTION OF PROPERTY...
DON'T FORGET WHAT THEY DID TO MY GNOMES!
WE'RE SORRY! WE'LL CLEAN IT ALL UP, WE SWEAR! SO WE JUST SNUCK OUT TO HAVE SOME FUN.
ONE LAST HALLOWEEN BEING KIDS TOGETHER...
THANK YOU FOR ADMITTING YOUR GUILT, JAMES.
YOU'LL RETURN WITH US TO THE CHURCH WHERE WE'LL DISCUSS A SUITABLE PUNISHMENT WITH YOUR PARENTS.
AND WHAT ABOUT YOU, RORY? ANYTHING TO SAY?

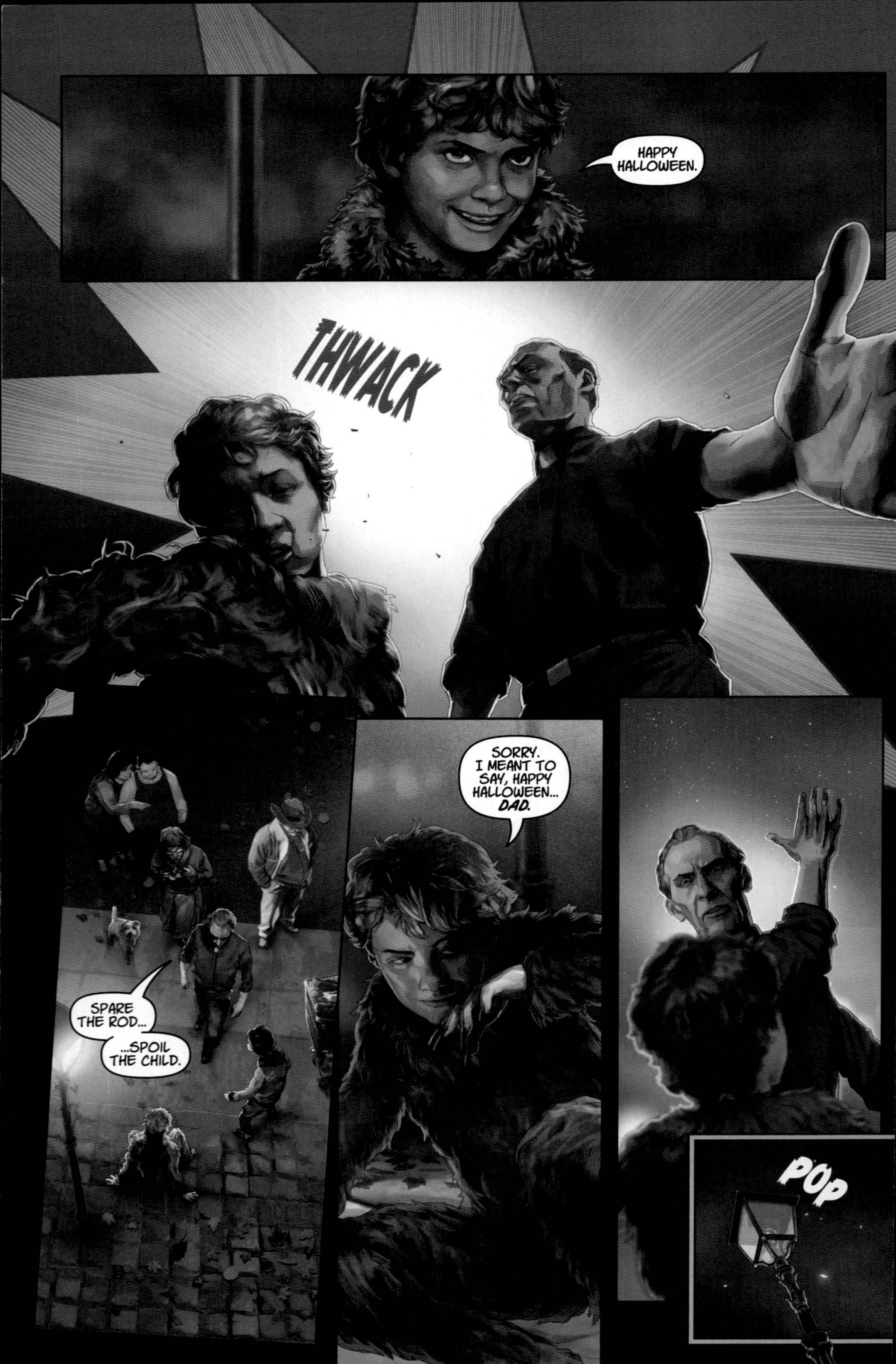
HAPPY HALLOWEEN.
THWACK
SPARE THE ROD...
...SPOIL THE CHILD.
SORRY. I MEANT TO SAY, HAPPY HALLOWEEN... DAD.
POP

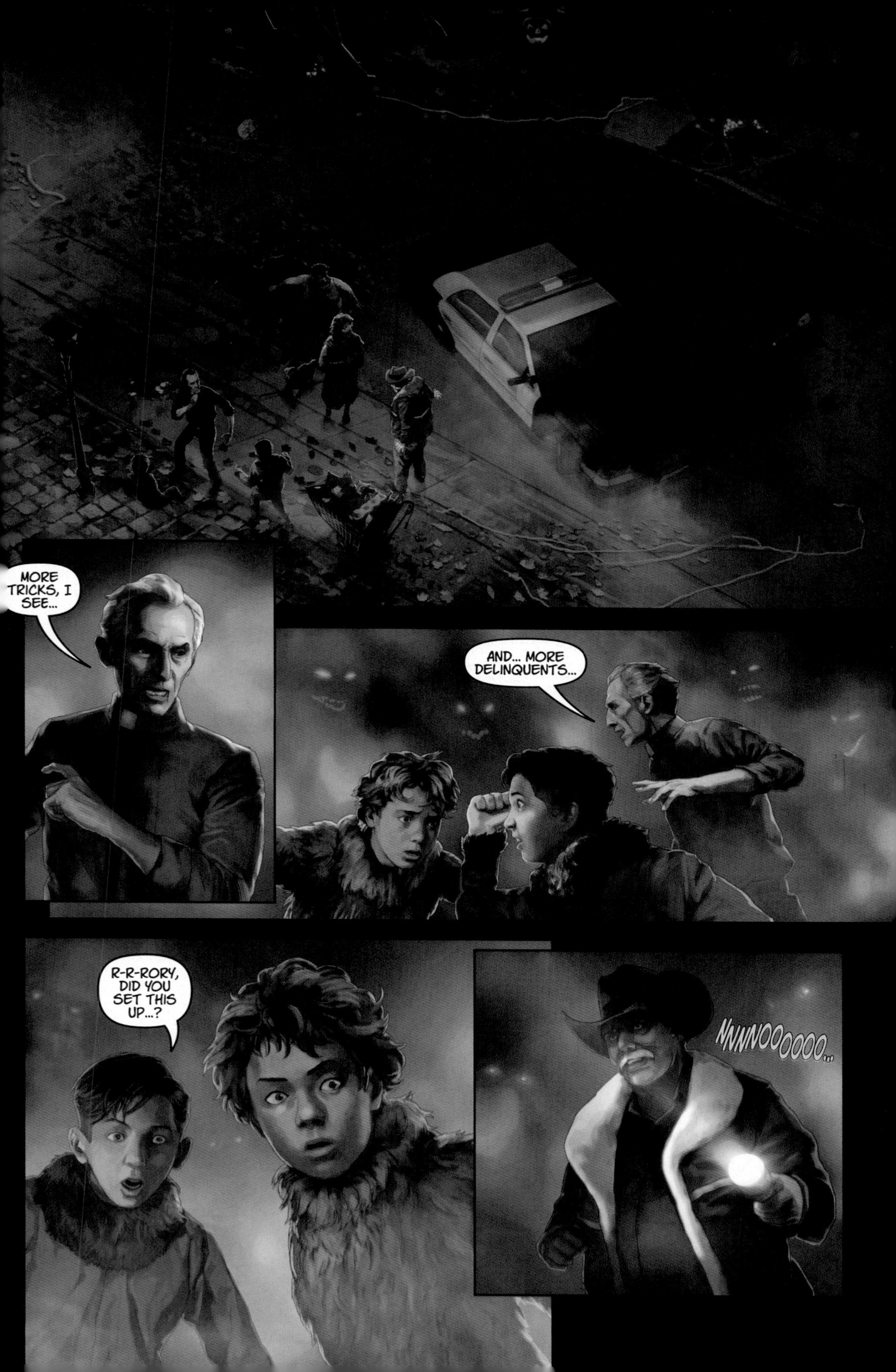
MORE TRICKS, I SEE...
AND... MORE DELINQUENTS...
R-R-RORY, DID YOU SET THIS UP...?
NNNNOOOOOO...

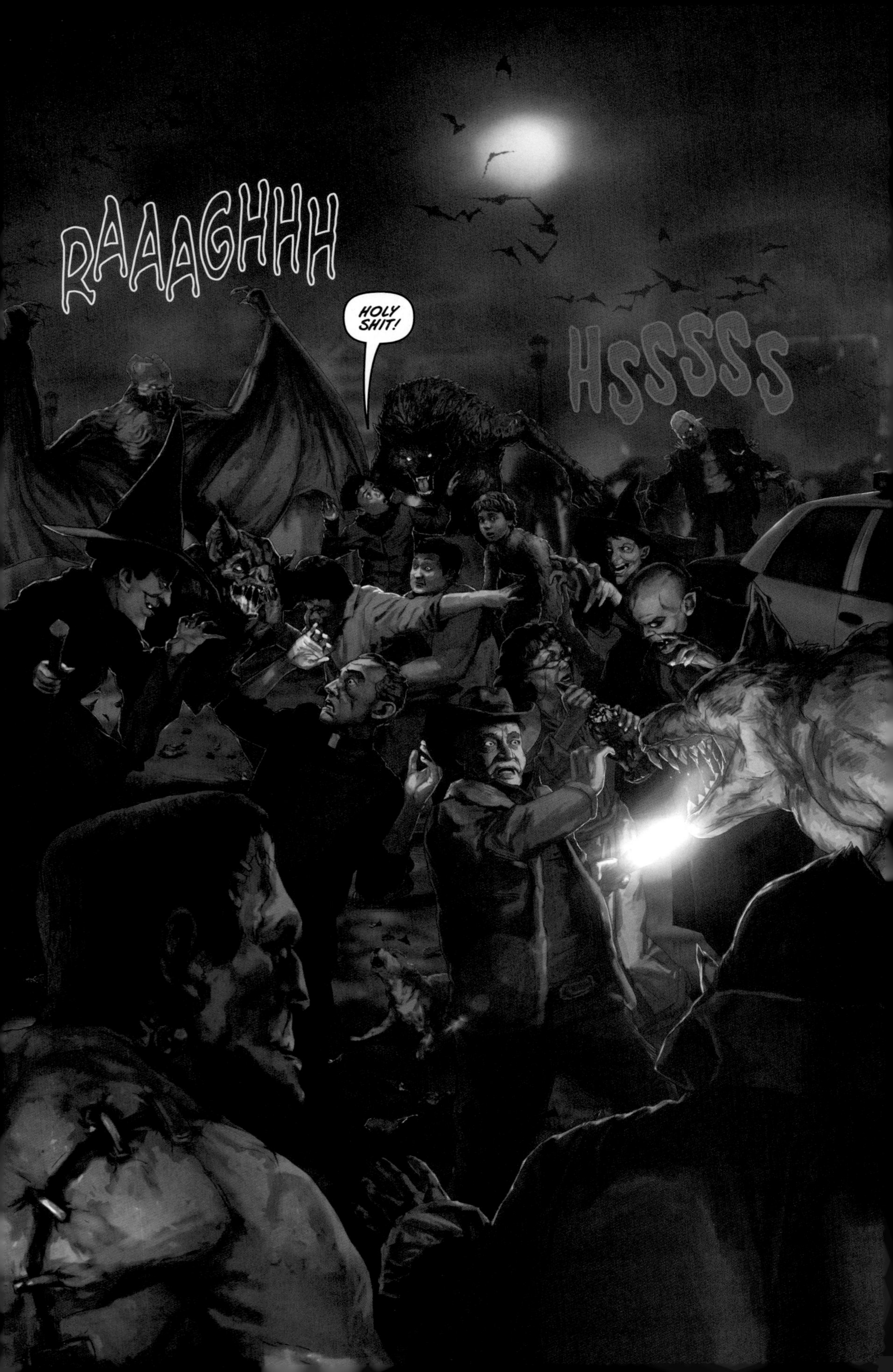
RAAAGHHH
HOLY SHIT!
HSSSSS

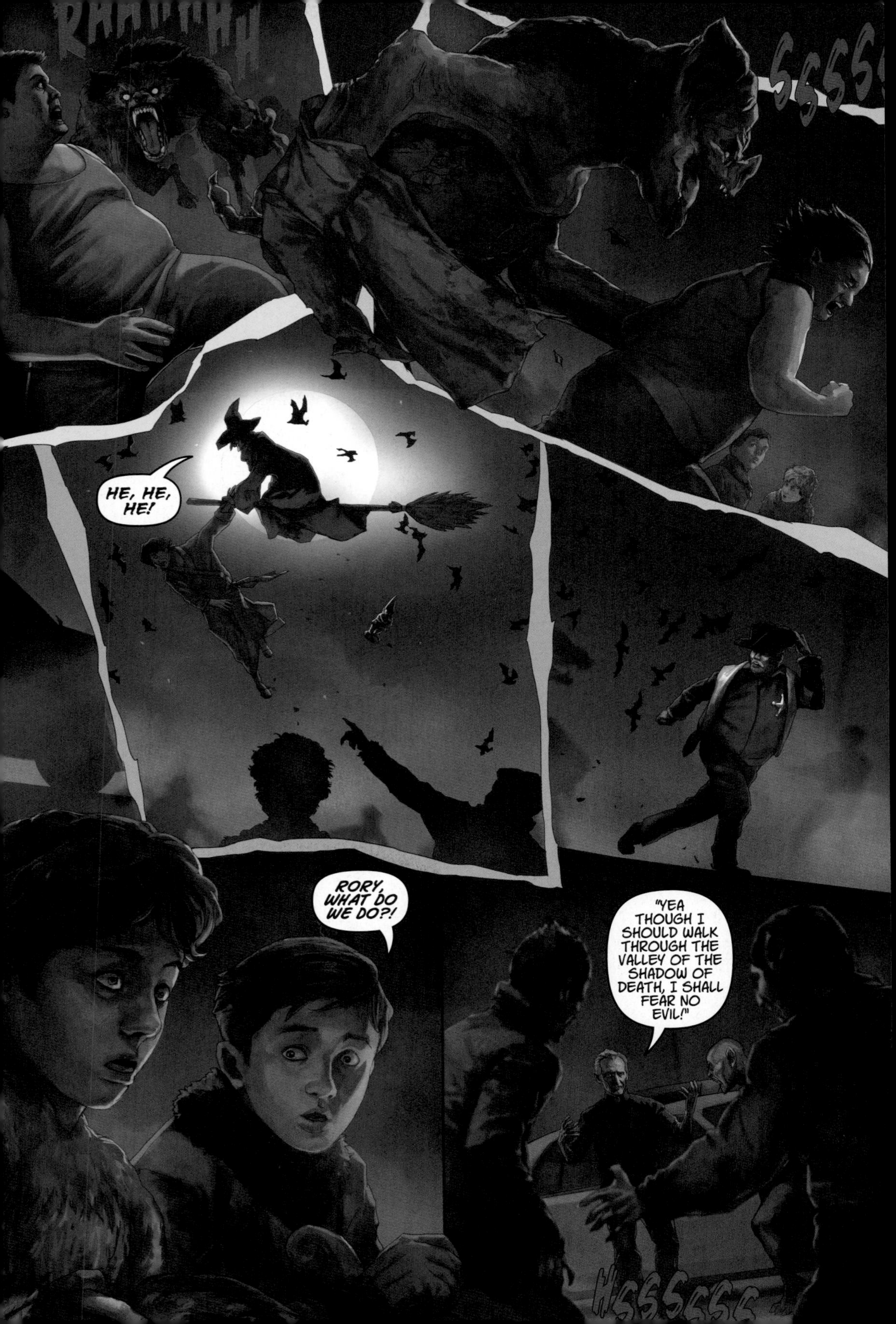
HE, HE, HE!
RORY, WHAT DO WE DO?!
"YEA THOUGH I SHOULD WALK THROUGH THE VALLEY OF THE SHADOW OF DEATH, I SHALL FEAR NO EVIL!"

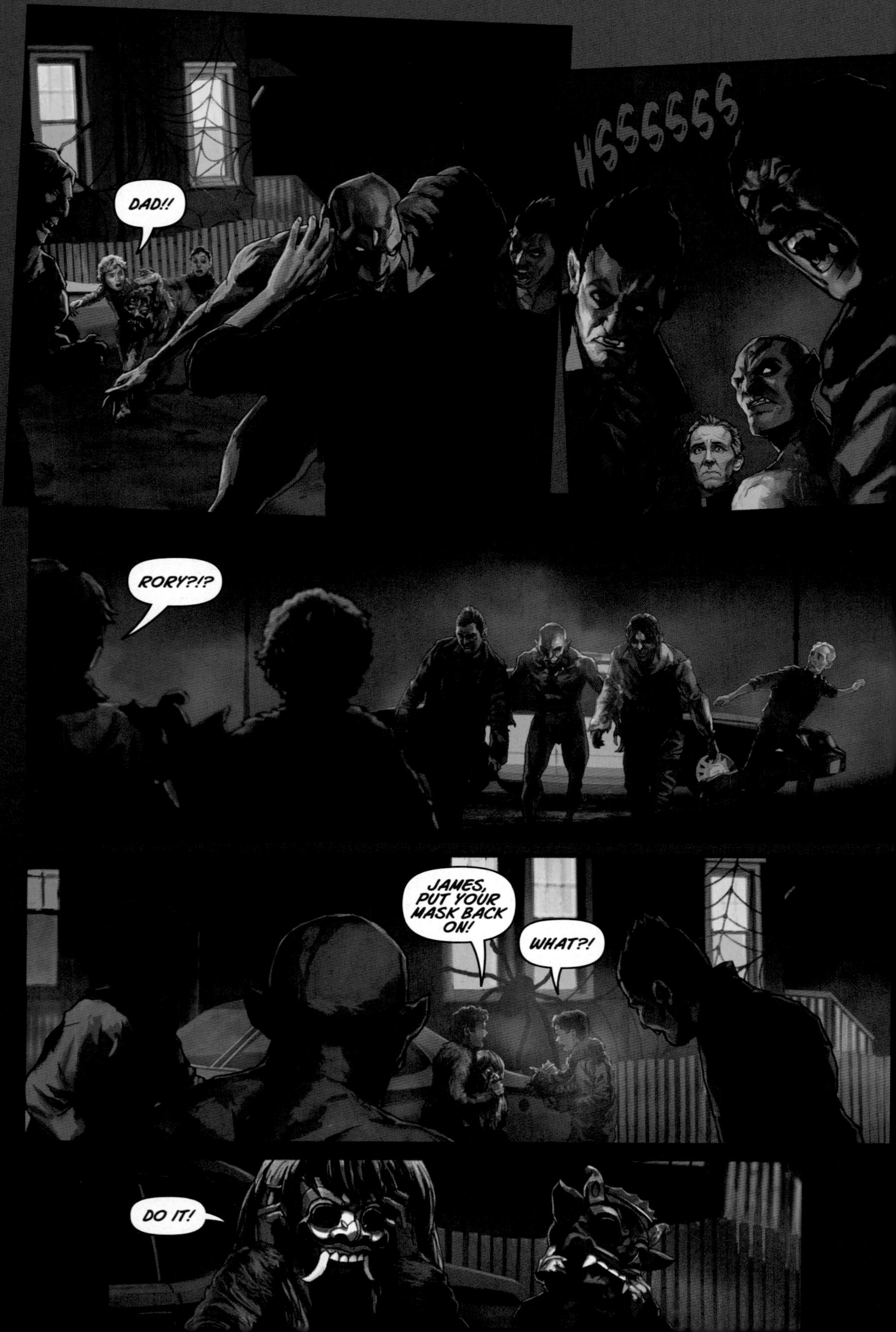
DAD!!
HSSSSSS
RORY?!?
JAMES, PUT YOUR MASK BACK ON!
WHAT?!
DO IT!

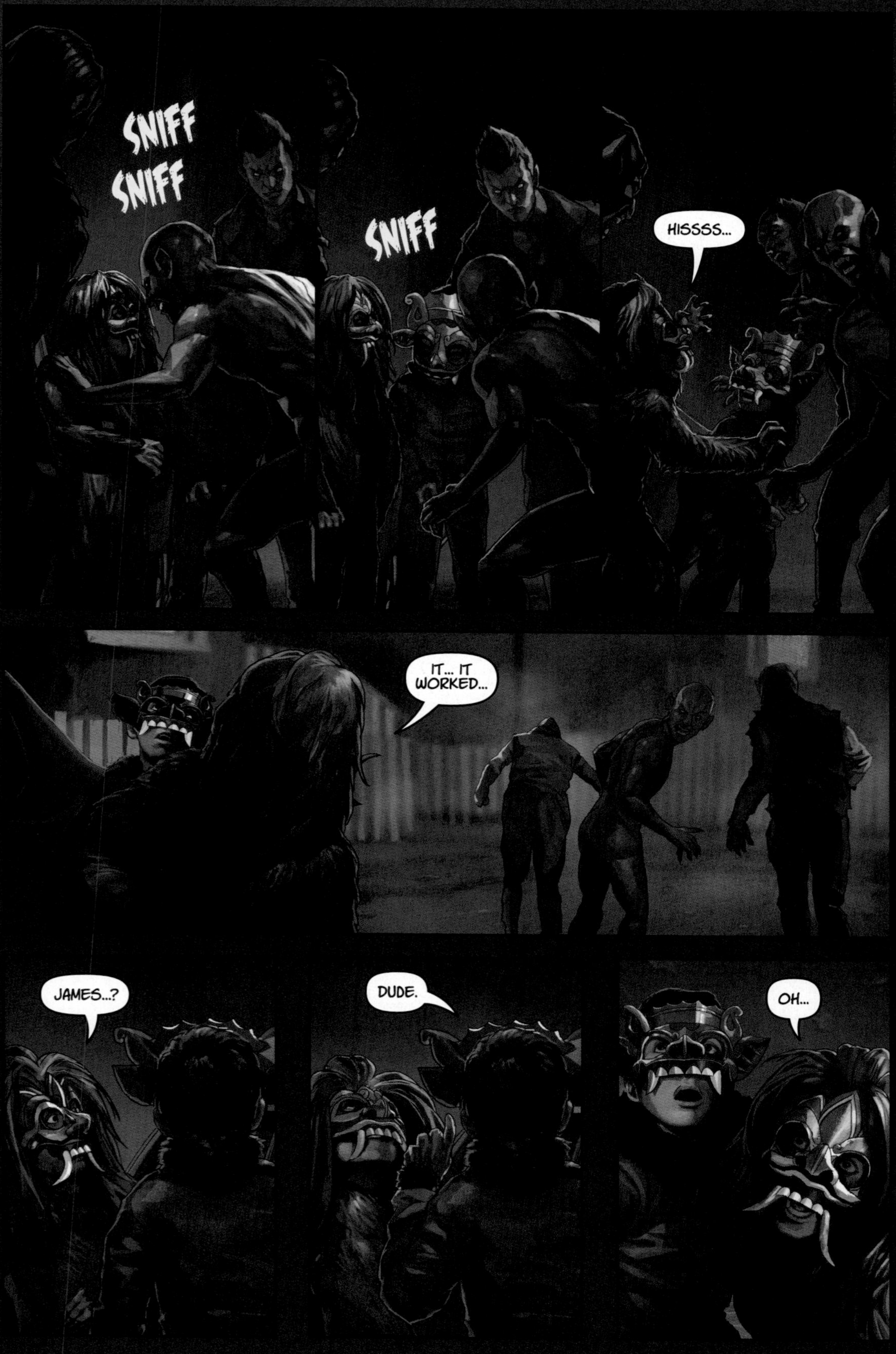
SNIFF
SNIFF
SNIFF
HISSSS...
IT... IT WORKED...
JAMES...?
DUDE.
OH...

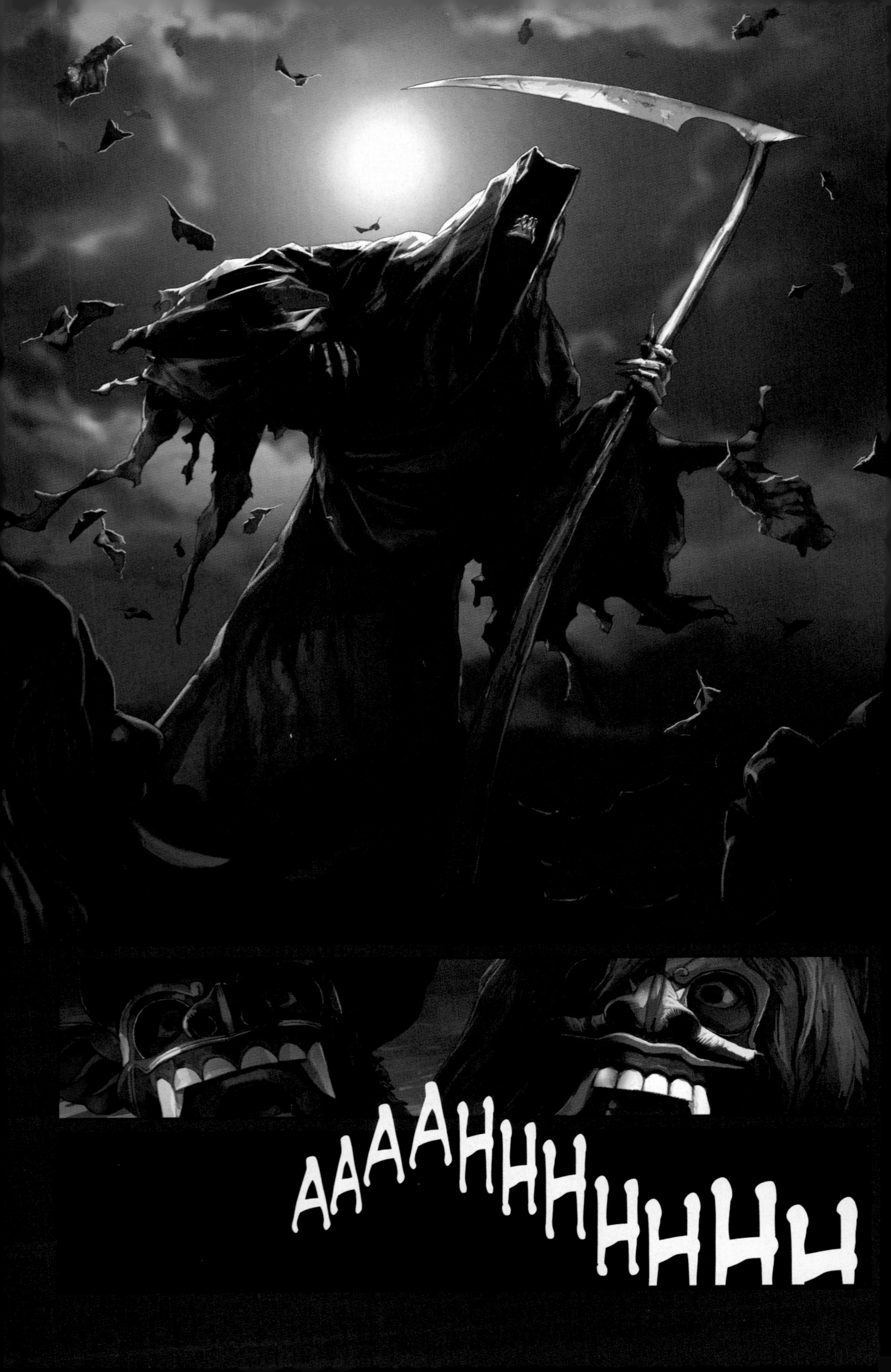
AAAAHHHHHHU

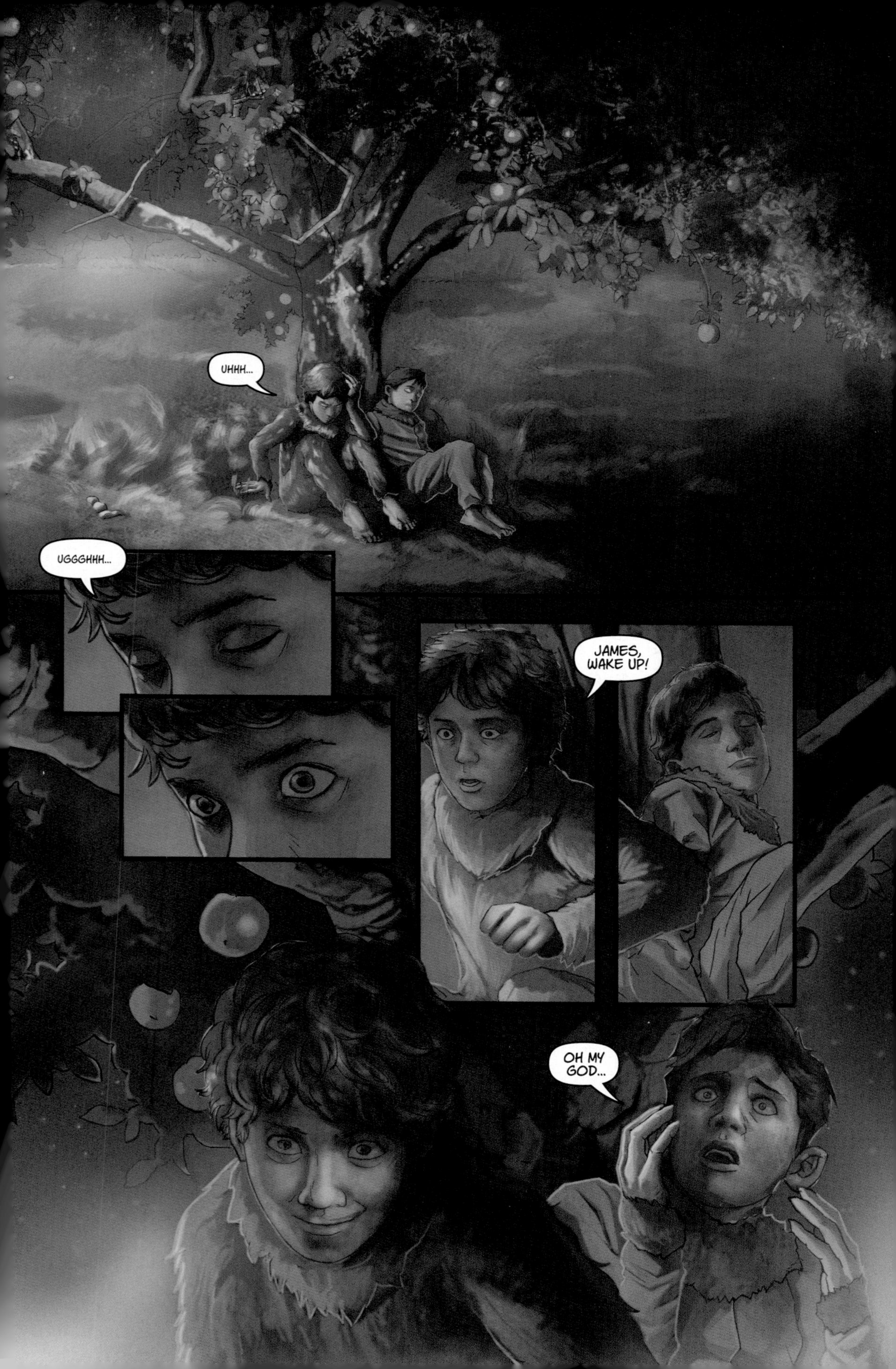
UHHH...
UGGGHHH...
JAMES, WAKE UP!
OH MY GOD...

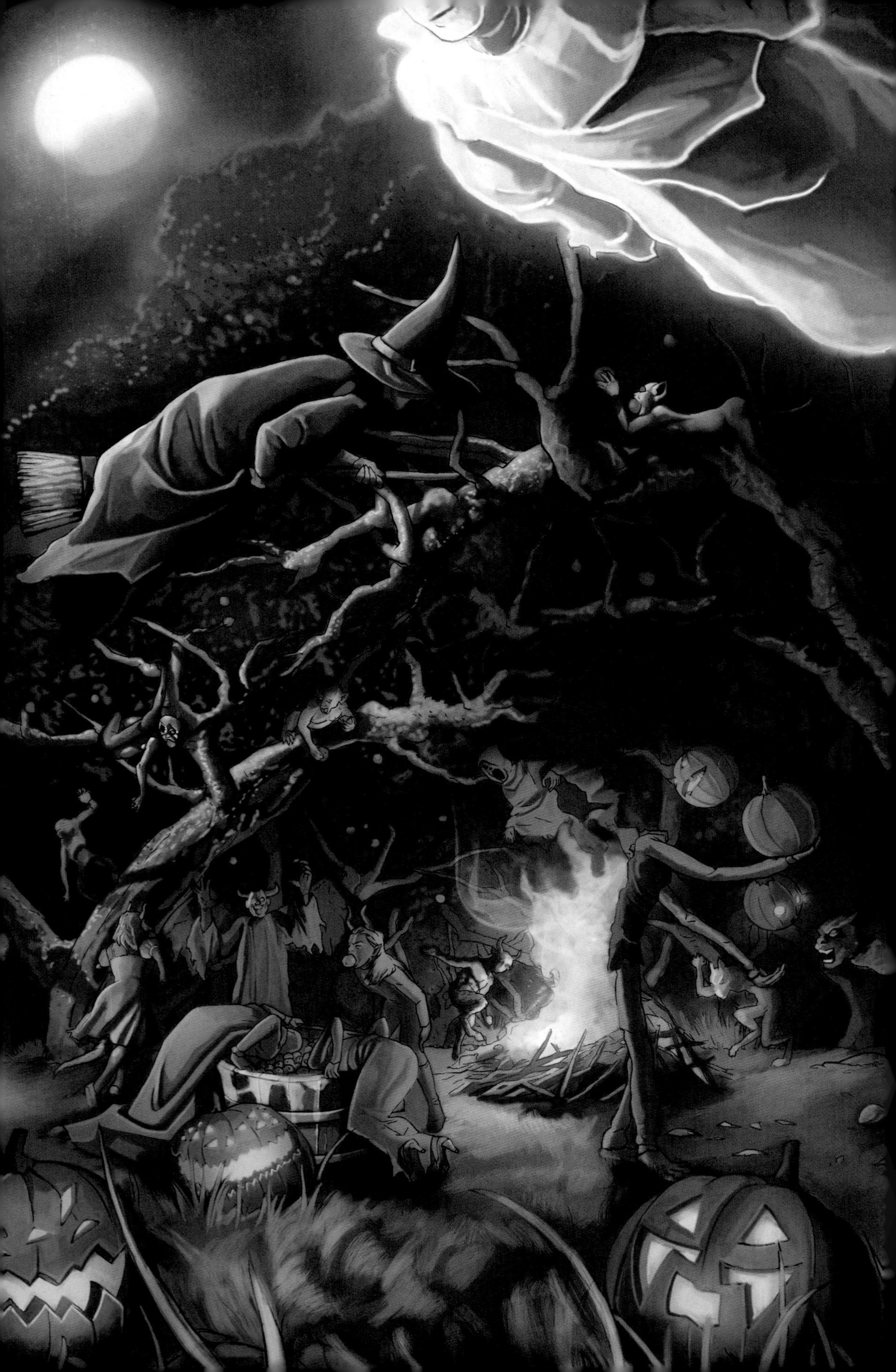

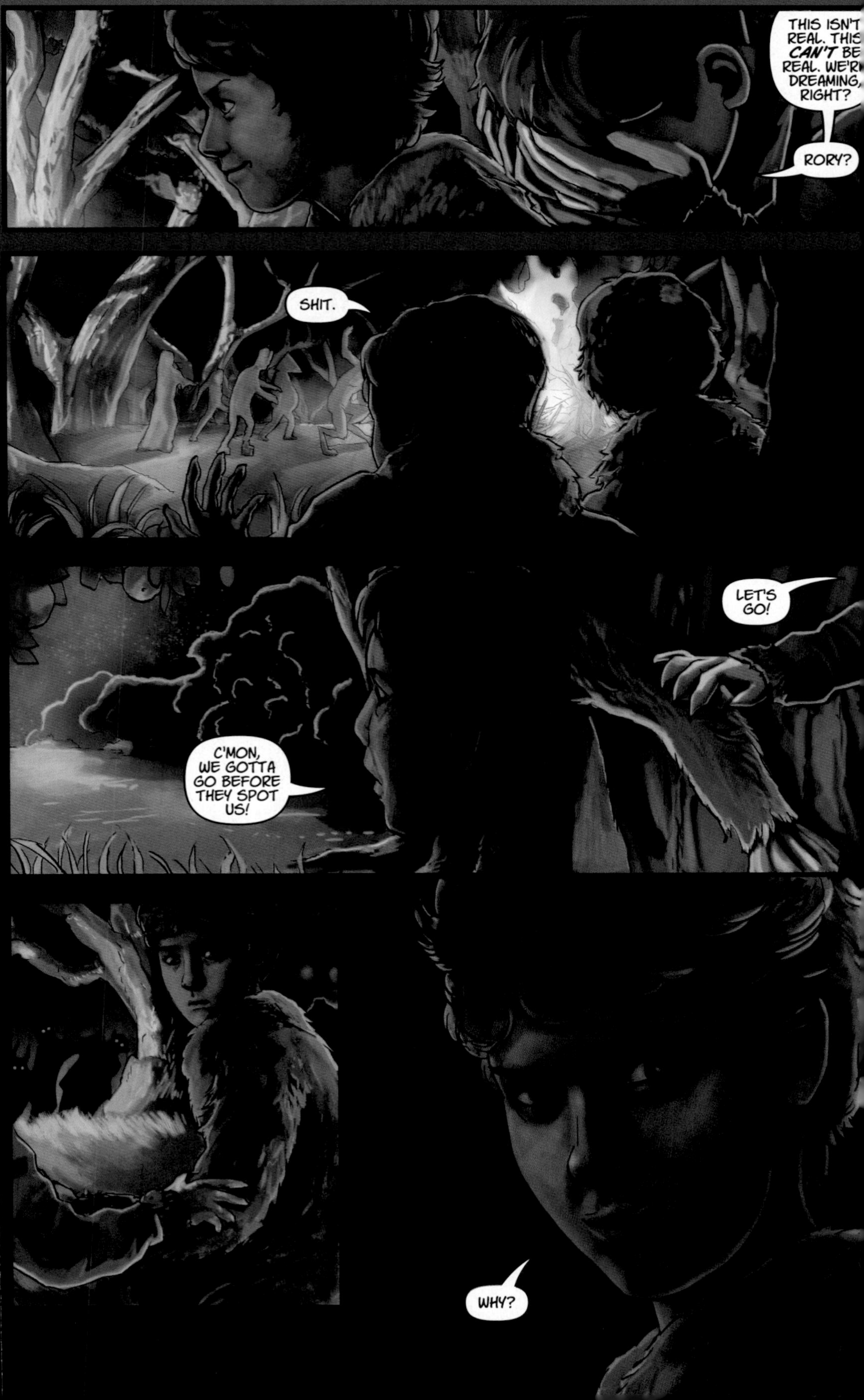
THIS ISN'T REAL. THIS *CAN'T* BE REAL. WE'R DREAMING, RIGHT?
RORY?
SHIT.
LET'S GO!
C'MON, WE GOTTA GO BEFORE THEY SPOT US!
WHY?

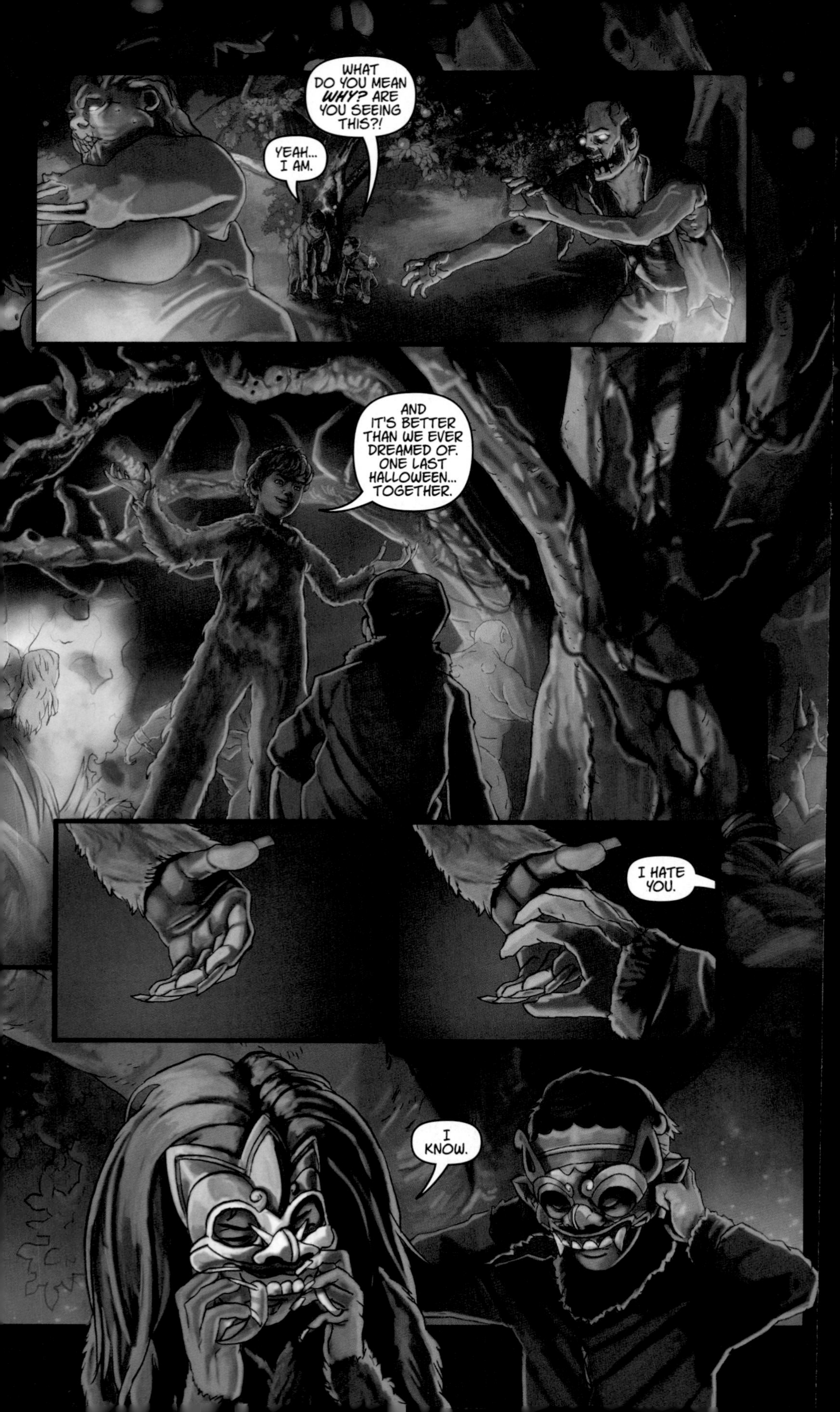

WHAT DO YOU MEAN *WHY?* ARE YOU SEEING THIS?!
YEAH... I AM.
AND IT'S BETTER THAN WE EVER DREAMED OF. ONE LAST HALLOWEEN... TOGETHER.
I HATE YOU.
I KNOW.

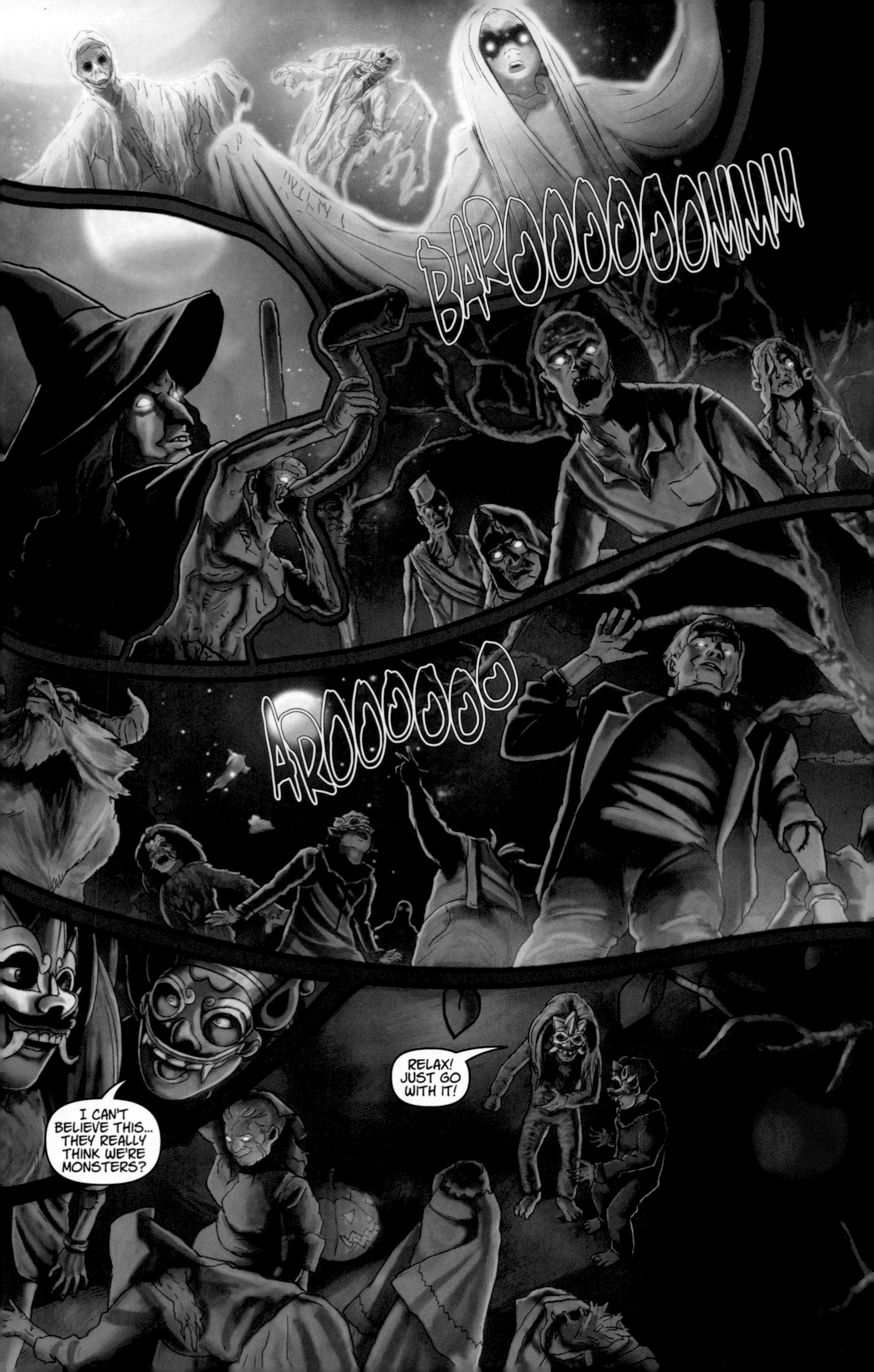
BAROOOOOOOMMM
AROOOOOO
I CAN'T BELIEVE THIS... THEY REALLY THINK WE'RE MONSTERS?
RELAX! JUST GO WITH IT!

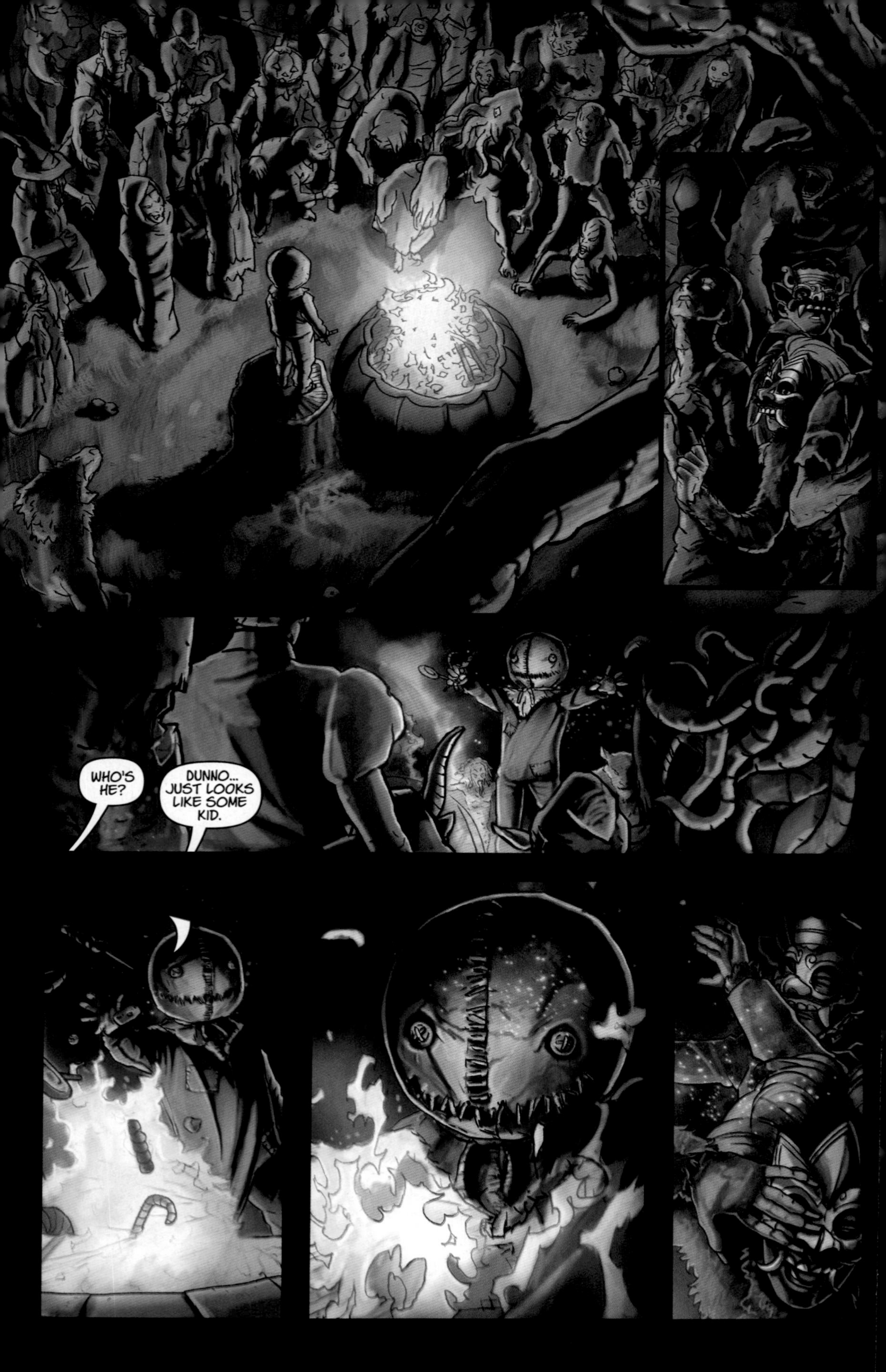
WHO'S HE?
DUNNO... JUST LOOKS LIKE SOME KID.

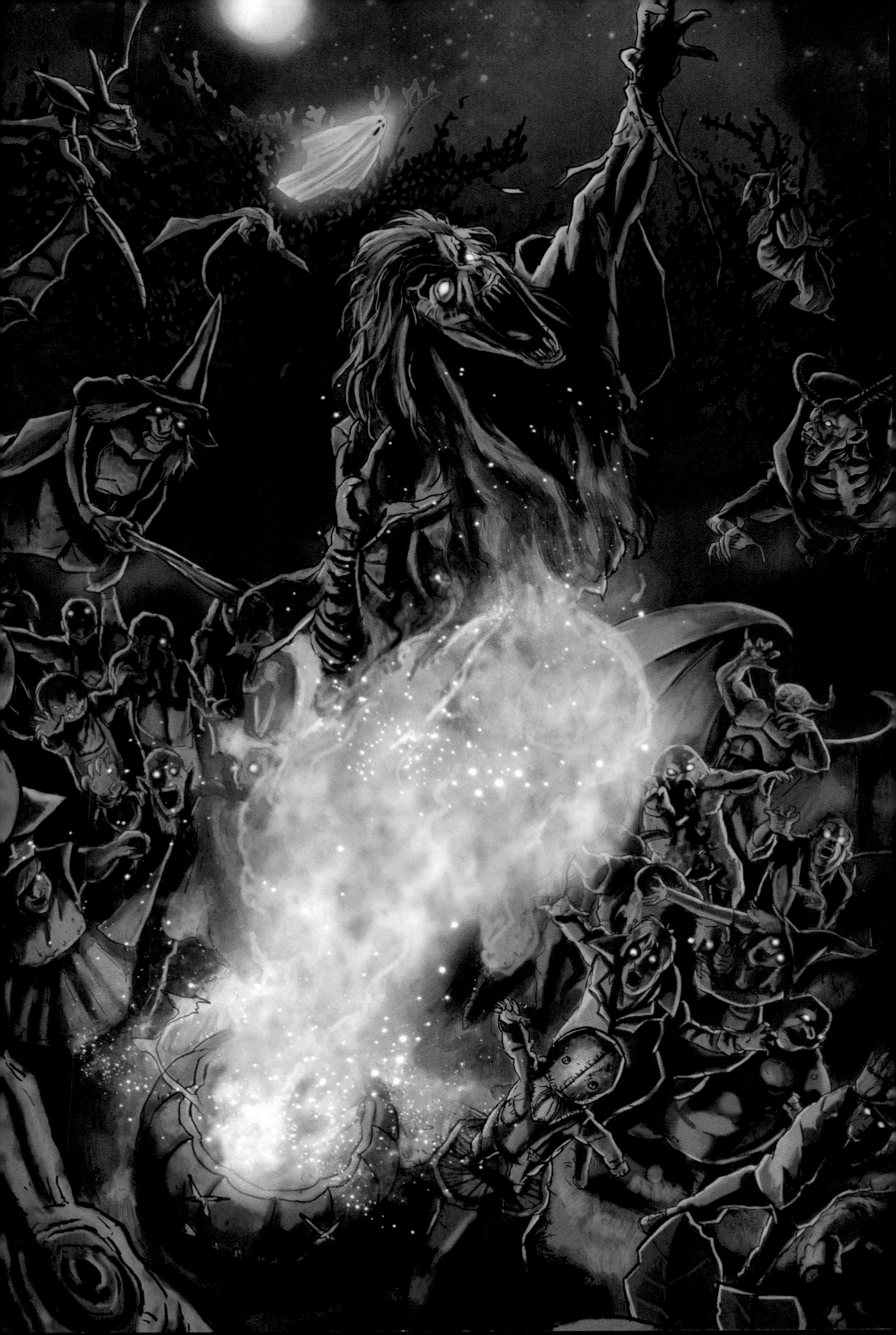

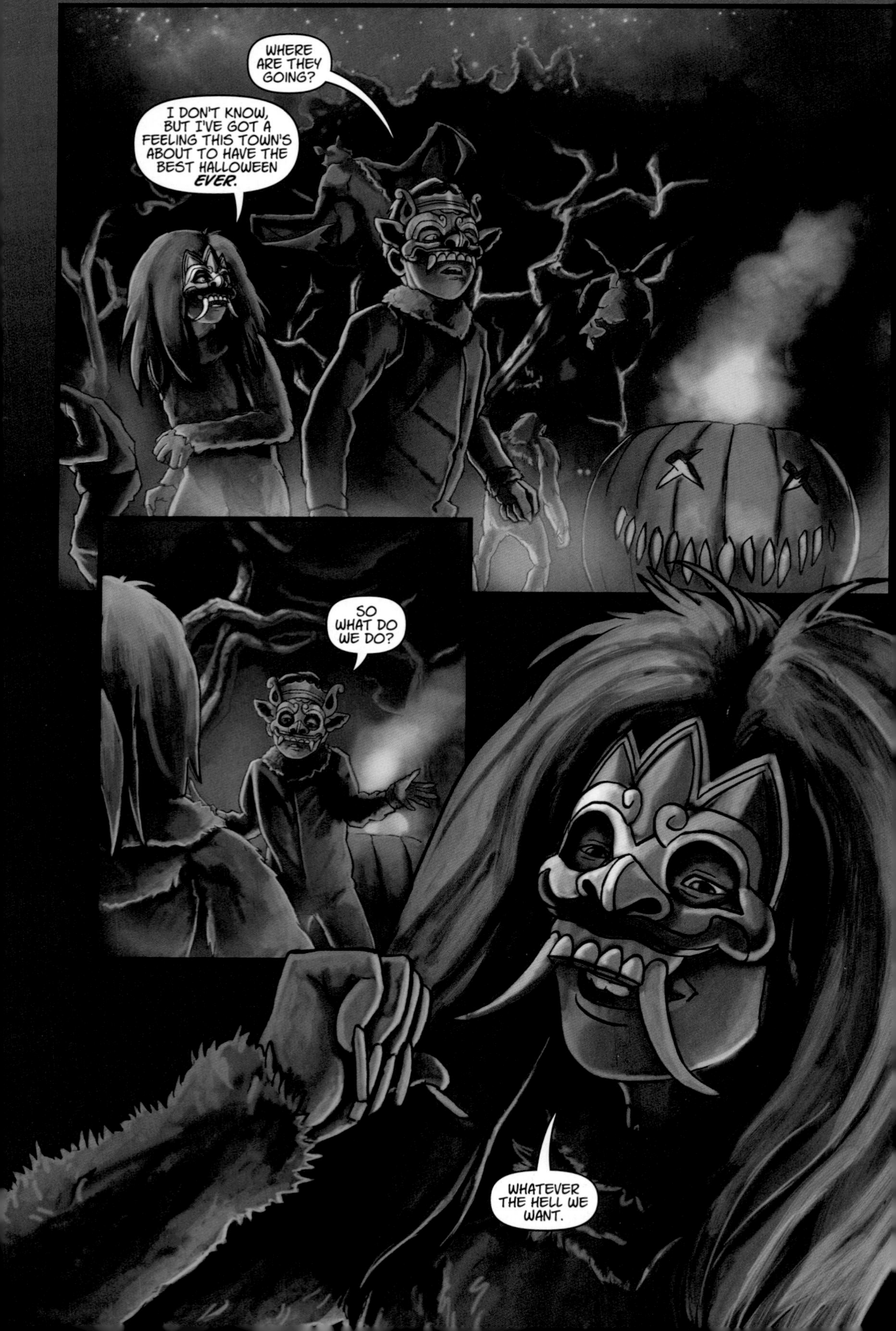
WHERE ARE THEY GOING?
I DON'T KNOW, BUT I'VE GOT A FEELING THIS TOWN'S ABOUT TO HAVE THE BEST HALLOWEEN ***EVER***.
SO WHAT DO WE DO?
WHATEVER THE HELL WE WANT.

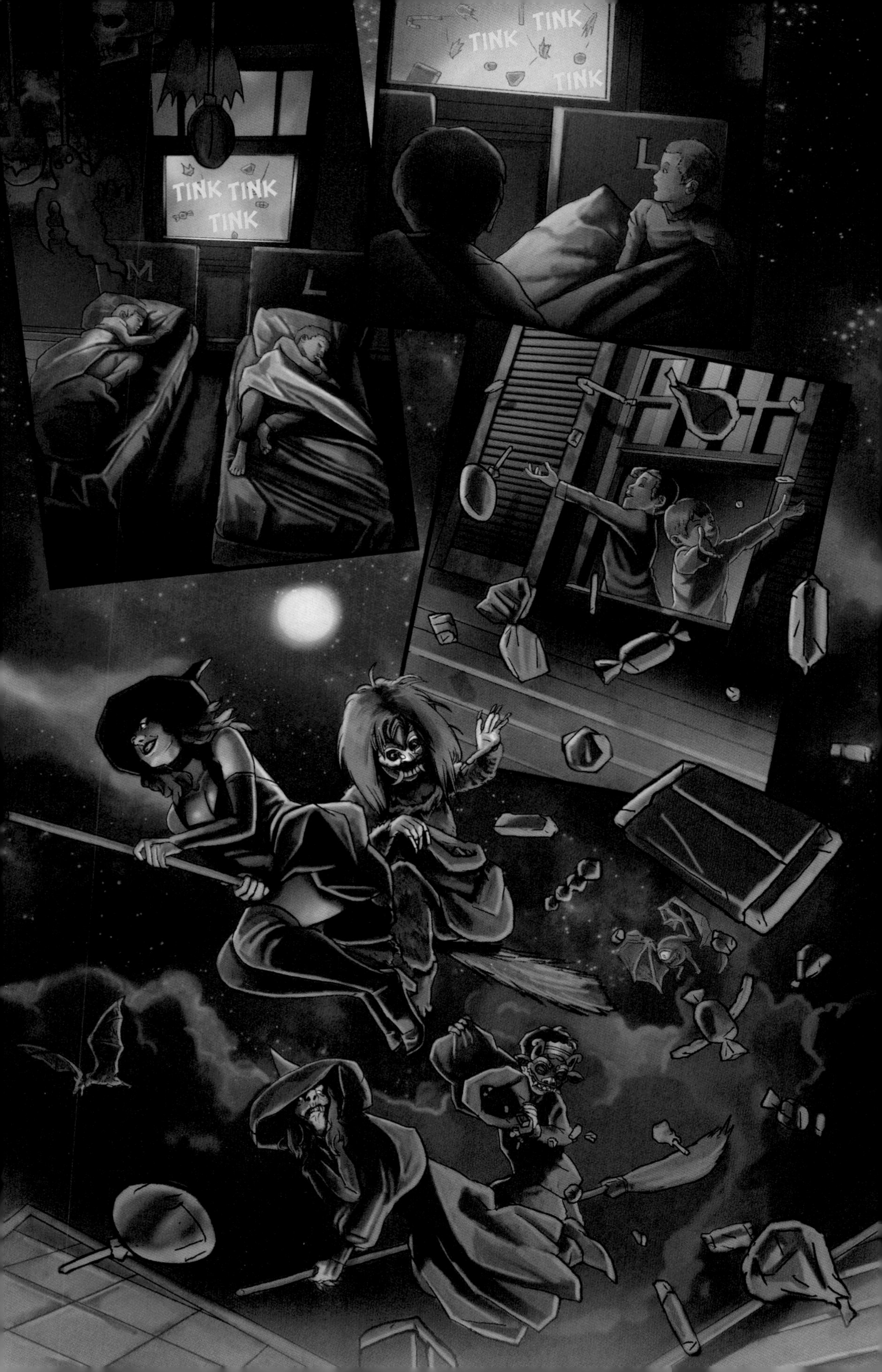
TINK TINK
TINK
M
L
TINK TINK
TINK
L

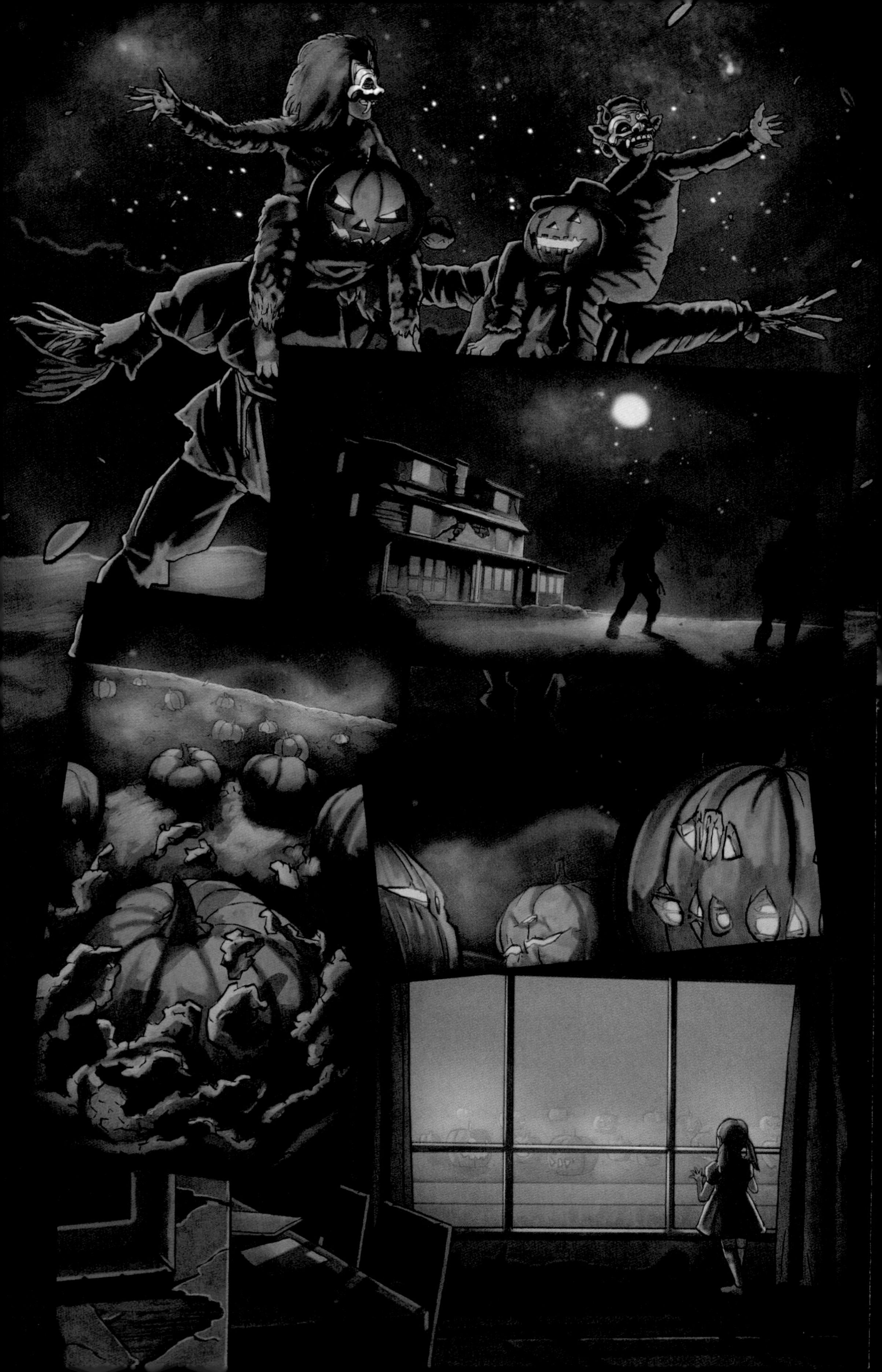

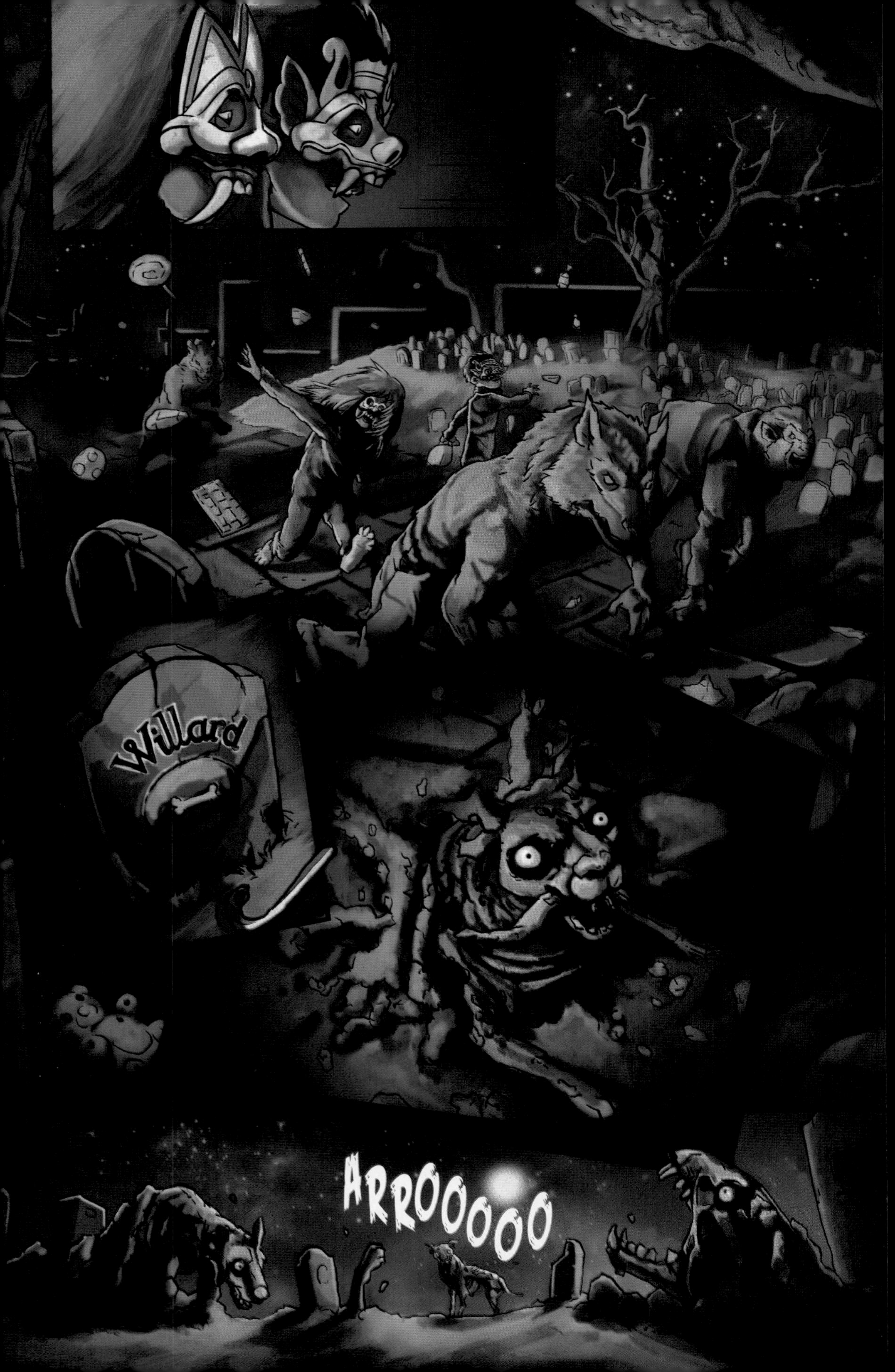
Willard
ARROOOOO

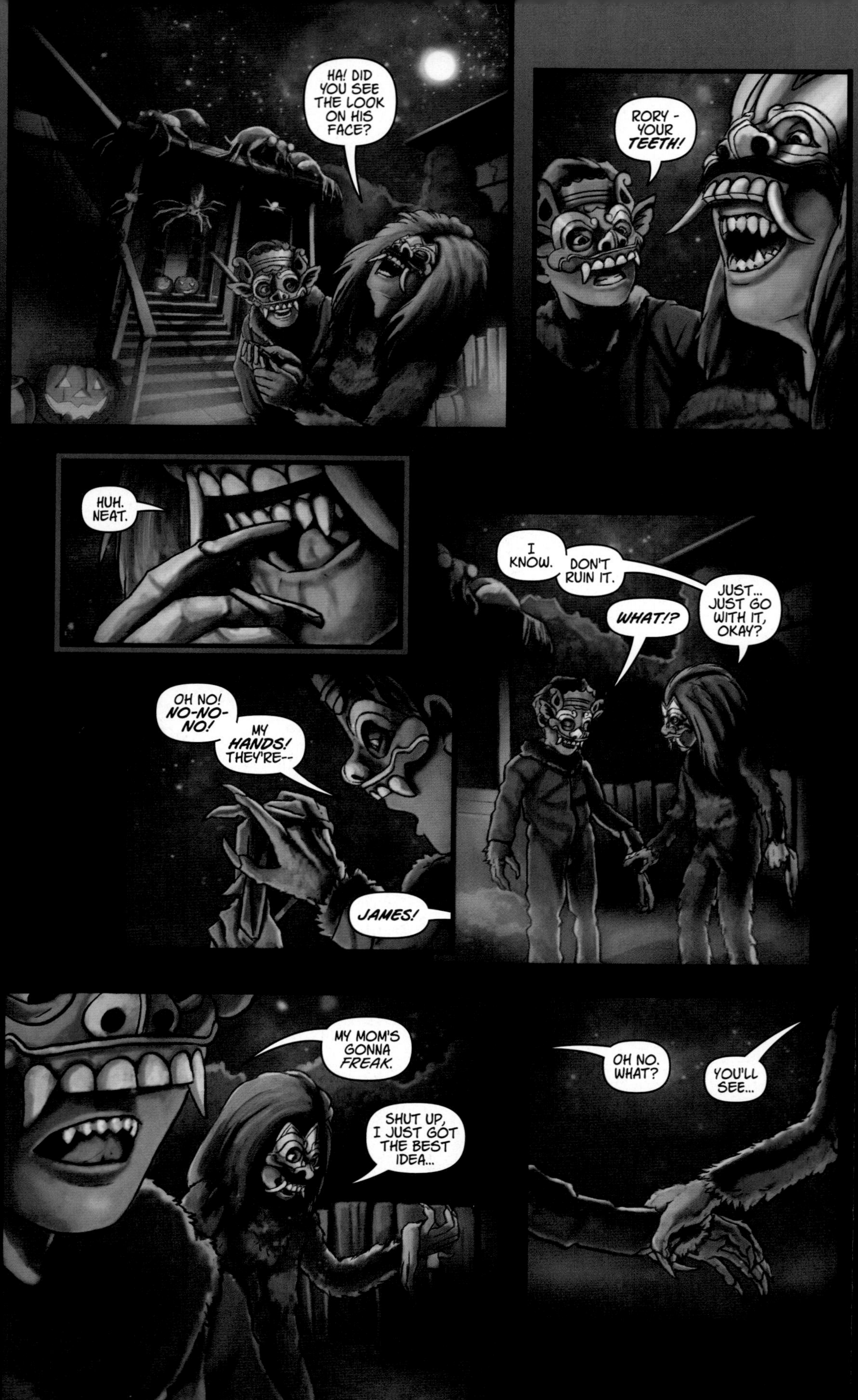
HA! DID YOU SEE THE LOOK ON HIS FACE?
RORY - YOUR *TEETH!*
HUH. NEAT.
I KNOW.
DON'T RUIN IT.
WHAT!?
JUST... JUST GO WITH IT, OKAY?
OH NO! *NO-NO-NO!*
MY *HANDS!* THEY'RE--
JAMES!
MY MOM'S GONNA *FREAK.*
SHUT UP, I JUST GOT THE BEST IDEA...
OH NO. WHAT?
YOU'LL SEE...

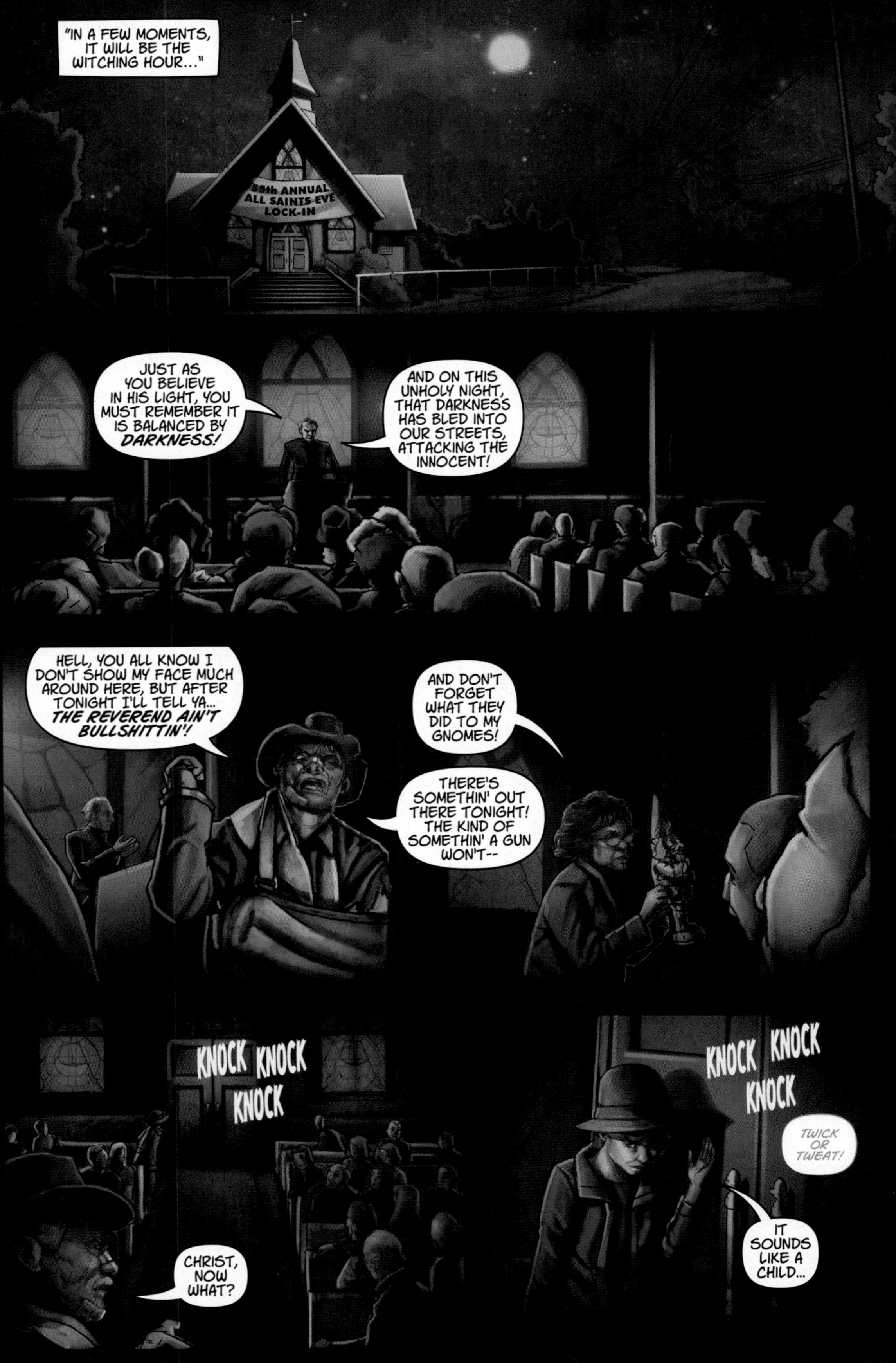
"IN A FEW MOMENTS, IT WILL BE THE WITCHING HOUR..."
55th ANNUAL ALL SAINTS-EVE LOCK-IN
JUST AS YOU BELIEVE IN HIS LIGHT, YOU MUST REMEMBER IT IS BALANCED BY DARKNESS!
AND ON THIS UNHOLY NIGHT, THAT DARKNESS HAS BLED INTO OUR STREETS, ATTACKING THE INNOCENT!
HELL, YOU ALL KNOW I DON'T SHOW MY FACE MUCH AROUND HERE, BUT AFTER TONIGHT I'LL TELL YA... THE REVEREND AIN'T BULLSHITTIN'!
THERE'S SOMETHIN' OUT THERE TONIGHT! THE KIND OF SOMETHIN' A GUN WON'T--
AND DON'T FORGET WHAT THEY DID TO MY GNOMES!
KNOCK KNOCK KNOCK
CHRIST, NOW WHAT?
KNOCK KNOCK KNOCK
TWICK OR TWEAT!
IT SOUNDS LIKE A CHILD...

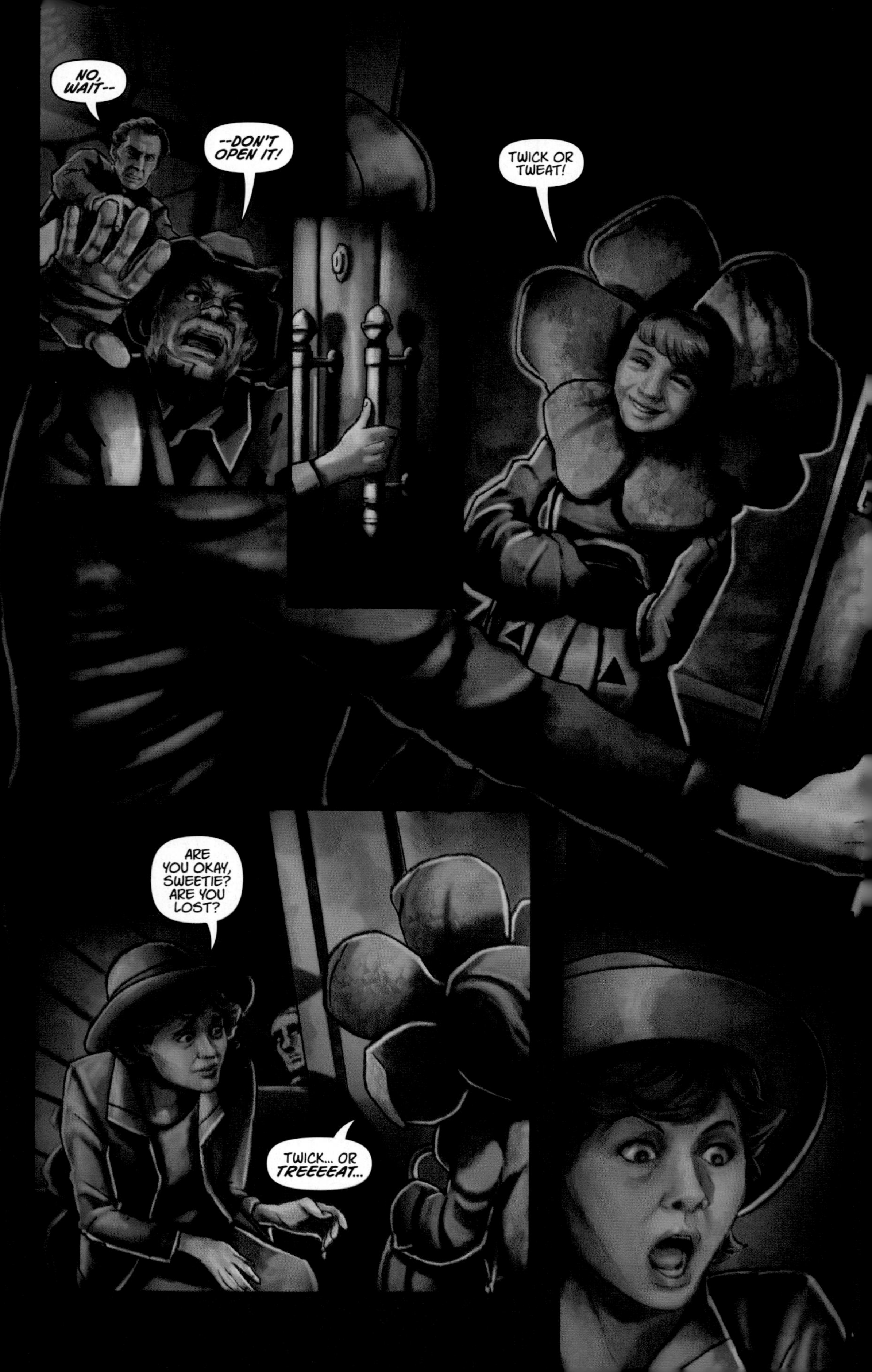
NO, WAIT--
--DON'T OPEN IT!
TWICK OR TWEAT!
ARE YOU OKAY, SWEETIE? ARE YOU LOST?
TWICK... OR TREEEEAT...

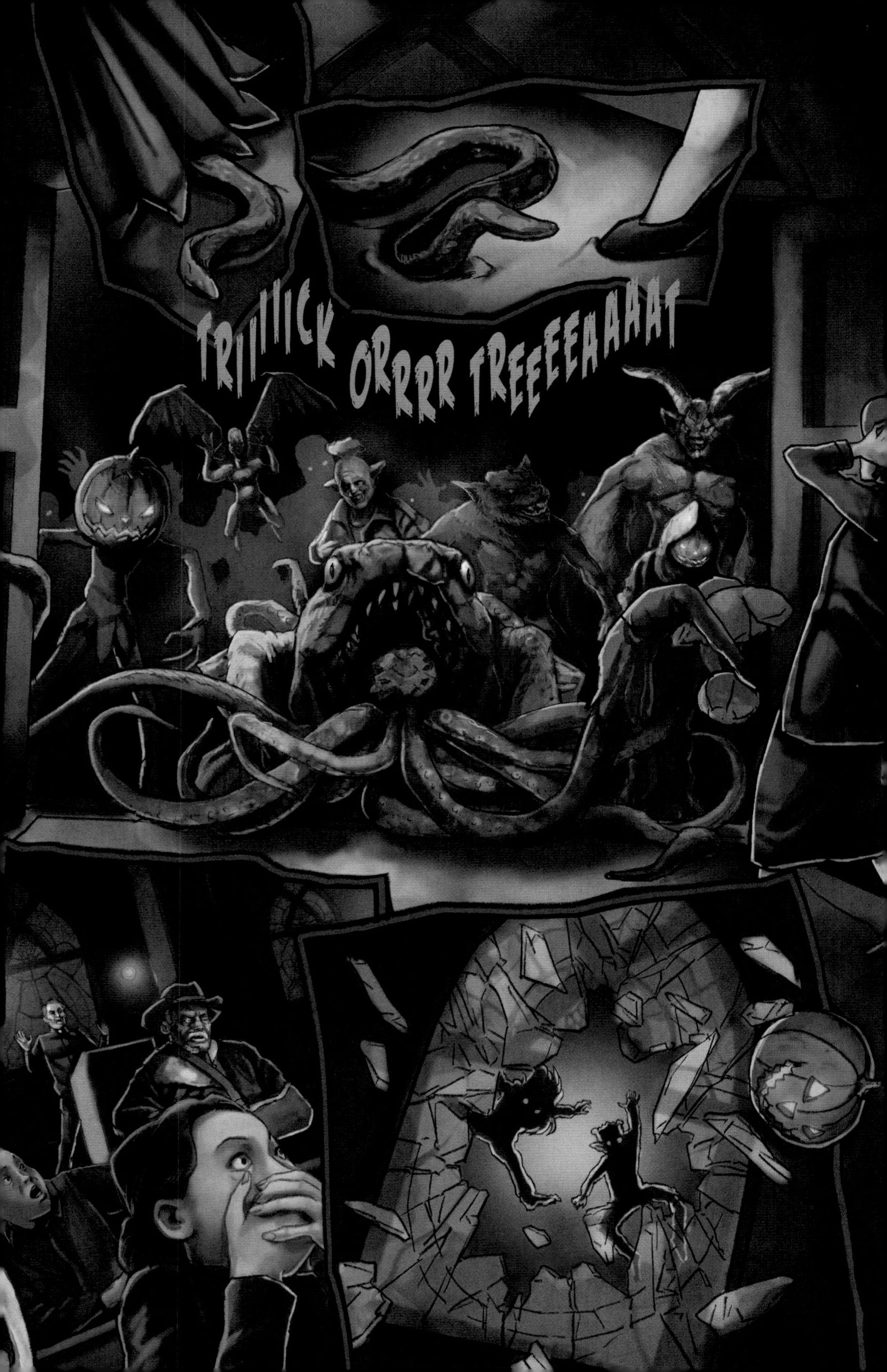
TRIIIICK ORRRR TREEEEAAAAT

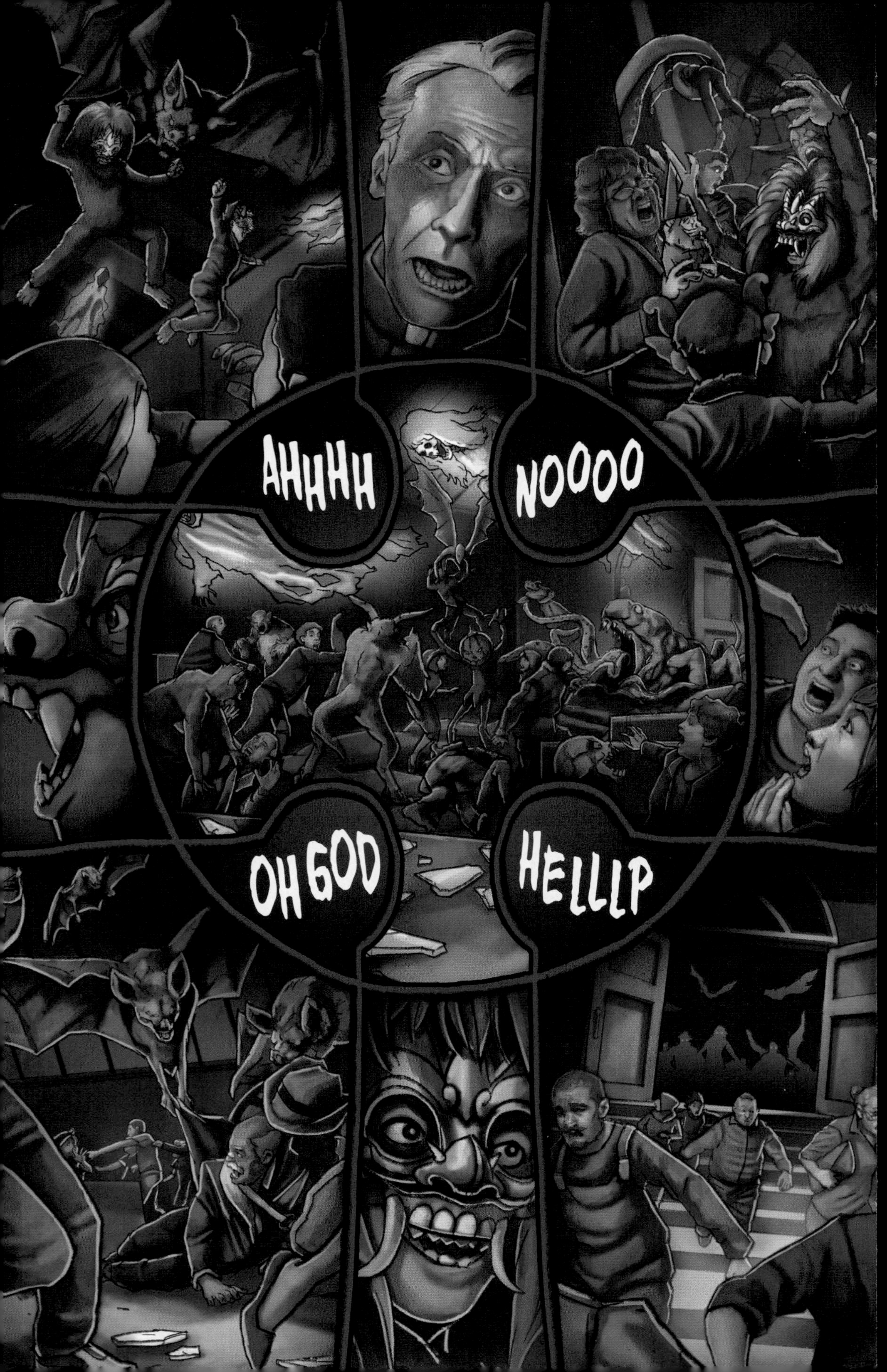
AHHHH
NOOOO
OH GOD
HELLLP

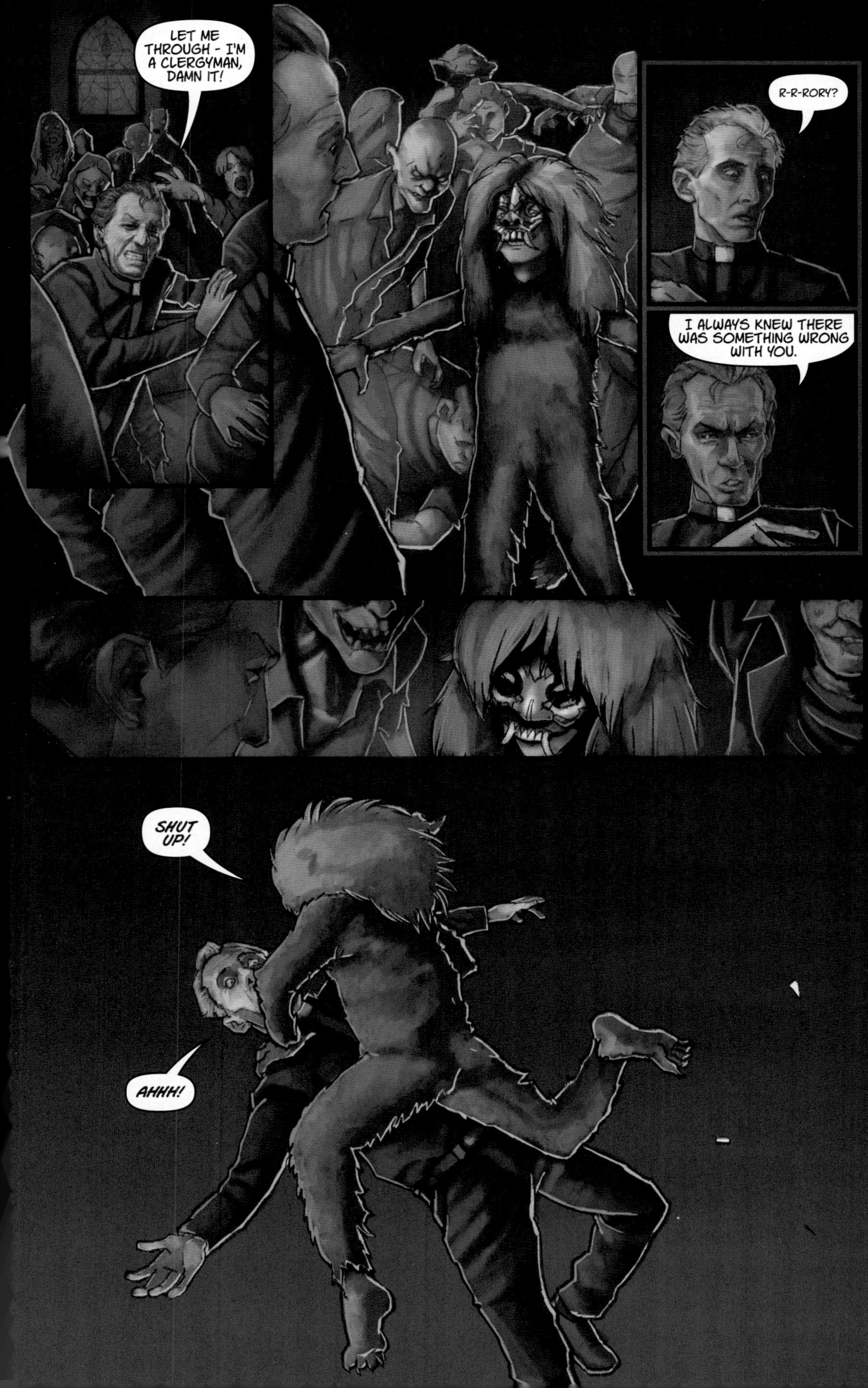
LET ME THROUGH - I'M A CLERGYMAN, DAMN IT!
R-R-RORY?
I ALWAYS KNEW THERE WAS SOMETHING WRONG WITH YOU.
SHUT UP!
AHHH!

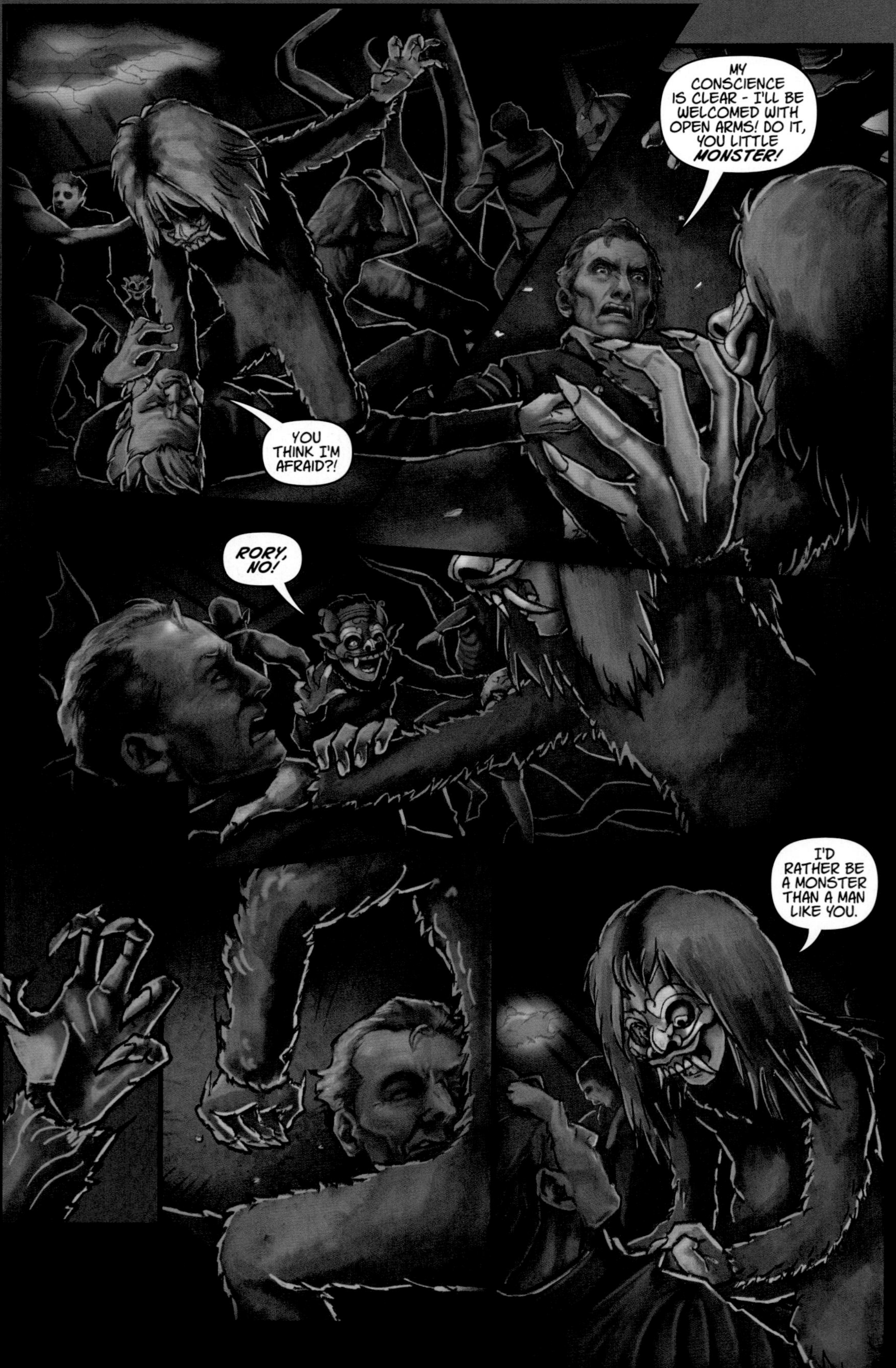
MY CONSCIENCE IS CLEAR - I'LL BE WELCOMED WITH OPEN ARMS! DO IT, YOU LITTLE *MONSTER!*
YOU THINK I'M AFRAID?!
RORY, NO!
I'D RATHER BE A MONSTER THAN A MAN LIKE YOU.

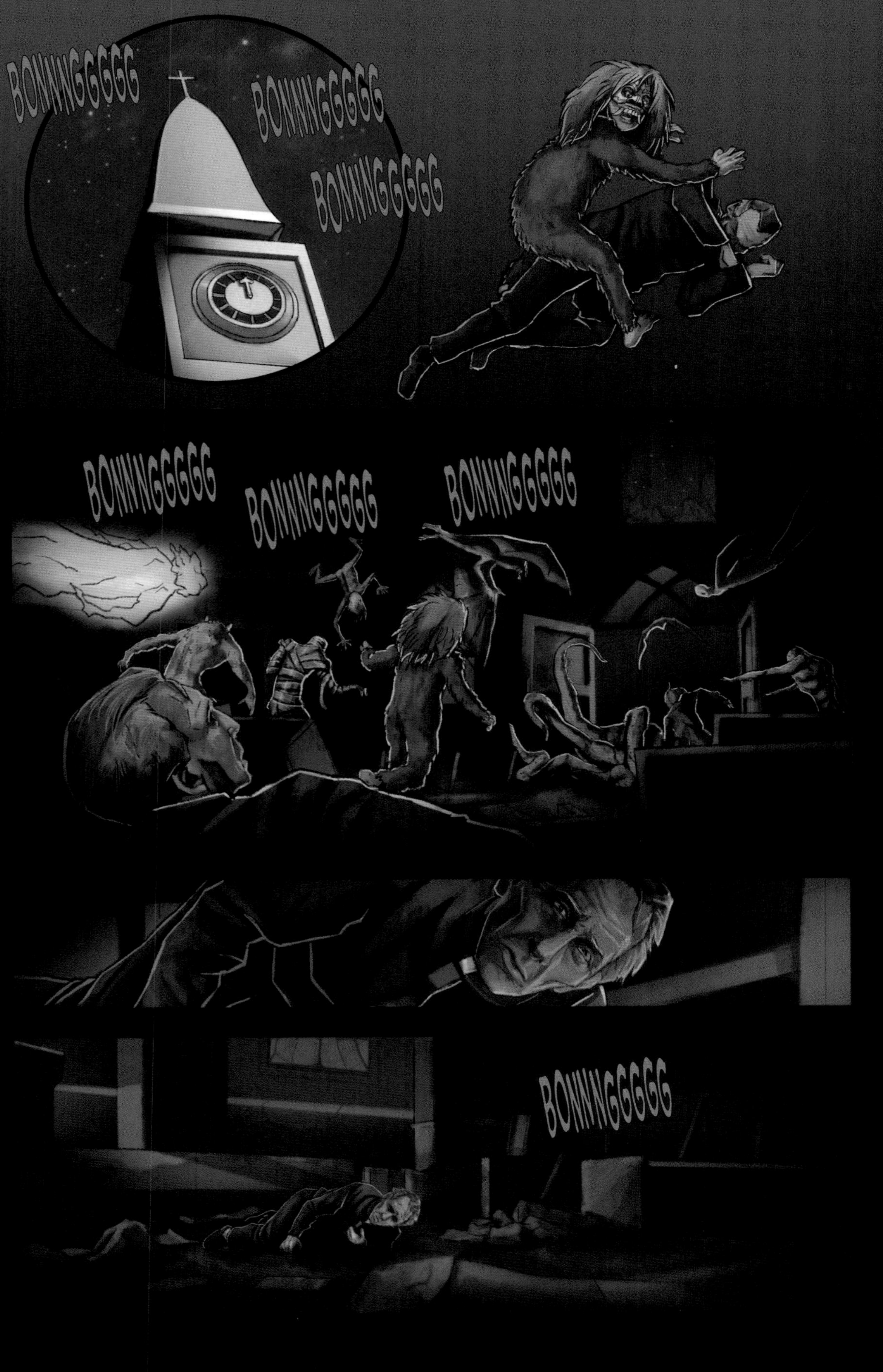
BONNNGGGGG
BONNNGGGGG
BONNNGGGGG
BONNNGGGGG
BONNNGGGGG
BONNNGGGGG
BONNNGGGGG

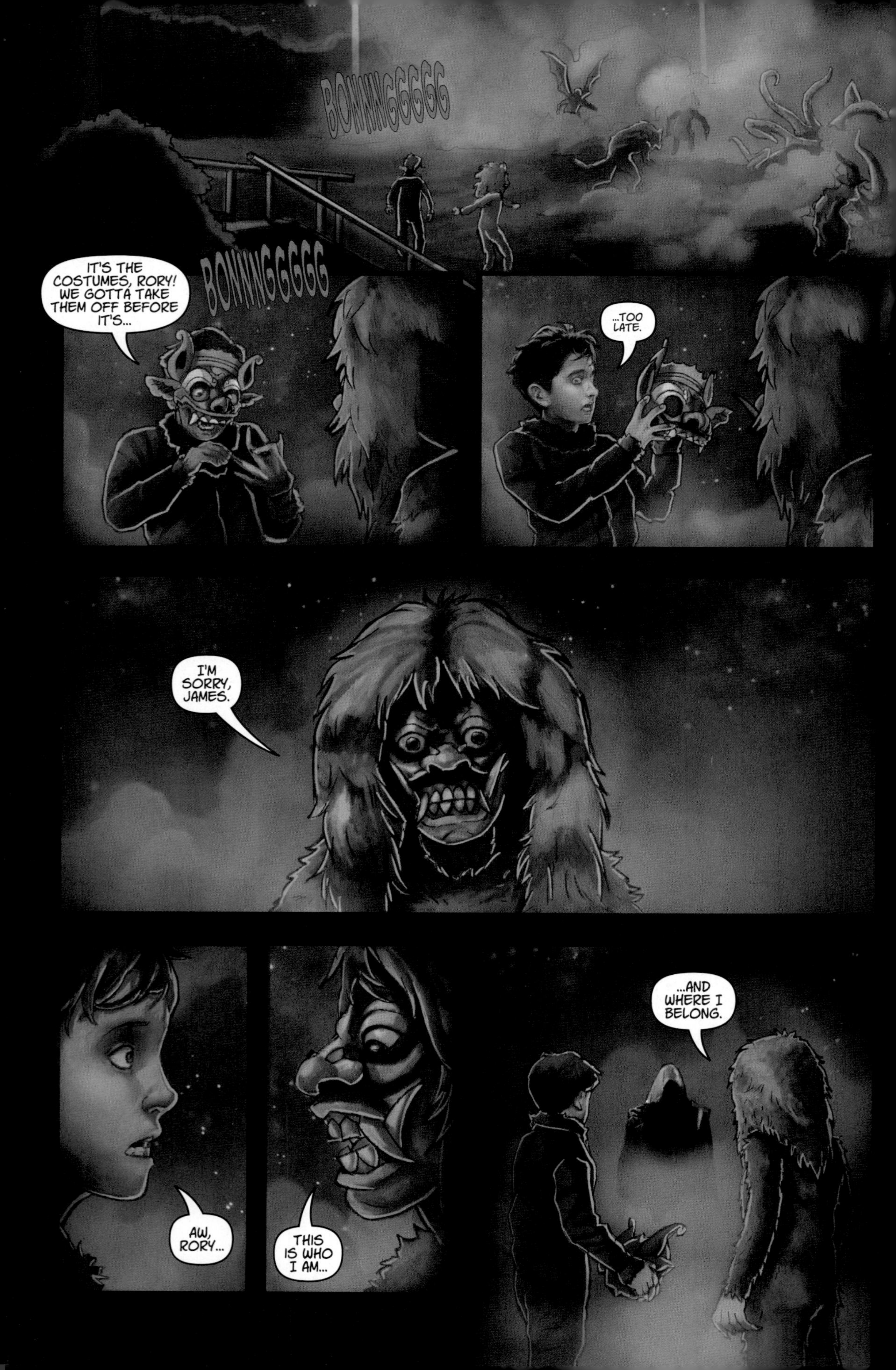
BONNNGGGGGG
BONNNGGGGG
IT'S THE COSTUMES, RORY! WE GOTTA TAKE THEM OFF BEFORE IT'S...
...TOO LATE.
I'M SORRY, JAMES.
AW, RORY...
THIS IS WHO I AM...
...AND WHERE I BELONG.

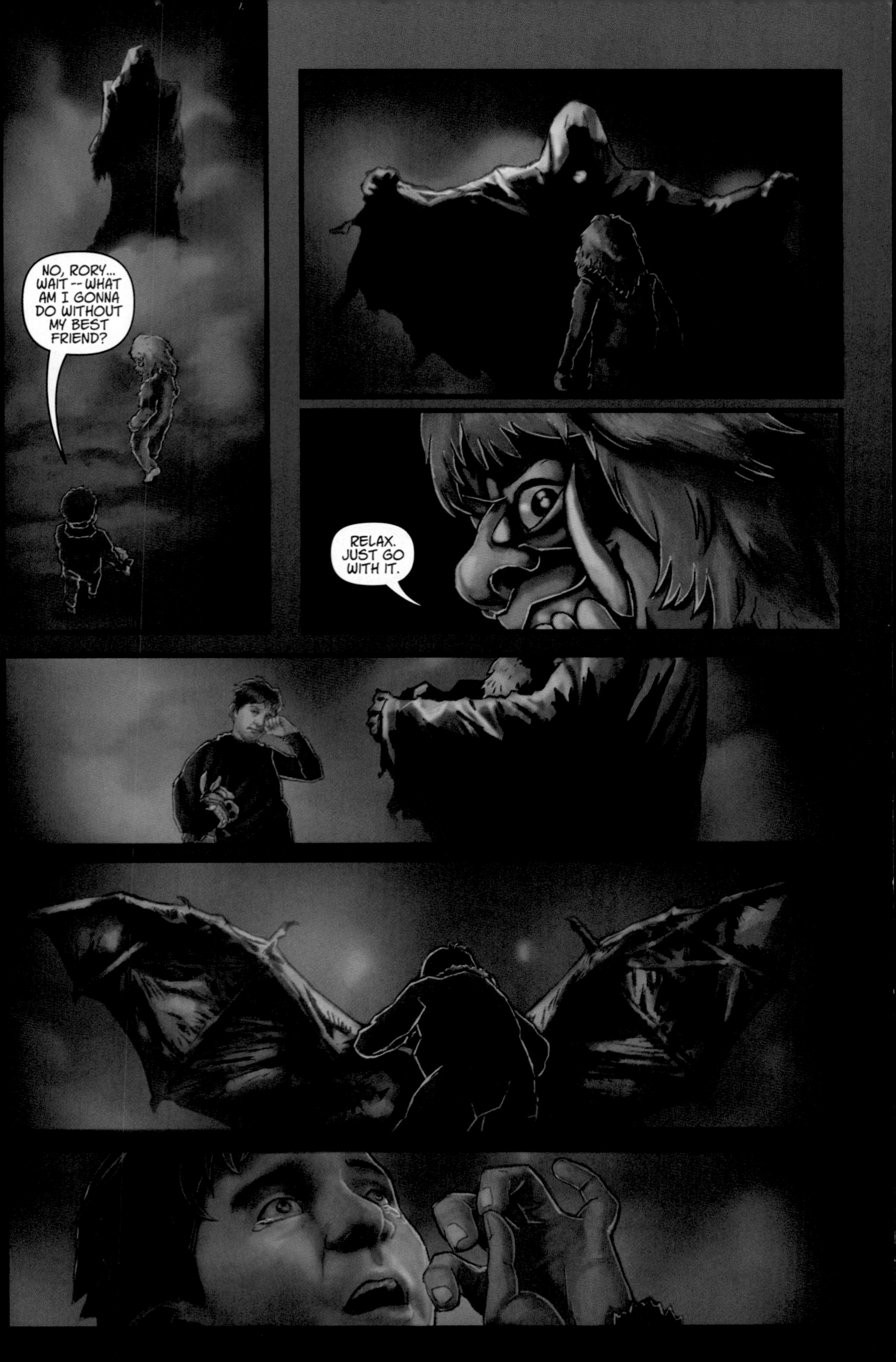
NO, RORY... WAIT -- WHAT AM I GONNA DO WITHOUT MY BEST FRIEND?
RELAX. JUST GO WITH IT.

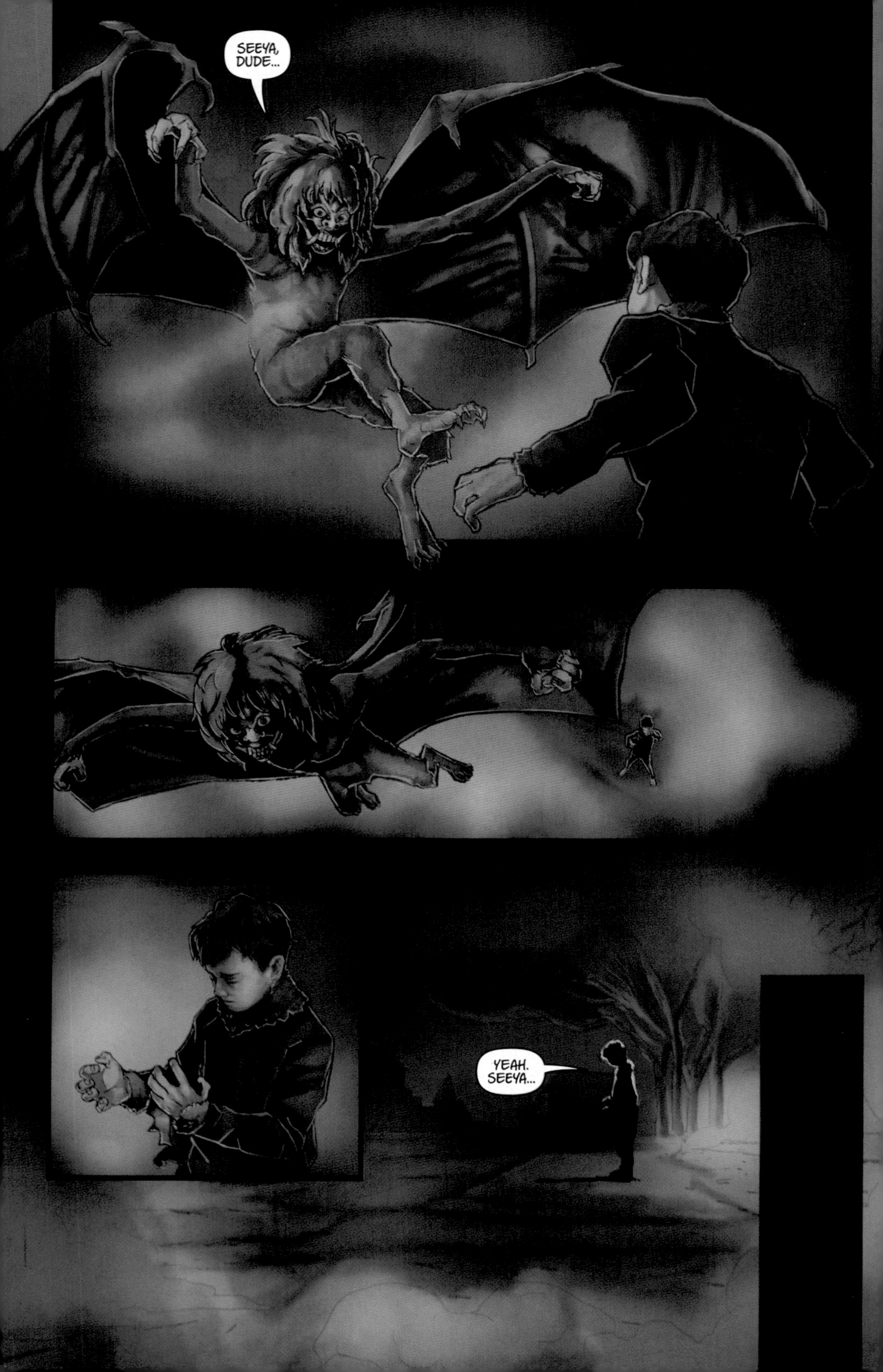
SEEYA, DUDE...
YEAH. SEEYA...

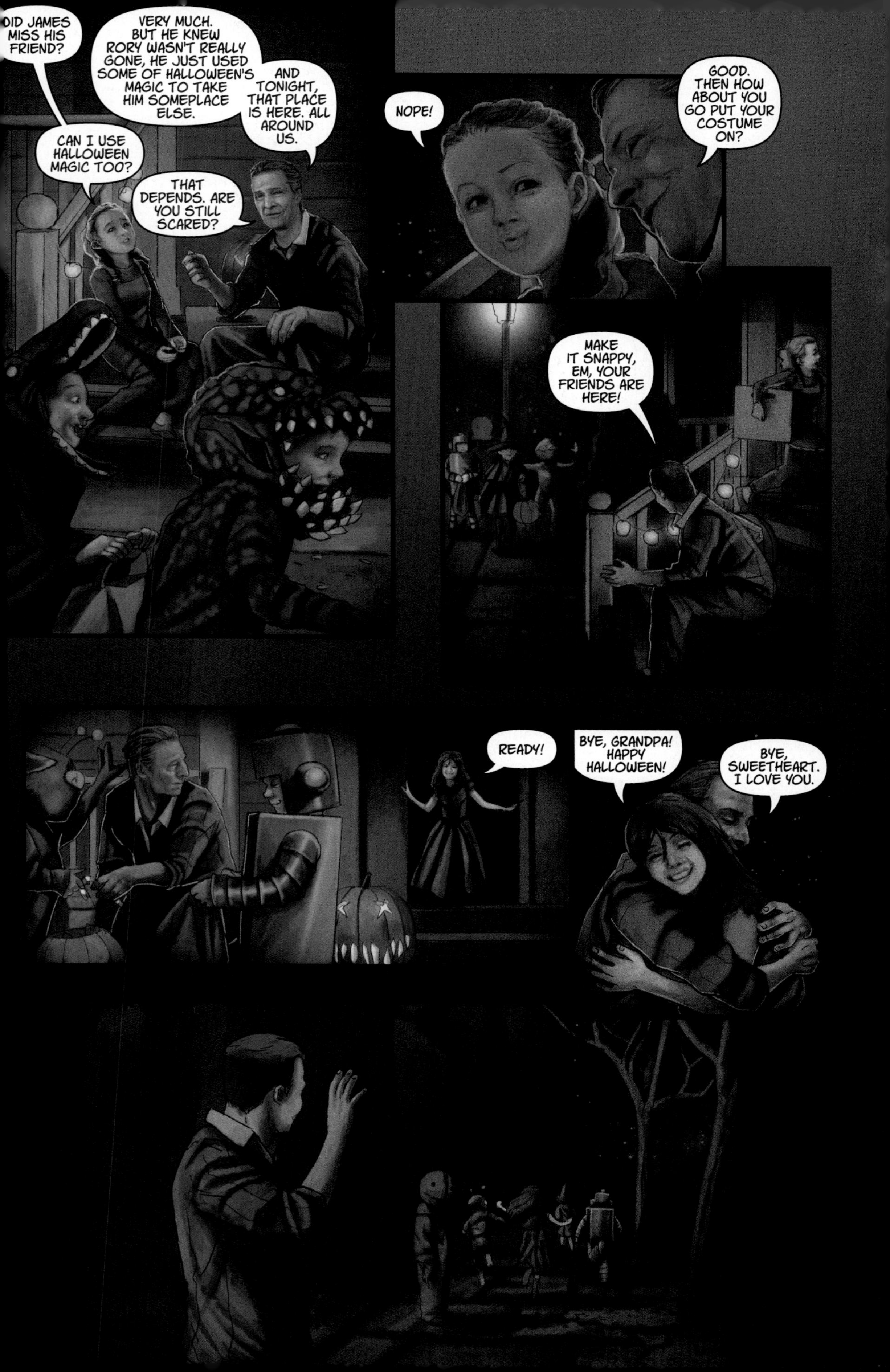
DID JAMES MISS HIS FRIEND?
VERY MUCH. BUT HE KNEW RORY WASN'T REALLY GONE, HE JUST USED SOME OF HALLOWEEN'S MAGIC TO TAKE HIM SOMEPLACE ELSE.
AND TONIGHT, THAT PLACE IS HERE. ALL AROUND US.
CAN I USE HALLOWEEN MAGIC TOO?
THAT DEPENDS. ARE YOU STILL SCARED?
NOPE!
GOOD. THEN HOW ABOUT YOU GO PUT YOUR COSTUME ON?
MAKE IT SNAPPY, EM, YOUR FRIENDS ARE HERE!
READY!
BYE, GRANDPA! HAPPY HALLOWEEN!
BYE, SWEETHEART. I LOVE YOU.

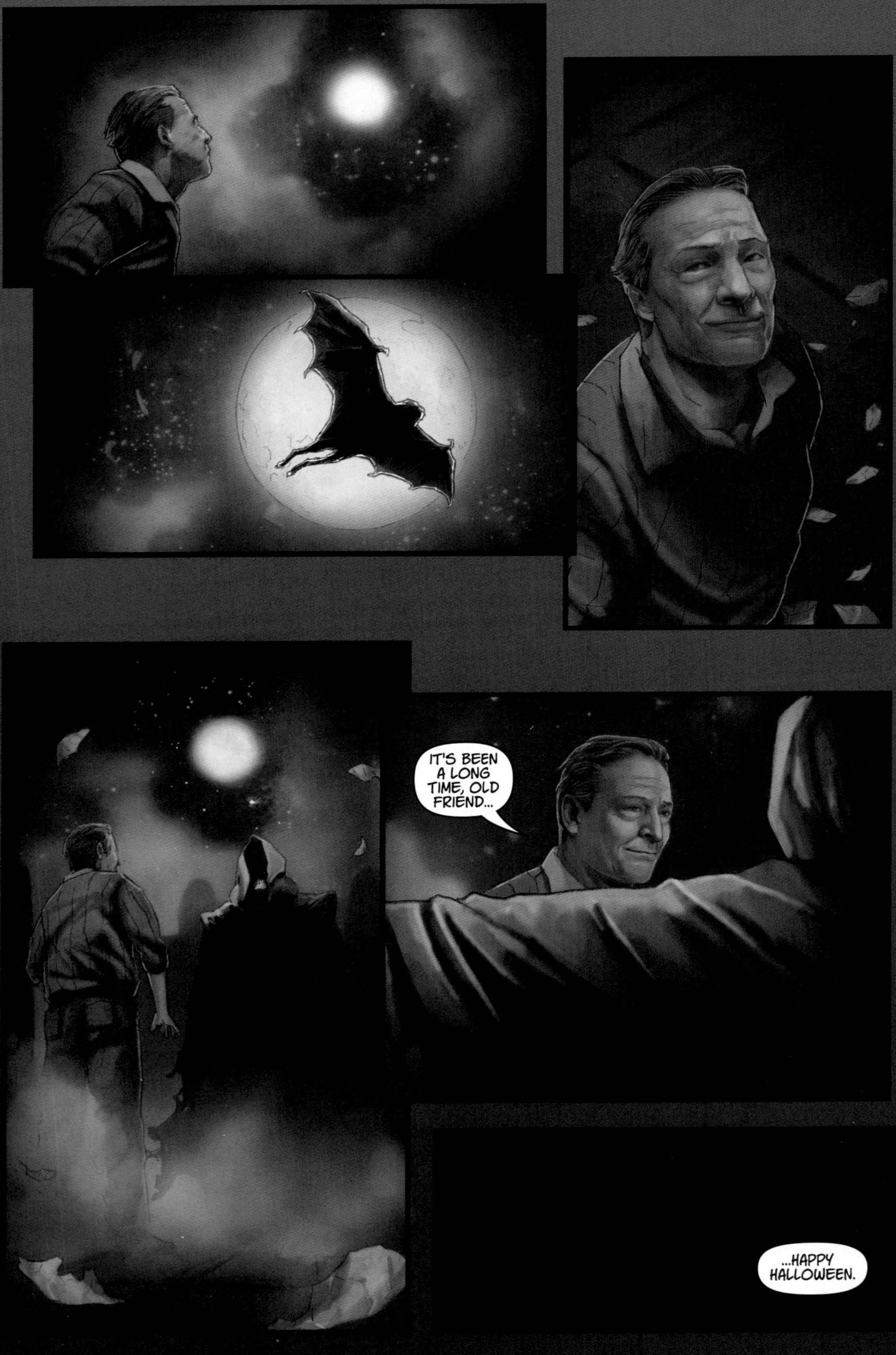
IT'S BEEN A LONG TIME, OLD FRIEND...
...HAPPY HALLOWEEN.

EXTRA TREATS

CORN MAIDEN pin-up by LEE FURGUSON

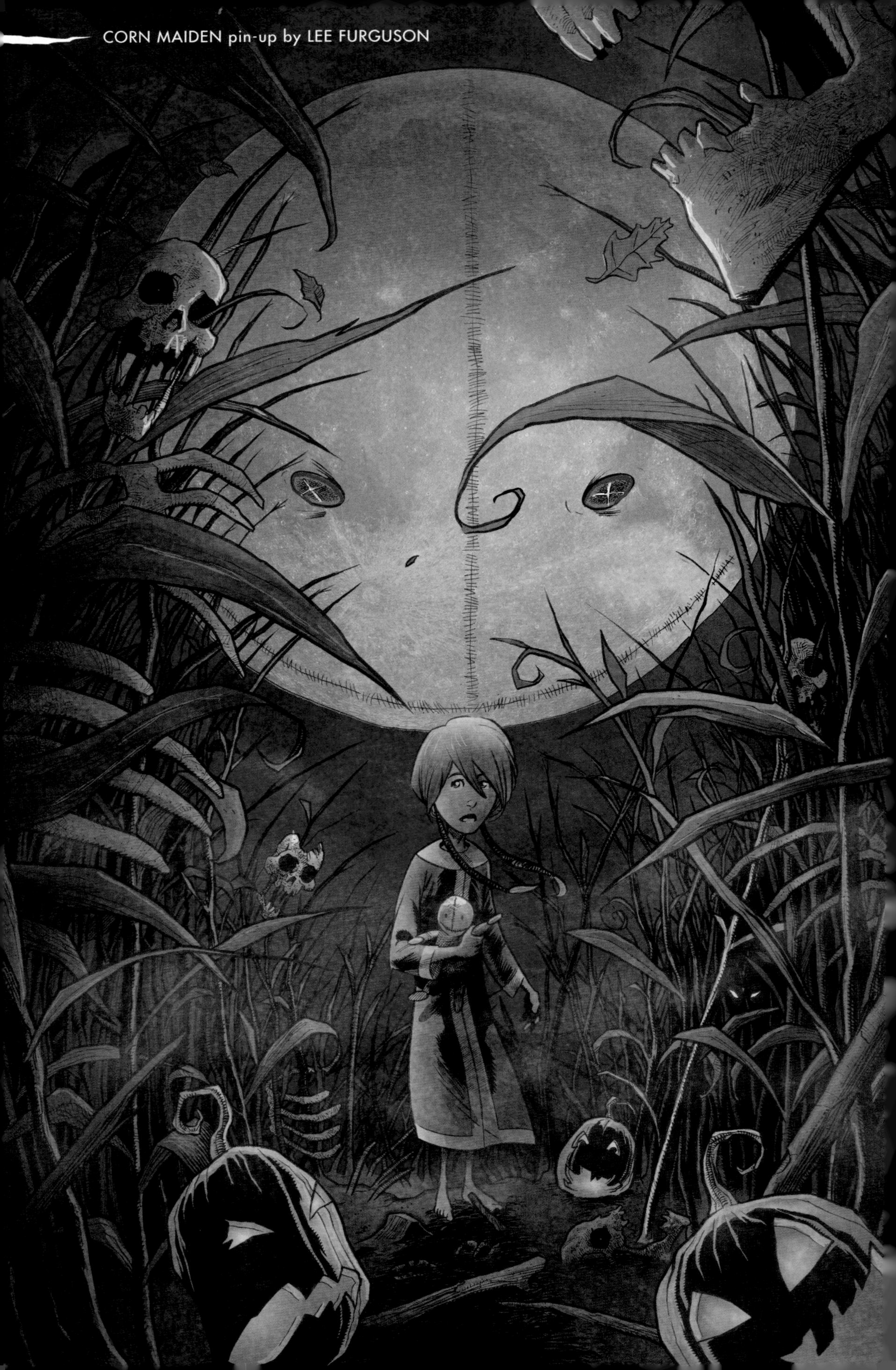

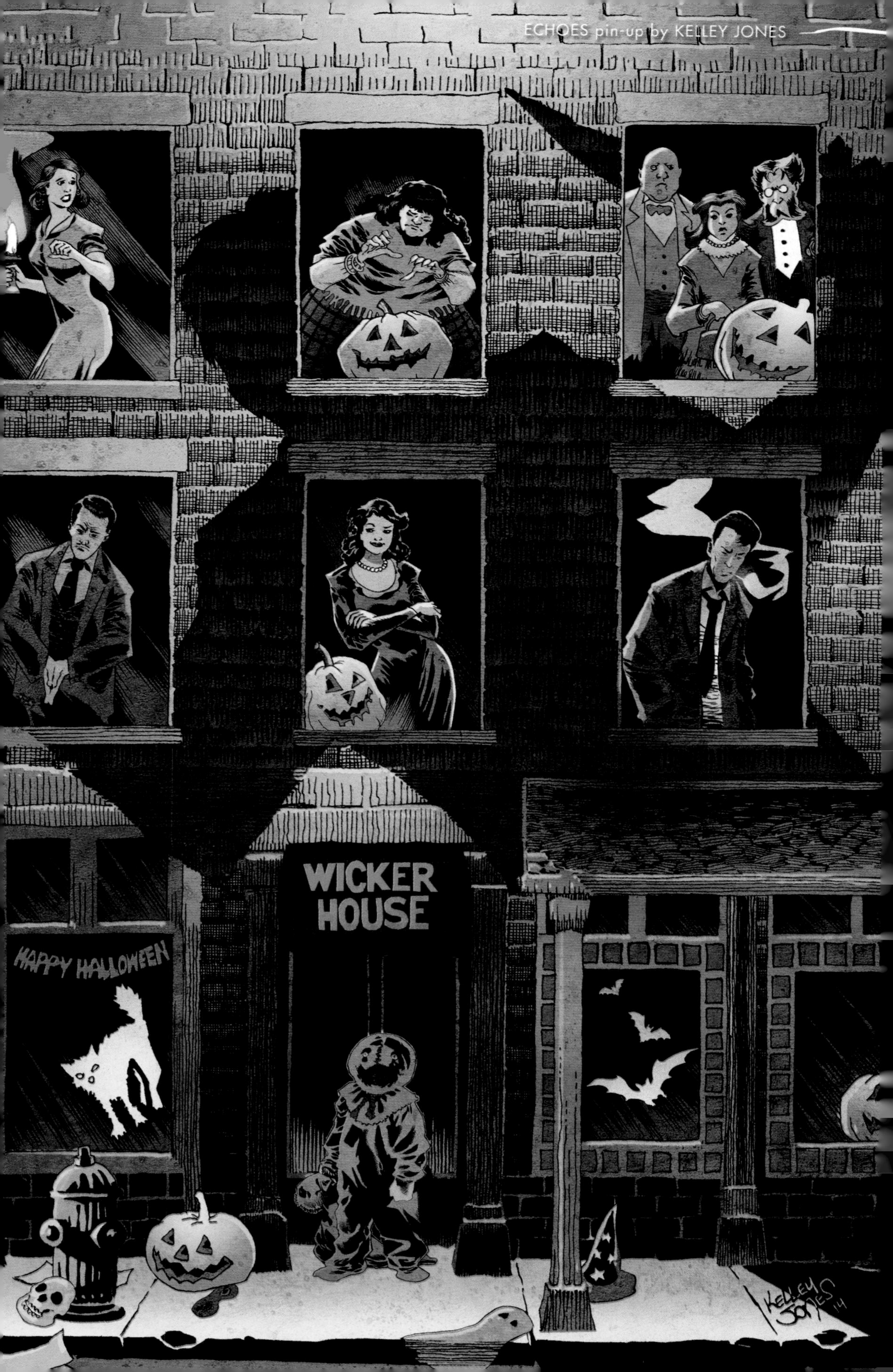
WICKER
HOUSE
HAPPY HALLOWEEN
KELLEY JONES '14

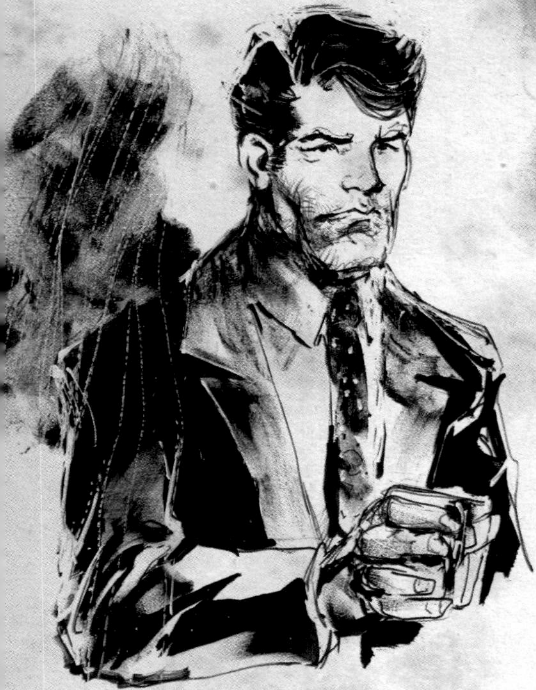

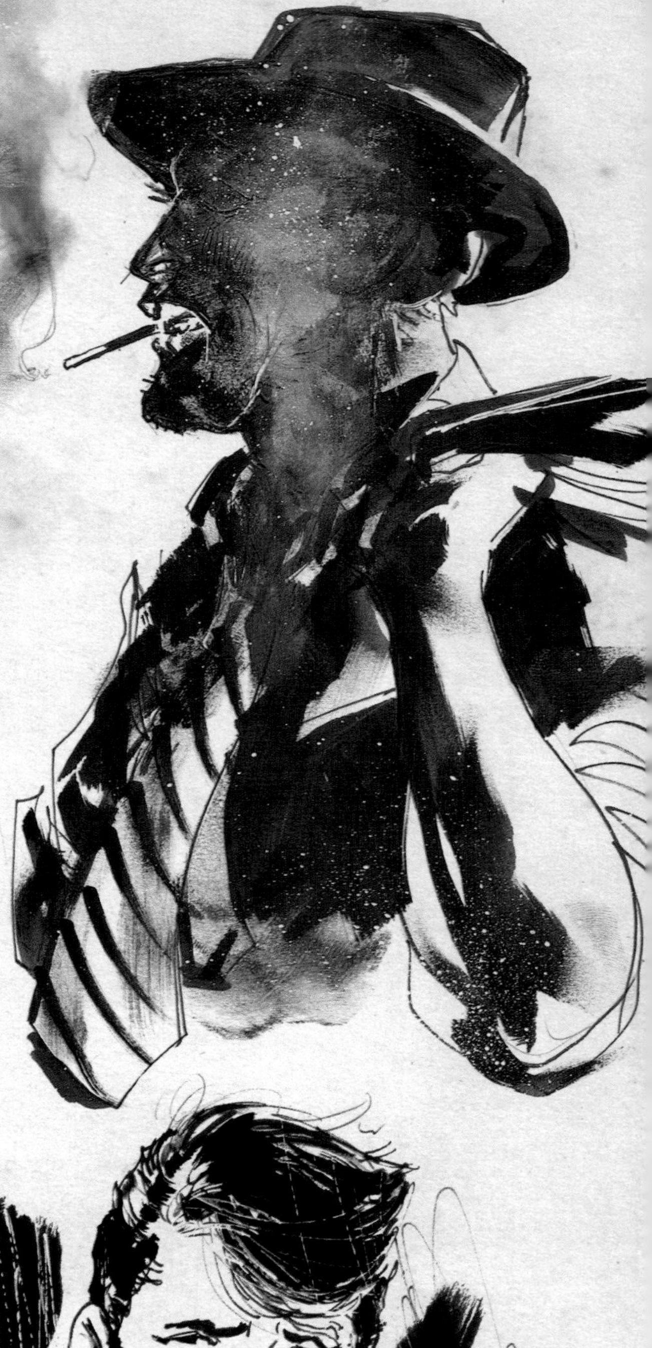

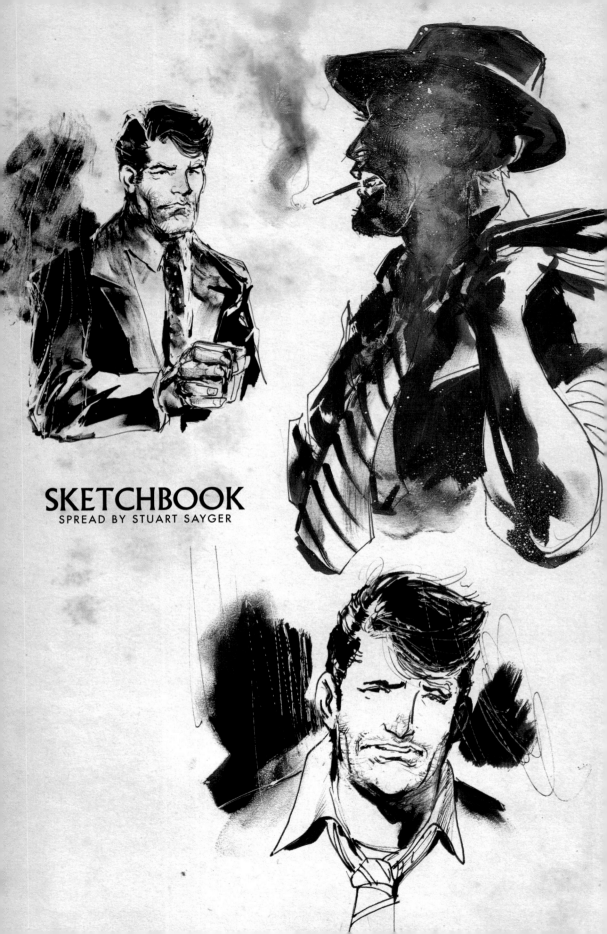

SKETCHBOOK

SPREAD BY STUART SAYGER

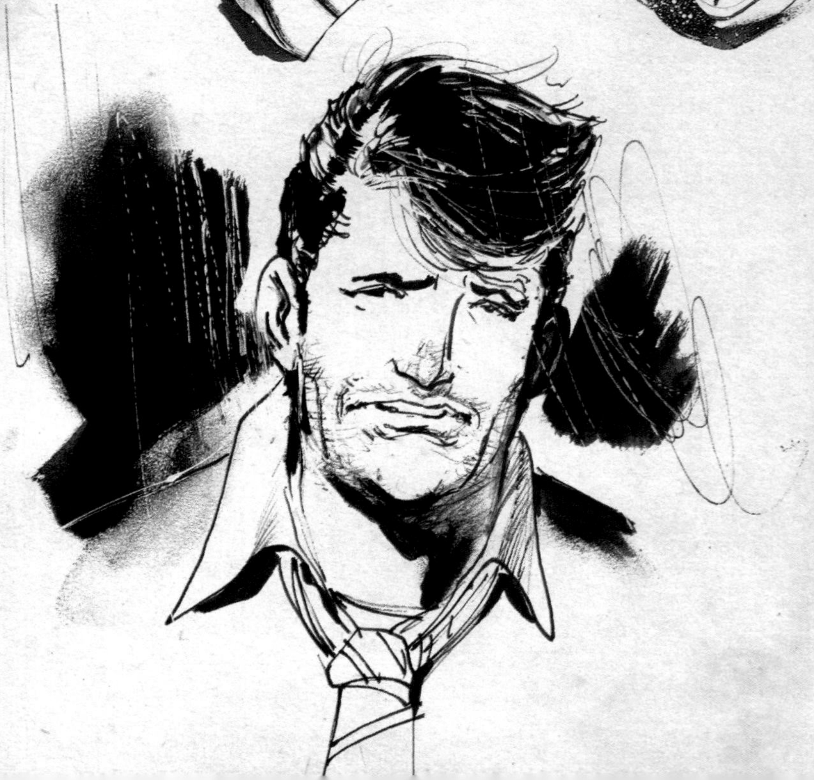

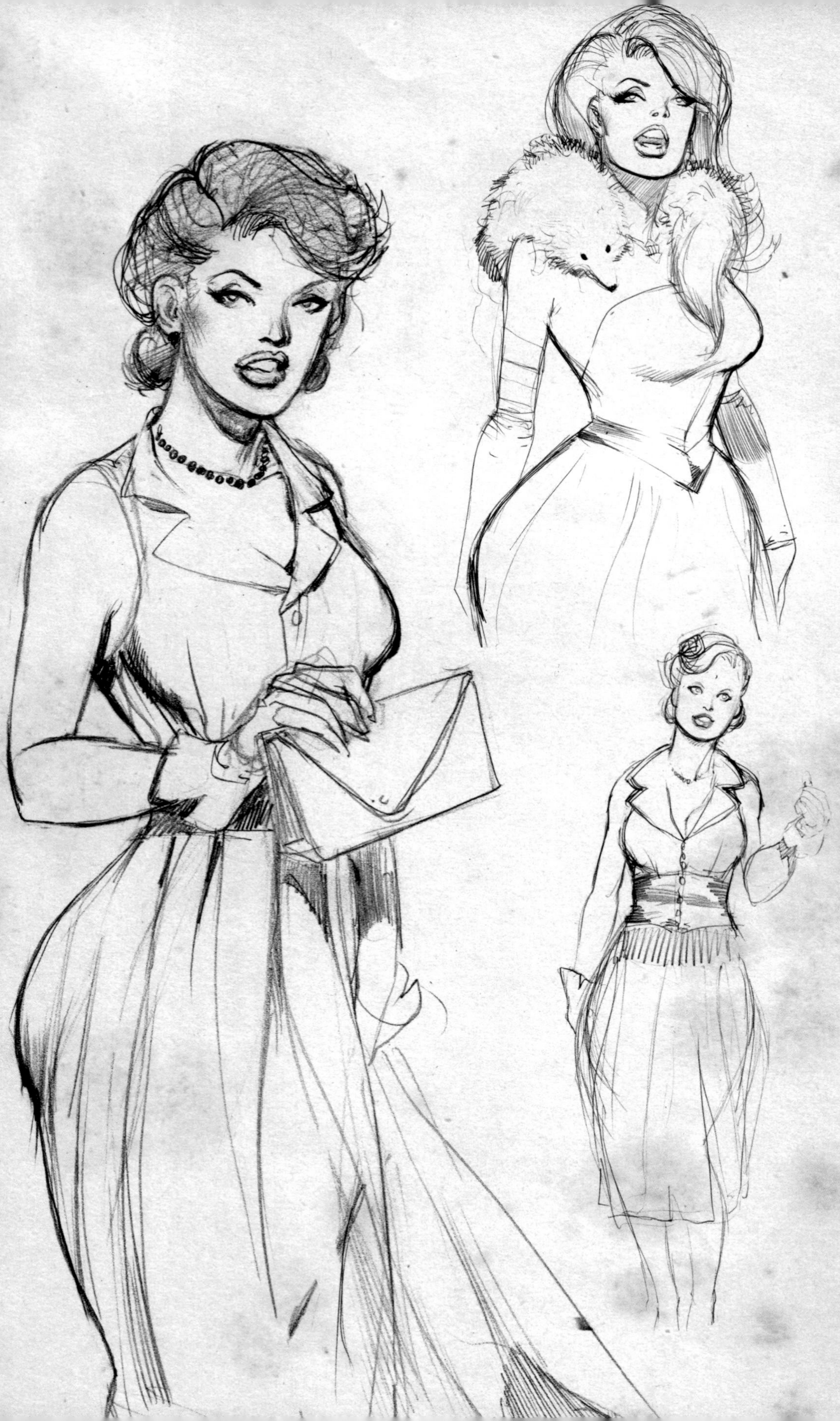

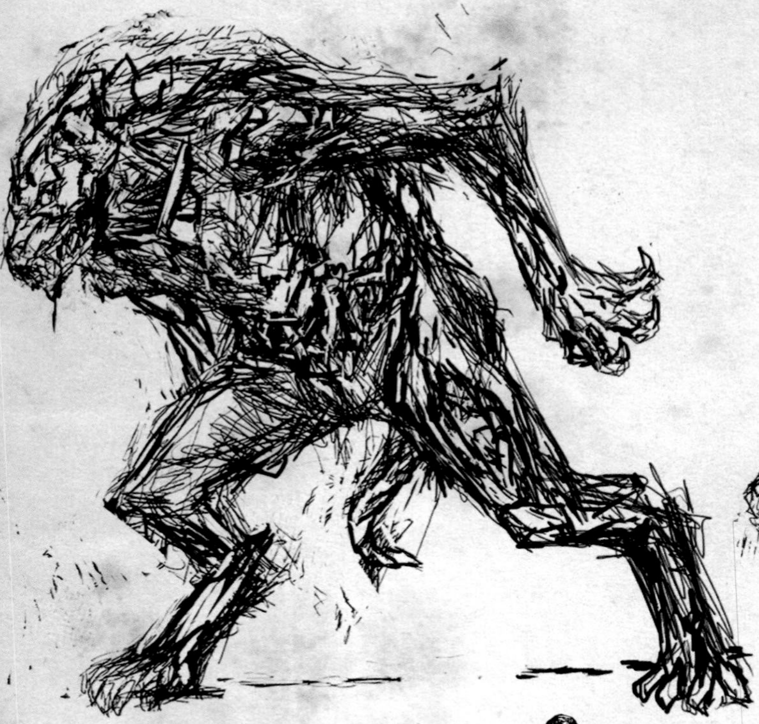

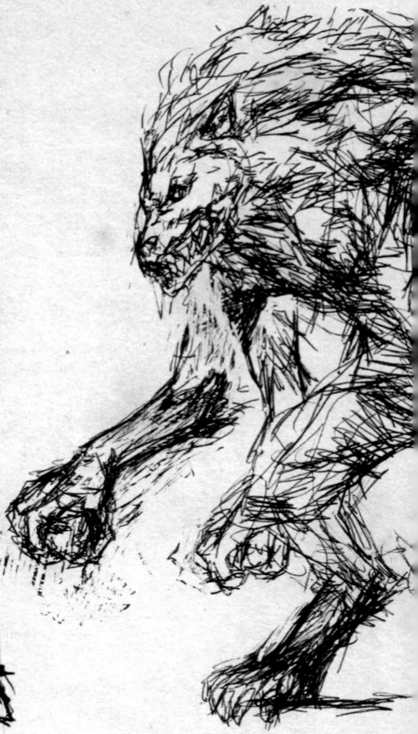

SKETCHBOOK

SPREAD BY ZID

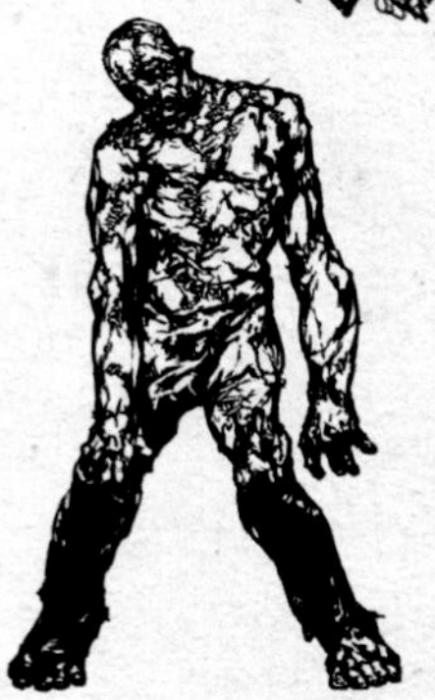

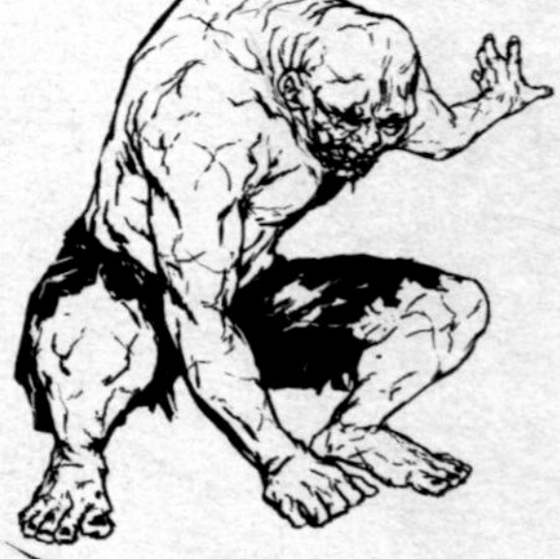

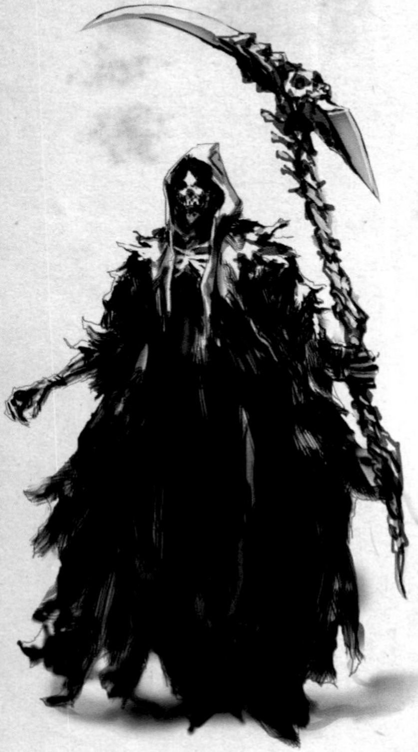

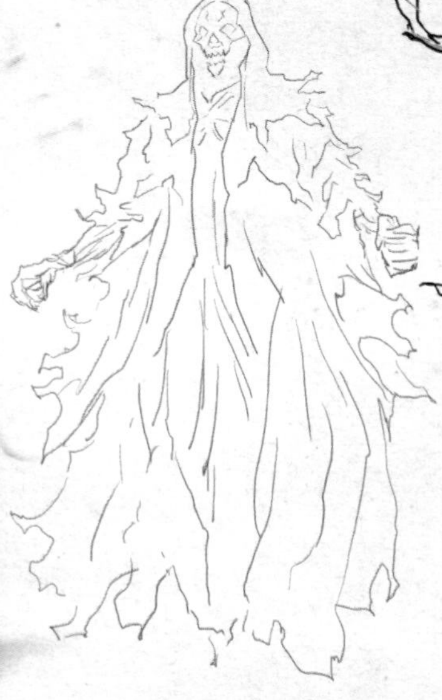

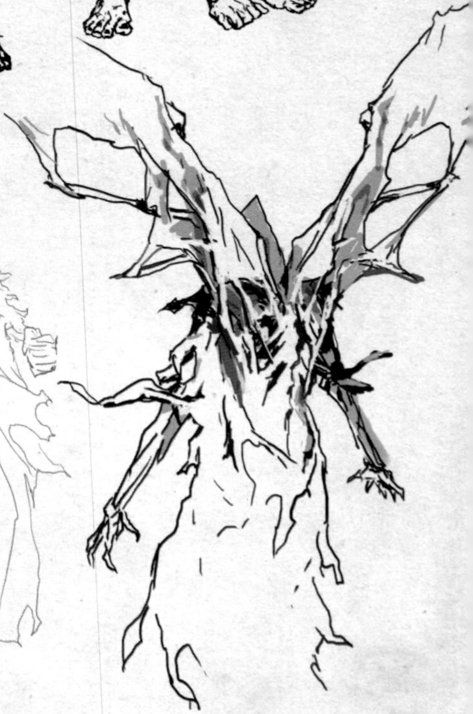

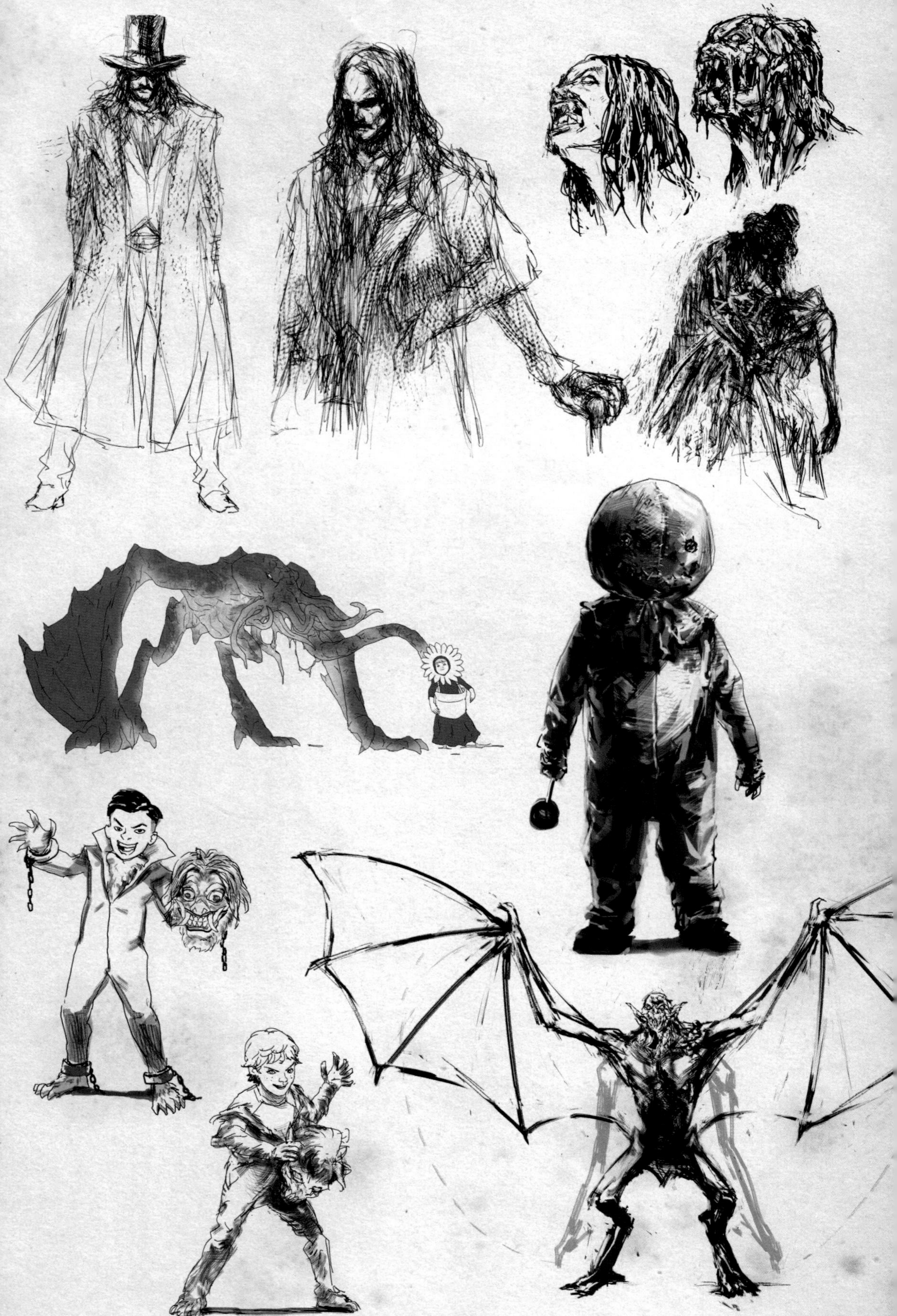

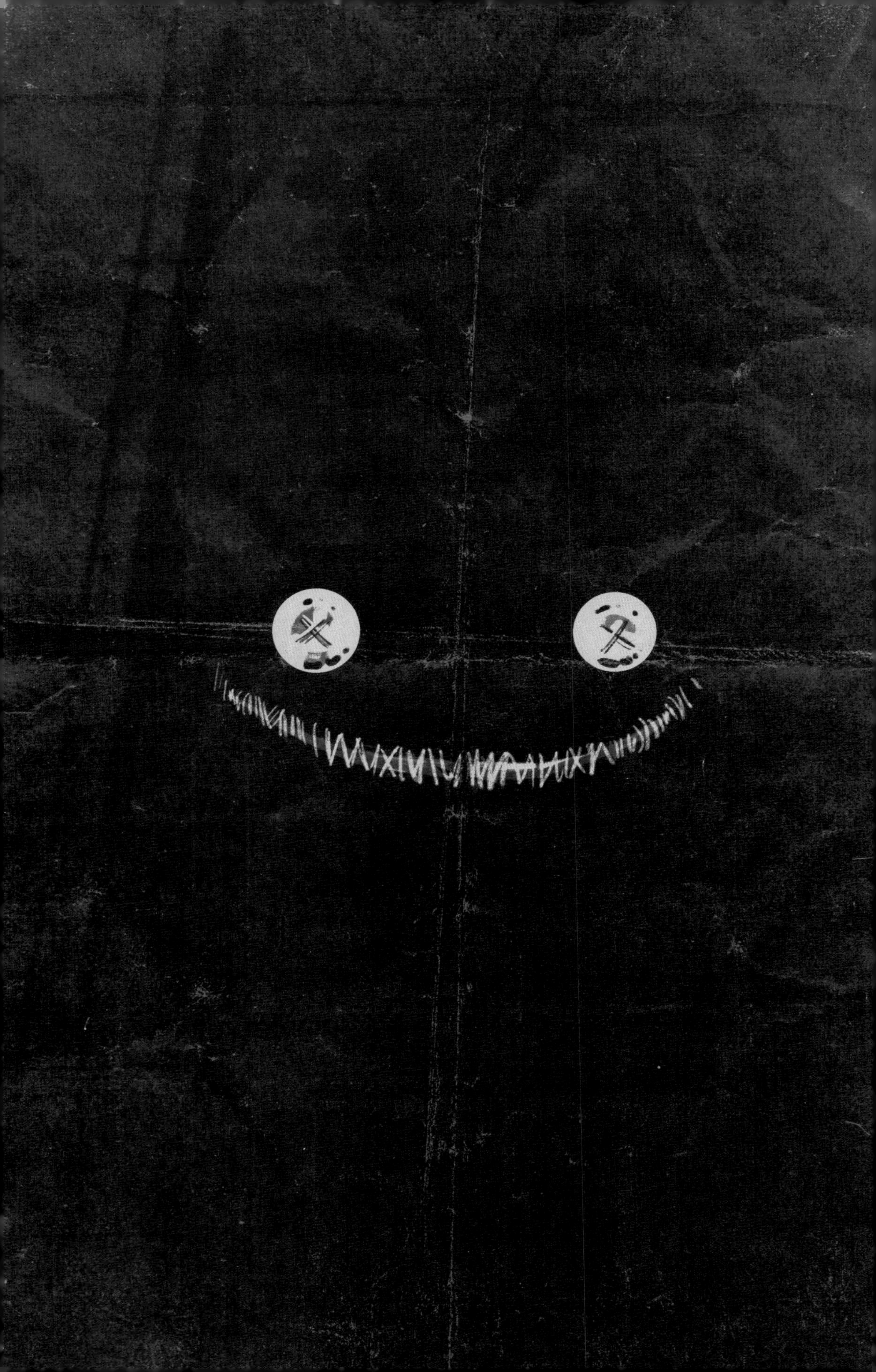